Increasing Legal Rights
for Zoo Animals

Increasing Legal Rights for Zoo Animals

Justice on the Ark

Edited by Jesse Donahue
Foreword by Nigel Rothfels

LEXINGTON BOOKS
Lanham • Boulder • New York • London

Published by Lexington Books
An imprint of The Rowman & Littlefield Publishing Group, Inc.
4501 Forbes Boulevard, Suite 200, Lanham, Maryland 20706
www.rowman.com

Unit A, Whitacre Mews, 26-34 Stannary Street, London SE11 4AB

British Library Cataloguing in Publication Information Available

Library of Congress Cataloging-in-Publication Data

Names: Donahue, Jesse, editor.
Title: Increasing legal rights for zoo animals : justice on the ark / Edited by Jesse Donahue ;
    Foreword by Nigel Rothfels.
Description: Lanham, Maryland : Lexington Books, 2017. | Includes bibliographical references and
    index.
Identifiers: LCCN 2017004289 (print) | LCCN 2017004786 (ebook)
Subjects: LCSH: Animal welfare--Law and legislation. | Zoo animals--Legal status, laws, etc.
Classification: LCC K3620 .I53 2017 (print) | LCC K3620 (ebook) | DDC 344.04/9--dc23
LC record available at https://lccn.loc.gov/2017004289

ISBN 9781498528948 (cloth)
ISBN 9781498528962 (pbk.)
ISBN 9781498528955 (electronic)

To Maia and Miles

Table of Contents

Foreword

Nigel Rothfels

On October 5, 1903, William Temple Hornaday, director of the still-quite-new New York Zoological Park (what is now usually referred to as the Bronx Zoo), wrote to a Mr. Rolker, the author of an article for *McClure's Magazine*. Hornaday was upset because a photograph he had provided the magazine of a female bison with her calf had been credited to the Central Park Zoo. "Hereafter," Hornaday writes, "we will never again, knowingly, furnish any photographs for publication, either in magazine, book or newspaper, wherein photographs of the Central Park Menagerie are to be used." "We are not in the class of the Central Park 'Zoo,'" he insisted, "and hereafter will do our best to prevent the appearance of being so."[1] Hornaday used "menagerie" and "zoo" to distinguish the older and in his mind somehow tawdry collection of exotic animals in Central Park from the modern, scientific, serious, educational, and culturally significant institution he was developing along the Bronx River. In a letter to another author for *McClure's* the following month Hornaday reemphasized that the word "zoo" was one that he and his colleagues particularly "despise" because it "always does more harm than good."[2]

In his pains to distinguish between the New York Zoological Park and the Central Park Zoo, Hornaday was repeating a line of reasoning that can be traced to the very beginnings of the public zoo movement in Europe in the late eighteenth and early nineteenth centuries. The proponents of the new, scientific, public zoological gardens consistently emphasized that whereas the old "menageries" arose from base curiosity and vain attempts at self-aggrandizement, modern zoological gardens, built by the rising middle class, were institutions committed to science and the edification of an increasingly urban and cosmopolitan public. In short, old zoos were bad, but new ones were good; zoos built for amusement were bad, but zoos built for science and education were good. The actors have changed, the term *conservation* has been added, but this same play continues to be rehearsed today. These days, "good" zoos are generally assumed to be those that receive accreditation from various professional associations like the Association of Zoos and Aquariums (AZA) or the World Association of Zoos and Aquariums (WAZA); the "bad" zoos are typically all lumped together among the other 90 percent of institutions that display animals as commercial and not-for-profit entities. Meanwhile, animal rights and animal welfare advocates continue to ask a question that can also be traced to the nineteenth century: no matter how good the zoo, isn't it somehow wrong to keep nondomestic animals captive in the first place, even for reasons of science or education? Partly in response to that question, the sanctuary movement (with its own accrediting bodies) has arisen to offer yet another elusory claim that there is some way of keeping animals in captivity that is better than . . . keeping animals in captivity.

Still, it remains intuitively and empirically clear that the conditions in which most (if not all) animals live in some zoos and sanctuaries are better than those at other facilities. Whether because of better spaces or climates, stronger finances, more well-trained staff, in-house and well-equipped veterinary supports, or mission-driven emphases on actual education, conservation, and welfare, a small number of undeniably better zoos have always essentially provided a justification for all the rest. These better zoos, the argument goes, suggest that it is not that zoos are bad in principle, but that some zoos are simply lagging behind because they lack sufficient resources. And, because the leading institutions have consistently resisted pushing for stronger governmental regulations on the whole industry, we are left with an essentially toothless self-accreditation system and a legal framework that, country by country, is so idiosyncratically implemented and so generalized, with zoos often being lumped together with all kinds of research, education, and entertainment institutions, that legal protections for zoo animals are much, much weaker than most people would likely believe.

With zoos of one form or another (and there is little rational reason to exclude "sanctuaries" for exotic animals under this title) clearly here to stay, the contributors to this collection seek to identify the legal frameworks in which zoos operate while also asking how one might improve the legal protections for animals and their audiences. Pointing out that both "wild" and "companion" animals typically have more legal protections than zoo animals, the scholars and zoo professionals assembled here point out that the leading institutions in the industry, the animals themselves, and the public could have much to gain by more clearly articulating the rights of zoo animals and our legal and moral obligations to them. An industry, for example, that increasingly locates its *raisons d'etre* in both serving as a genetic reserve and *in situ* conservation (deploying techniques of translocation and reintroduction) can find itself frustratingly constrained by generalized welfare laws that take no account of how, for instance, carnivores actually live in the world. Would it make sense to embrace possible expansions of companion animal laws to include zoo animals, whose lives, in most obvious respects, are more similar to those of companion animals than any of their "wild" conspecifics? Would it make sense to move federal oversight of American zoos out of the Department of Agriculture and into the Department of Justice? In what ways do recent efforts to reform legislation in New Zealand suggest alternatives to zoo regulations in other countries? What paths might exist to build robust international standards of law protecting zoo animals and encouraging zoos themselves to become stronger advocates of animal welfare and conservation? These and other critical questions form the background of this collection of timely essays. As the authors make clear, as debates about personhood status for nonhuman primates expand, as the public becomes increasingly concerned about the lives of cetaceans and elephants in captivity, and as the current "great extinction" accelerates, the stakes in reforming welfare laws for zoo animals will only increase. It is time for the industry itself, for its critics, and for the public to begin a long-overdue discussion about "justice on the ark."

NOTES

1. William Temple Hornaday to A. M. Rolker, October 5, 1903, New York Zoological Park, Office of Director, William T. Hornaday and W. Reid Blair Outgoing Correspondence 1895–1939.

2. William Temple Hornaday to Gilbert C. Lutz, November 4, 1903, New York Zoological Park, Office of Director, William T. Hornaday and W. Reid Blair Outgoing Correspondence 1895–1939.

Introduction

The Legal Landscape and Possibilities for Change

Jesse Donahue

The Malayan tigers at the Bronx Zoo in New York City live in over 100,000 square feet during the day and night. Scientists estimate that there are only about 250 of their kind left in the wild. They spend all day with a community of other tigers in their home called "Tiger Mountain," socializing and eating.[1] They are a highly bonded group with strong emotional attachments to one another. They are allowed to breed occasionally, but not to a great extent. It is likely that most, if not all, of their babies will be taken away and placed in other zoos when they are old enough. Throughout the day visitors look at, but they do not get to touch the tigers. Their cubs are kept out of the public's view periodically to make sure that their stress level is low. The tigers get time off at night when guests go home. Their keepers feed them, but interaction is limited for safety reasons. They have state-of-the-art veterinary care that is available throughout the day and night. The Wildlife Conservation Society, the parent organization that runs the Bronx Zoo, urges guests to sign a petition to Congress supporting the Multispecies Conservation Fund to help preserve these animals in the wild.[2]

Harley is a westhighland terrier and his living space in his Manhattan apartment is 1,500 square feet during the day, but at night he sleeps in a 3-foot long, by 2-foot wide crate that allows him to get up, turn around, and have a drink because he tends to have accidents at night. He is taken out for a short walk in the morning in Central Park where people look at him and then he goes back up to his owner's apartment where he will spend the rest of the day by himself. He gets at least two more walks during the day, once when his owner gets home at 5:00 p.m., and again in the evening before bed at around 9:00 p.m. Harley's owner loves him and interacts with him a few times each day depending upon his schedule. Each time Harley goes out people smile at him and sometimes pet him. Because he is a terrier, he has an enormous amount of energy that is only partly satisfied by short walks around Central Park. His owner bought him from a breeder located north of New York City. Harley's life is probably secure, but he can be given away or sold at any time. His owner has neutered him responsibly so he will never have any offspring and he lives entirely alone because his owner feels that the apartment is too small to include other dogs and cats. His owner does not have pet health insurance, but does take him to a good vet when needed and when he has time after work.

Which of these animals is better off and why? Almost all of the ethics literature on animal rights suggests that the dog is better off because he is not "imprisoned" in a zoo.[3] But the dog's mobility is curtailed dramatically. He exists in a very small indoor space by himself for hours at a time with only limited walks on a leash. He has no ability to reproduce or become a member of a permanent canine family. Like the tigers at the Bronx Zoo he is genetically preconditioned to want dramatically more outdoor activity than he gets. He has no interaction during the day with any of his kind. So why is it that that the zoo animal, who never experienced any time in the wild, is the prisoner and the dog is not?

The answer to the question about which kind of animal is better off is not a question of space, whether the animal could roam long distances or not, or who looks at it. The answer revolves around which one has more legal rights. Humans in the United States are better off than their animal coresidents because they have more legal rights. Companion animals in the United States are better off than zoo animals to a large extent because they have more rights. So the answer to our question is that the dog is better off because he is a companion animal and as such he is better off than the zoo animal even though he is just as confined in his home. The question then, is how to give zoo animals and other exotic captive animals as many rights as possible? And if so, which rights? Or, the animal legal scholar David Favre would ask, how can we give them increased legal respect and accommodate them better within the legal system?[4]

Currently zoo animals in the United States primarily fall under the legal framework of the Animal Welfare Act, or AWA (created for laboratory animals 1966 and amended in 1970 to include exhibition animals), the Marine Mammal Protection Act (1972), the Endangered Species Act (1973), and the Convention on the International Trade of Endangered Speceis of Flora and Fauna (CITES in 1973). All of these acts to some extent focus on animal welfare, the Marine Mammal Protection Act, for example, stops people from taking (harassing) these animals in the wild. So preventing harassment is a form of promoting animal welfare. But the act that most directly impacts animals living in zoos is the AWA because it established regulations covering the transportation, purchase, sale, housing, handling, and treatment of zoo animals. It sets minimum requirements for the daily care of the animals including housing, feeding, watering, and shelter from extreme weather conditions. Zoos must get licenses from the United States Department of Agriculture (USDA) to stay open and keep a variety of records about the animals including information on their purchase, sale, transportation, and previous owners.[5] The Animal and Plant Health Inspection Services (APHIS) located in the Department of Agriculture enforces the act through its Animal Care division that makes unannounced annual inspections to the extent that they can given the number of organizations that house exotic captive animals. The USDA, however, never wanted the job of enforcing animal welfare at zoos. Because it is the federal agency whose work focuses on farmers, policing exotic animals was not something they wanted to do. Despite their initial objections Congress tasked them with the work and so this is the US federal agency enforcing zoo animal welfare. Critics point to the extent to which APHIS has failed to realize the goal of high-quality welfare for all zoo animals, but what this misses is that the law itself sets the minimum standards for animal space, for example, very low. Because the USDA was primarily a public agency devoted to farms, its employees had no real knowledge of how much space exotic animals needed or how to ensure their best care so they turned to the only group at that time that had that kind of information: zoo directors. On the one had it was true that this group knew the most about keeping exotic animals alive. On the other they felt the need to protect small and outdated zoos with inferior space requirements because they were members of their profession and sometimes members of what was then known as the American Association of Zoological Parks and Aquariums (now known as the Association of Zoos and Aquariums or AZA). These zoo directors worked with the Department of Agriculture to both help set regulatory requirements and to police their own members to a limited extent through internal accreditation. Given the modest nature of what they could require of poor older zoos, they kept the regulations fairly minimal and the AWA has been criticized ever since. Critics point to the Act's failure to cover all animals (it omits cold-blooded animals including fish, reptiles, and amphibians); APHIS' tendency to give violators of the AWA too many chances to redeem themselves prior to punishment; the fact that the agency only keeps records for three years which makes it difficult for Administrative Law Judges to punish repeat offenders. So, how could laws work better for animals in zoos if the AWA has significant weaknesses?[6]

Steven Wise, the legal scholar, presents one such approach to increasing legal rights for captive exotic animals. His organization, the Nonhuman Rights Project, is attempting to help primates in research institutions gain personhood status, a fundamental and crucial legal right.[7] He is working through the courts to liberate chimpanzees from tiny cages and lives of complete isolation by using habeaus corpus to get at least one judge in the state of New York to give chimpanzees legal personhood. Because New York allows unlimited appeals he and his organization hope to find a judge who will agree that they have the same legal status as humans. Wise points out that other entities like corporations have personhood status in the law and thus it is possible that a judge will finally agree and confer this status on chimpanzees. Although he has primarily focused on primates in research institutions in recent years, his previous attempts to help animals get legal standing included focusing on dolphins. In both cases Wise argues that these captive exotic animals are excluded from our basic human protection of liberty, which includes at a minimum, protecting us from restraint against our will and the right not to have others touching us without consent. He believes that certain animals should have "the right to move about unless one is in danger to oneself and others, which would certainly be the case for chimpanzees or bonobos in the U.S., but certainly not the case for, say, Atlantic bottlenose dolphins along America's East and Gulf coasts."[8] Where, then do we place the captive animals if they might do themselves or others harm? According to Wise, we should not place them in zoos, but instead they "could be placed in sanctuaries in which they would have some reasonable degree of bodily liberty."[9]

How likely it is that this will benefit all zoo animals? It is certainly possible that a judge will confer personhood on chimpanzees. It is less likely that a common law judge will bestow that status on all animals in the United States or even most of the rest of animals in zoos. So, given that lack of realistic sweeping change, how might we go about increasing legal rights for as many possible zoo and aquarium animals? Are there ways that we could extend existing laws that could temporarily increase their legal rights while waiting for their status of personhood? Are there rights that other animals have that could be used by captive exotic animals as well? And what about other countries in which captive exotic animals have even fewer rights? What could we do in those countries where animals are even less likely to receive the rights of personhood in their courts?

These are the kinds of questions that this book addresses primarily by examining zoo animal law and politics in the United States but also by asking some of the same questions about zoos in Southeast Asia and New Zealand. The book discusses the kinds of legal rights zoo animals have, whether we can increase them, and if so, in what ways? Underlying this search is the motivating question of how we can increase justice for all exotic captive animals, but particularly those in zoos, aquariums, and sanctuaries.

This focus on zoo animal legal rights is a completely different approach than currently exists in the field. Zoo critics are typically animal ethicists or animal welfare activists whose primary focus is on increasing attention and compassion for the plight of research, farm, and abandoned companion animals. These scholars largely ignore zoos even though some of their ideas are applicable to zoo animals.[10] This failure to research or thoroughly examine zoos is mimicked by animal rights groups and shared on their websites. Here again zoos are not the primary focus. Activists are often mainly concerned about the historically sad plight of farm and research animals who have been killed and mutilated in these industries by the billions.[11] Although this is crucial work, these same groups also unfortunately feel compelled to add vague, unsubstantiated statements about zoos on the argument that zoos are commercial organizations that deal in animals, therefor they must all be bad. The Friends of Animals website informs guests that "Babies are produced [at zoos] to amuse customers and cover the zoo's overhead costs. Older and disabled animals often just disappear one day."[12] This is an important point and is true, as we shall see, at some zoos around the world. But which zoos are we talking about? Where are these zoos?

Other criticisms by anti-zoo proponents focus on the animals' lack of freedom. If they are wild animals, then they should be in the wild. Friends of Animals, argues that zoos "remove animals from their natural birthplaces and companions, and confine them in unnatural surroundings."[13] An academic critic states that zoos are "taking animals out of their native habitats and keeping them in alien environments."[14] Here again we wonder which zoos are doing this and how often is it happening? Which kinds of animals are collected from the wild and where? We know that this is not the case today for accredited zoos in the United States today and even cursory research would have revealed this. Zoo directors, curators, and keepers invite people to visit and want them to see the animals. They place webcams in animal enclosures rather than locking concerned citizens out through gag order legislation like the kind that we find protecting farms and animal research centers. If accredited zoos in the United States were collecting new orangutans from the wild, for example, we would notice their sudden appearance through the web cams placed a many zoos around the country.

Zoos in the United States and the rest of the world did collect animals from the wild in the 1800s, but people let their dogs roam wild in the streets of New York in the same period as well. By the 1980s, moreover, zoos in the United States had almost entirely stopped collecting animals from the wild. To take one example, Gary Clark, the director of the Topeka Zoo (KS) in the 1980s received one tree shrew from the Lincoln Park Zoo (IL), a Przewalski's horse loaned from the San Diego Zoo, and a yellow anaconda through an open exchange from the San Diego Wild Animal Park. The zoo did not collect a single animal from the wild.[15] Accredited zoos in the United States rarely collect animals from the wild today both because they oppose doing that for reasons other than to save endangered species and because it is much cheaper to get the animals either through a loan or by purchasing them from another zoo. The Association for Zoos and Aquariums, hereafter referred to as the AZA, is the largest zoo interest group in the United States and keeps track of the number of animals collected from the wild. According to them, zoos collect about 5 percent of their animals from the wild, but they do so to rescue them from extinction, breed them to sustainable levels, and return them to the wild. Moreover, these are overwhelmingly small animals like toads and frogs who are not drawing large crowds to zoos.[16]

Another zoo critic complaint is that zoos are not educating visitors well enough. One critic, for example, claims that "hunters and fisherman" among other groups of people who kill animals for sport are more knowledgeable than zoo guests about animals, which he feels justifies the closing of zoos. Although he acknowledges that some education happens in zoos, he insists that it would be better if people got that through "films, slides, and lectures."[17] Critics who make this argument sometimes feel confident that the feelings of their children should determine the interests and behavior of all others. A writer for *Out Door Magazine* recently shared that his son watched a *Nature* documentary and was "glued to the screen," so, comparing this to zoos he wondered "whether there are any good arguments for keeping animals in artificial enclosures, that are at best, only a fraction of the size of their natural habitats?"[18] His hope and the hope of other critics is to close them all down.

But what should we do with the animals who are in zoos if they are all closed? The answer for zoo critics is to stop allowing the animals to breed and move them all to sanctuaries. The word *sanctuary* seems very appealing. It sounds like nirvana and conjures images of expansive grounds, constant high quality attention, enrichment, and never-ending financially stability. One writer opines, for example, that it is time to move all "legitimately conservation-oriented breeding programs to spacious sanctuaries and preserves where the public can still view the animals."[19] He argues that zoo animals sometimes experience stress that they would not suffer at sanctuaries because of their greater space. Here again, this may be a legitimate point for some kinds of animals at some well-funded sanctuaries. But is this the case for all sanctuaries? Are animals always better off in sanctuaries? It would be very difficult to argue that all big cat sanctuaries around the world offer the animals more space.[20] What about the zoos that now call themselves sanctuaries? The Wildlife Conservation Society, formerly the Bronx Zoo (NY), for example, calls itself a sanctuary. The only legal right that a captive animal at a sanctuary has that a zoo animal does not have is the right not to breed. However, we can say that in the reverse as well. Zoo animals can breed and breeding is a natural part of all animals lives, but sanctuary animals are always prevented from breeding and therefore also have less liberty.

Zoo animals in accredited zoos in the United States have problems, but they are not the frequently repeated ones in much of the literature that attacks them. What the critics have missed is that we are on the precipice of momentous legal changes for animals that may in the near future give some of them citizenship rights. Zoos animals should benefit from that revolution as well. Unintentionally marginalizing them through criticisms of their entire institutional life support system particularly when it is at its best, will not aid them in that quest. Sending all zoo animals to sanctuaries to help them die off is a recommendation that sounds a lot like the proposals of some nineteenth-century American abolitionists who proposed sending African Americans back to Africa rather than integrating them into our society and affording them as many legal rights as possible.

To help zoo animals take advantage of the coming revolution in animal legal rights we first need to recognize that by their presence they are co-citizens with us. At a minimum citizenship includes residing in a place. A baby born in the United States cannot vote, but he or she is a citizen in our country. Regardless of where they originally came from, zoo animals live among us because we brought them here and made them vulnerable by keeping them. Zoo animals are here, they have a right to stay, and we ought to help them thrive. We owe them morally to appreciate who they are and make their lives as fulfilled as possible. The contributors to this volume, however, are not all of one voice on how many rights zoo animals need. As zoo-focused scholars and zoo directors from different countries, we differ in our understanding of the kinds of problems zoo animals face and our recommendations for what kinds of changes we could make in the legal systems to rectify them. To a large extent those differences reflect the complex reality that captive exotic animals face in different parts of the world.

At one extreme we have the United States that we cover in chapters 1 through 3, and to a certain extent again in chapter 6. In chapter 1 I show how zoo animals could take advantage of the increasing rights of companion animals across a variety of areas. I suggest that zoo animals might need a name change to better reflect their real status in our communities. Many zoo animals will never be reintroduced into the wild for a variety of reasons. There is sometimes nowhere for them to go because their habitat is overrun by development or poaching. Other times they were rescued exotic companion animals and they would face certain death by returning to the wild because they lack the skills necessary to survive. As a result, the author suggests that the name *wild public companion animal* be given to zoo animals instead of the current name of *wild animal*. Using the current name *wild animal* is a double-edged sword. It is useful because it suggests the animal's historic background and its potential for human harm. It is also critical legally because the major pieces of legislation impacting zoo animals—the Animal Welfare Act, the Endangered Species Act, and the Marine Mammal Protection Act—allow zoos to exhibit *wild* animals. It is unhelpful in the ways illustrated by the confusion of the critics. Because they are called *wild animals*, the critics are assuming that they are always actually wild animals who were caught and placed in enclosures that are much smaller than the ones that they recently experienced in the wild. By renaming them *wild public companion animals*, zoos could acknowledge that these animals may have a lifelong relationship with people who visit them in their homes in zoos.

In addition to changing their name to help them take advantage of the momentous legal changes on the way, I suggest resurrecting the idea of a small federal agency aimed entirely at their needs. Currently zoo animals in the United States have strong watchdogs in the form of animal welfare groups that bring lawsuits against practices that they feel violate the spirit or letter of the major pieces of legislation that govern them. But their political representation through federal agencies is so fractured that their needs fall through the cracks in the United States. And I illustrate how zoo animals could use the increasing rights that companion animals are getting in the areas of redress against physical harm, rights conferred from working, and inheritance laws that could be applied to them. Zoo animals are effectively both companion animals and employees: Hence the often-heard name given to them is *ambassadors*. Companion animals now have the right to have trusts that zoo animals should have as well. Mandating that each zoo animal had its own money that followed it for life and protected it from disasters of various kinds would help eliminate the suspicion that zoo animals are sold to hunting ranches. Giving them the right to have time off from the stress of visitors and retire to a private space at some point seems just as important if there is any evidence that being around humans is a stressful experience for them

In chapter 2, we examine the issue of reintroductions. Zoo directors and other zoo employees would like to reintroduce as many animals as possible. They want to repopulate the wild with endangered species. A zoo director of a major national zoo who participated in reintroduction programs reviews some of those reintroductions and reflects on the technical and legal pitfalls that they face. How do zoo biologists navigate the difficult terrain of reintroducing a predator animal on its way to full release when that means killing other animals that enter its temporary enclosure? Do the scientists in charge of that project need to protect the welfare of those animals? Predator animals need to master the skill of hunting live prey to feed themselves in the wild. Predators with permeable barriers kill other animals, but this violates legal requirements of the Animal Welfare Act that restricts wild animal ingress in to captive animal homes. In addition, he shows that the designation of endangered species also poses problems for animals who are in release programs. Zoo directors have to redesignate animals as nonessential experimental populations so that they can bring them back into captivity if they get injured in the release process. Is this how this process should work? Or should all animals in the process of reintroduction automatically be eligible for additional help if they need it before attempting release again? How does one reintroduce animals when hunting for species who look like them is legal? This is the case, as we shall see, with red wolves, a reintroduced species from zoos in North Carolina. They look like coyotes, particularly at night, so they are inadvertently killed by hunters. Zoo directors do not have the legal authority at this point to stop all hunting just because they have a species conservation plan that includes reintroductions. The zoo director argues that we need laws that stop the hunting on animals who look similar to any animal involved in a reintroduction program in a state. Much of the public is very supportive of animal reintroductions, as is the zoological community. But he shows us the difficulty of keeping those animals alive once they are released given the current state of hunting laws in the United States.

But what about using zoo animals in research? If the chimpanzee held at a research institute gets sent to a zoo, will it be subject to more invasive research? This would certainly defeat the purpose of rescuing the animal from the research lab if that were the case. As we shall see from chapter 3, that is not the case. In this chapter a biologist and zoo animal researcher reviews the history of animal research at zoos to illustrate that the vast majority of research on zoo animals is noninvasive and typically voluntary on the part of the animal. Zoos primarily focus on education and conservation and less on research. Today most zoo research involves observational studies in which biologists from either the institution or universities stand outside of the animals' homes observe them and record behaviors. In other cases they collect fecal samples left in their homes to monitor stress hormones so that they can determine how best to minimize any discomfort the animals are experiencing. When they draw blood or conduct other physically invasive tests they do those when the animals are anesthetized for annual medical procedures so the animal is not in any pain. The one area in which zoo animal research is more invasive involves breeding for conservation purposes. Here animals are given hormone injections, for example to enhance the chances for successful insemination.[21] But these efforts are for animal conservation, not for human benefit. She also shows that and animal welfare research requirements by the Association of Zoos and Aquariums (AZA) in the United States, far exceed those in required by the Animal Welfare Act that, for example, omits certain animals like mice from coverage and allows painful research on animals if it is expressly for the purpose of studying pain. This is a case then, in which the AWA falls short of the welfare work ongoing in zoos and should be amended to eliminate pain studies.

In chapter 4 we move outside of the United States and an animal welfare scholar from New Zealand considers the individual case of his country. Zoo animals there are regulated by the Animal Welfare Act (2000) that was inspired by the Five Freedoms recommended by the Farm Act in the United Kingdom. To a certain extent this has increased zoo animal welfare because it has created a dialogue about what constitutes normal patterns of behavior and what it means to be free from pain and distress. The Act was amended in 2015 to recognize animals as sentient, which hints at ways at which animal rights could be headed in an expansive direction. As in the United States, zoo animals in New Zealand are regulated by an agency whose primary purpose is not their welfare. They are under the jurisdiction of the National Welfare Advisory Council, which is the same group that works on farm animal issues. The National Welfare Advisory Council has to get approval from the Ministry of Primary Industries. As a result, zoos in New Zealand are effectively regulated as commercial institutions. As a result, the rights of zoo animals are dragged down by the attempts by the agency and its farm supporters to keep rights for farm animals at a minimum. Zoo animals are also regulated under new organism containment laws that are primarily designed to prevent new life forms from overtaking the island. Here again, however, the interests of captive animal welfare are not paramount. Instead the focus is primarily on stock animal and wild animal health. Unlike the United States, companion animals in New Zealand are not gaining the kinds of rights that could be given to zoo animals. As a result, the author recommends that zoo animals in New Zealand who are exhibiting stereotypical behavior be sent to sanctuaries where perhaps their lives will be improved. He also suggests that the best way for captive exotic animals to increase their rights in New Zealand is to have a stand-alone governing body entirely focused on captive exotic animal rights so that their needs are not subsumed by those of farm or research industry interests.

In chapter 5 the book considers the entire region of Southeast Asia. Here we clearly see the problems that zoo critics talk about when the condemn zoos all zoos all over the world. Although this is clearly not the only region of the world where these problems exist they provide a good lens into where zoo activists should be placing their emphasis. Here a zoo director and scholar from the region outlines the significant challenges that animal welfare advocates in Southeast Asia face. We find the illegal animal capture and importation of both endangered and nonendangered animals. Endangered animals including rhinos, for example, are caught in South Africa and shipped to Southeast Asia. We find social animals like nonhuman primates placed in tiny cramped cages sometimes completely on their own in zoos. Then there is the constant use of animals as entertainment, often at zoos and resorts. Southeast Asia as a region faces the problem of western environmental tourists who go to see the animals and have more direct contact with them then they are allowed to in the United States, Europe, or Canada. Riding elephants for example, is a common reason for traveling to some Southeast Asian countries. Like exotic captive animals in the United States and New Zealand, their fellow animals in Southeast Asia are typically governed by agencies that whose primary purpose lies elsewhere including agencies focused on agriculture, natural resources, and commerce. The countries differ in the extent to which the small number of regulations are enforced, but zoo animals in all of the countries need significantly more rights. Some of the countries like Cambodia and Myanmar have to start from scratch to create better laws for their animals. Others like Singapore, Taiwan, and Malaysia have to enforce their laws better. The author recommends creating a single agency within each country focused solely on captive exotic animal issues and creating laws that prohibit animals in entertainment. The failure of regional zoo associations to motivate zoos to increase the size of zoo animal homes makes him recommend that countries adopt laws on enclosure sizes that are based on the recommendations by animal scientists. And he recommends laws that will require zoo directors to make sure that animals are placed with their own kind and not housed by themselves. He suggests using a percentage of ticket revenue to fund the enforcement of these laws and proposes that a voluntary police force could be deputized to report animal welfare abuses to the agency in charge of regulating zoos and aquariums.

Finally, we consider the question of whether we should simply place all zoos in sanctuaries as some critics suggest. Recall that Stephen Wise suggests placing the chimpanzees he rescues into sanctuaries, not zoos. Is this really always in the best interest of the animals? The author of this chapter who is a both a zoo director and a board member of one of the successful sanctuaries in the world provides us with the most comprehensive study of sanctuaries undertaken to date and shows that some of them are excellent institutions that afford the best care for animals and some are not. Sometimes sanctuaries, contrary to their names, are poorly funded, cramped institutions with at best volunteer labor to take care of the animals. They might be better than research labs, but they would be significantly worse for the animals than an expansive home at a zoo. The author of this chapter also focuses on another issue that is missed by advocates who suggest that sanctuaries should replace zoos, which is that there are too many animals in need of rescuing. There are thousands of nonhuman primates and large carnivores held as companion animals in the United States alone. In addition, most animal welfare advocates would like to see research animals placed in sanctuaries. As a result, there is no way that the small number of sanctuaries in the United States and the rest of the world could take in all animals in need of rescuing from private homes, exotic animal dealers, research labs, and zoos, even if they wanted to.

When we return then to the question of which kind of animal is better off, the tiger or the terrier, we suggest that the west highland terrier has the better life, but not because he has more space, can roam in a way that fits the physical requirement of his species, or can socialize with members of his own kind. He is better off because the law is increasingly on his side and because his life is recognized as worthwhile and defended by dog interest groups. He coexists in human society in a prominent way that suggests the path that zoo animals need to take. They need more rights both inside any captive animal facility and once they leave the bounds of the institutions and return to their home in what Irus Braverman calls the "managed wild."[22] Before we embark on the challenging task of thinking through how to increase justice for zoo animals and give them the same consideration that we are increasingly giving companion animals, it is worth noting that criticism that is fair and truthful is good for institutions. People and the institutions they work in can always improve. And it is to that effort that we turn now.

NOTES

1. I wish to thank Erik Trump for his thoughtful editorial suggestions for portions of this book.

2. For a brief description of the tigers see http://bronxzoo.com/updates/a-tale-of-two-tigers or http://bronxzoo.com/exhibits/tiger-mountain. Accessed August 12, 2016. For the petition see http://www.wcs.org/our-work. Accessed November 22, 2016.

3. We frequently use the word "zoo" to stand for both zoos and aquariums in this book.

4. David Favre, "Integrating Animal Interests into Our Legal System," *Animal Law*, 10 (2004): 87–97, 90–91.

5. For a discussion of how zoos became regulated by the AWA, see Jesse Donahue and Erik Trump, *The Politics of Zoos: Exotic Animals and And Their Protectors* (Dekalb: Univerisity of Illinois Press, 2006), 28–32. For a discussion of the Animal Welfare Act see the Department of Agriculture's web site https://www.nal.usda.gov/awic/animal-welfare-act. Accessed October 5, 2016.

6. For a discussion of the limits of the AWA, see Kali S. Grech, "Detailed Discussion of the Laws Affecting Zoos," at https://www.animallaw.info/article/detailed-discussion-laws-affecting-zoos. Accessed March 4, 2016. For a dicussion of how zoos could enhance animal welfare through the AWA, see James F. Gesualdi, *Excellence Beyond Compliance: Enhancing Animal Welfare Through the Constructive Use of the Animal Welfare Act* (Anna Maria, FL: Maurice Bassett Press, 2014).

7. See the Nonhuman Rights Project website at www.nonhumanrightsproject.org. Accessed April 3, 2016.

8. Steven Wise, "Rattling the Cage Defended," in *Boston College Law Review*, 43, 3 (2002): 623–96, 638–39.

9. Steven Wise, "Rattling the Cage Defended," 639.

10. For an example of this see Sue Donaldson and Will Kymlicka, *Zoopolis: A Political Theory of Animal Rights* (Oxford: Oxford University Press 2011). Despite the promise of the book's name the longest discussion of zoos occurs in a footnote in which the authors discuss the reproductive rights of zoo animals briefly, but provide no guidance of any kind for all of the other ethical and legal questions involving zoo animals. See page 283, note 45.

11. There are many important books on this topic. See for example, Peter Singer, *Animal Liberation* (New York: Harper Collins, 2002); Peter Singer, ed., *In Defense of Animals* (New York: Basil Blackwell 1985); Gail Eisnitz, *Slaughterhouse: The Shocking Story of Greed, Neglect, and Inhumane Treatment Inside the U.S. Meat Industry* (New York: Prometheus Press, 2007).

12. See the Friends of Animals website at http://friendsofanimals.org/node/6256. Accessed 3/27/15.

13. See the Friends of Animals website at http://friendsofanimals.org/node/6256. Accessed 3/27/15.

14. Dale Jamieson, "Against Zoos," in Peter Singer, ed., *In Defense of Animals* (New York: Basil Blackwell, 1985), 109, 111, 112, 115. For more recent academic and activist critiques of zoos see Ralph R. Acampora, ed., *Metamorphoses of the Zoo: Animal Encounter after Noah* (Lanham, MD: Lexington Books, 2010).

15. Interdepartmental Communication to MDL from Gary Clark, May 20, 1981. Gary Clark Archive, Saginaw Valley State University.

16. Interview with Don Moore, PhD, Animal Care Director for the Association of Zoos and Aquariums, May 20, 2015.

17. Dale Jamieson, "Against Zoos," 111–12.

18. Tim Zimmerman, "Don't Fence Me In: It's Time for Zoos to Close Their Doors Once and For All," *Out Door Magazine*, March 2015, 28.

19. Tim Zimmerman, "Don't Fence Me In: It's Time for Zoos to Close Their Doors Once and For All," *Out Door Magazine*, March 2015, 28. See Irus Braverman, *Wild Life: The Institution of Nature* (Stanford, CA: Stanford University Press, 2015).

20. For a visual image of some tiger sanctuaries that will illustrate the weakness of assuming that sanctuaries are always better than zoos see http://www.tigercreek.org/ or http://www.bigcat.org/.

21. These are more invasive studies and zoo veterinarians and directors should help minimize any pain or distress that accompanies this process. For a thoughtful discussion of the problems of these animal experiences see Mathew Chrulew, "Managing Love and Death at the Zoo: The Biopolitics of Endangered Species Preservation," in Deborah Bird Rose and Thom van Dooren, eds., "Unloved Others: Death and the Disregarded in a Time of Extinction," Special issue, *Australian Humanities Review* 50 (2011): 135–57.

22. Irus Braverman, *Wild Life: The Institution of Nature* (Stanford, CA: Stanford University Press, 2015).

BIBLIOGRAPHY

Acampora, Ralph R. Edited. *Metamorphoses of the Zoo: Animal Encounter After Noah* (Lanham, MD: Lexington Books, 2010).

Braverman, Irus. *Wild Life: The Institution of Nature* (Stanford, CA: Stanford University Press, 2015).

Chrulew, Mathew. "Managing Love and Death at the Zoo: The Biopolitics of Endangered Species Preservation," in Deborah Bird Rose and Thom van Dooren, eds., "Unloved Others: Death and the Disregarded in a Time of Extinction," Special issue, *Australian Humanities Review* 50 (2011): 135–57.

Donahue, Jesse and Erik Trump. *The Politics of Zoos: Exotic Animals and Their Protectors* (Dekalb: Univerisity of Illinois Press, 2006).

Donaldson, Sue and Will Kymlicka. *Zoopolis: A Political Theory of Animal Rights* (Oxford: Oxford University Press 2011).

Eisnitz, Gail. *Slaughterhouse: The Shocking Story of Greed, Neglect, and Inhumane Treatment Inside the U.S. Meat Industry* (New York: Prometheus Press, 2007).

Favre, David. "Integrating Animal Interests into Our Legal System," *Animal Law*, 10 (2004): 87, 87–97.

Gesualdi, James F. *Excellence Beyond Compliance: Enhancing Animal Welfare Through the Constructive Use of the Animal Welfare Act* (Anna Maria, FL: Maurice Bassett Press, 2014).

Grech, Kali S. "Detailed Discussion of the Laws Affecting Zoos," at https://www.animallaw.info/article/detailed-discussion-laws-affecting-zoos. Accessed August 16, 2016.

Jamieson, Dale. "Against Zoos," in Peter Singer, ed., *In Defense of Animals* (New York: Basil Blackwell, 1985).

Singer, Peter. *Animal Liberation* (New York: Harper Collins, 2002).

———, ed. *In Defense of Animals* (New York: Basil Blackwell 1985).

Wise, Steven. "Rattling the Cage Defended," *Boston College Law Review*, 43, 3 (2002): 623–96.

Zimmerman, Tim. "Don't Fence Me In: It's Time for Zoos to Close Their Doors Once and For All," *Out Door Magazine* (March 2015): 28.

ONE

Zoo Animal Citizens

Jesse Donahue

Marius, a healthy two-year-old reticulated giraffe at the Copenhagen Zoo who unfortunately did not have the right genetic makeup, was lured by zoo employees into a secluded area, anesthetized, and then shot in the head with a bolt gun. Once he was dead, Danish school children watched his dissection because zoo employees claimed that they would learn important educational lessons about the giraffe's body and about the cycle of life and death.

Is this what we owe giraffes in zoos? Or for that matter, what do we owe any animals in zoos? When zoo directors, curators, and keepers talk about animal welfare, they typically focus on the size of enclosures, enrichment programs, excellent veterinary attention, the ongoing professional training for zookeepers, and healthy nutrition for the animals. All of these are crucial issues, but they miss the important questions about Marius' fundamental rights. To state the painfully obvious, if Marius were human, this would never have happened, which suggests that we owe him a lot more than a few more acres of enclosed space. We owe him his life. But who is going to guarantee that in a world in which zoo animals have so few guaranteed rights? What would those rights look like and how can we understand them in the context of our own lives? Are zoo animals represented politically in any way? Should they be represented more than they currently are? What if we reimagined them as fellow citizens? How would that change their rights and obligations? What if we gave them the same rights as companion animals? These are the questions that this chapter examines.

Drawing primarily from recent scholarship by citizenship theorists and the legal rights of companion animals in the United States, I argue

1

that zoo animals are already fellow citizens who live interconnected lives with humans. As a result of making their lives vulnerable by placing them in zoos or aquariums, we have a range of legal responsibilities to them. As animals with a subjective sense of good and the ability to feel emotion, who are also entirely dependent upon humans, they should be included in our political system. To an important extent zoo animals already have political representation through animal welfare interest groups, attorneys, zoo employees, and federal agency workers. However, they could have significantly more legal rights if we rethought some fundamental ideas about who they are and where they belong in our community. To give them more rights, we need to consider renaming them.

THE POLITICS OF A NAME

The zoological profession calls zoo animals in its care "wildlife" or some-times "ambassadors." The San Diego Zoo (CA) describes itself as an "expansive wildlife sanctuary," the Wildlife Conservation Society (the Bronx Zoo) has a name that clearly states who it represents and its mission, and the Sacramento Zoo (CA) has an "ambassadors program" for animals who participate in wildlife stage shows and animal encounters.[1] Why do these institutions call their animals "wildlife" when they are not living in the wild? The answer is complex and has a long history that is worth thinking about because it has real political implications.

At the simplest level the zoological profession calls their animals wildlife partly from the clear and understandable recognition that most zoo animals (in raw numbers), are not tame. A tiger may spend its whole life in captivity, but still kill a human if it is provoked, as three young men learned when their friend was killed on Christmas in San Francisco in 2005.[2] Zookeepers can work with many animals to get them to move or sit for a veterinary exam, but untrained people would not be so success-ful. Thus, part of the explanation for why zoos stress the "wild" aspect of their animals' nature is for the safety of the visitors and workers. Many of the animals are not trained; some are only minimally taught to submit to human care for their health.

Zoos also emphasize the "wild" nature of their animals to increase their attraction to visitors at the same time that they discourage exotic pet ownership. Zoos are generally commercial institutions and need to at-tract visitors so that the institutions can afford to pay to keep the animals alive. The idea is to go on a trip and see a somewhat dangerous attrac-tion. "Wild" is synonymous with fun, unusual, and exciting. Zoos also emphasize the dangerous nature of some of their animals to discourage guests from creating their own wild animal menageries that they are not equipped to handle and removing endangered species from the wild for the pet trade. One of the Wildlife Conservation Society's projects, for example, includes increasing the wild numbers of two-foot eastern hell-bender salamanders native to Western New York because they are captured for pets. The Detroit Zoo reminds visitors to their website that "unfortunately millions of exotic animals become victims of the pet trade each year [because] well-meaning individuals often purchase the exotic animals with good intentions." Sadly, they note, this often results in a situation in which animals "suffer and many stories are reported about the dangerous and frequently deadly outcomes when people keep exotic animals as pets."[3] Zoos, clearly try to name the animals in their care differently from typical companion animals partly out of a well-meaning attempt to protect people and animals from encounters that they are not equipped to handle with their current level of education, training, and resources.

And finally zoo employees also stress the wild nature of their charges because of a clear political motive of species conservation. Beginning in the 1980s zoo employees began to consciously engage in deanthropomorphizing animals. Zoos animals were described as members of species not beloved pets. They could be interchanged with one another for breeding purposes if required for the good of the species. Accredited zoos in the United States and around the world participate in species preservation programs for endangered and threatened animals. Successful examples of animal reintroduction programs for endangered species include black-footed ferrets, California condors, freshwater mussels, golden lion tamarins, Oregon spotted frogs, red wolves, and wyoming toads, among others.[4] All of these animals were nearly decimated in the wild, but because of successful breeding programs by several zoos in the United States and cooperation with federal agencies, these animals now have sustainable populations in wild habitats. For this group of animals who have been returned to the wild, the term *wildlife* accurately captures their nature and their future place in the world.

Finally zoo animals are frequently called "ambassadors" for their species. They are political representatives designed to elicit good will for the animals zoos want protect. Sometimes these are animals that have no chance of reintroduction into the wild either because the animal is not endangered (and so is not placed in a conservation category), or because they are members of a group that is difficult to reintroduce for a variety of political reasons related to the geographical range that they inhabit. As a result, this is the name that gets closest to what they really are. They are not completely wild even though they have the genetic makeup of some wild animals. Many of them are not dangerous, and the reality is that zookeepers frequently develop kinship bonds with the animals analogous to the kind that family members have with pets.

To help ensure the most legal rights possible for zoo animals under American law, zoo animals need a name change that better reflects who they are. Zoo animals are really *wild public companion animals* rather than *wild animals*. The truth is that they are not completely wild animals. They have genetic material in common with wild animals, they may return to the wild at some point, but while they are living in our communities, housed by people, fed by people, and medicated by people, they are not wild.[5] They are not companion animals, however, belonging to a single individual. They are typically owned, for example, either by a private, nonprofit zoological society or a city government. An analogy that fits here is the name for feral cats given by IndyFeral, a group that spays and neuters feral cats in the Indianapolis area. Lisa Tudor, the founder of the organization calls these cats "community cats" because they do not reside in anyone's home. She does not call them "wild cats" because sometimes feral cats do make the transition from living on their own to living with people. Zoo animals are arguably less wild than feral cats, squirrels, chipmunks, and birds—the so-called liminal animals that live among us and benefit from our presence, but come and go as they please. Zoo animals, in contrast, are very definitely living with people and are members of our community.[6] Their designation as wild community companion animals should give them access to the limited rights that companion animals currently have under the law in the United States even if they are in reintroduction programs. Although they may return to the wild at some point, they are currently companion animals while they reside in the zoo.

Although zoo animals do not currently have the same legal rights afforded companion animals, they are represented politically by animal welfare groups, zoo professionals, and federal agency workers. These groups have represented zoo animals to varying degrees of success in the courts and in public agencies.

THE COURTS

Animal welfare groups have repeatedly represented zoo animals in court and typically lost the battle, but succeeded in bringing publicity to the situation. The vast majority of court cases have failed because attorneys have been unable to get legal standing for the plaintiffs. The legal challenges have typically focused on the major pieces of animal legislation that allow zoos to collect and exhibit animals.[7] Animal welfare groups have tried to use the courts in many ways to ensure the well-being of zoo animals. Groups like the Humane Society of the United States, and the Fund for Animals have brought a variety of court cases against zoos over the years, shedding light on the practices of zoos and testing the legal boundaries of the central pieces of legislation that govern zoo animals: The Animal Welfare Act (1966 amended to include exhibition animals in1970), the Endangered Species Act (1973), and the Marine Mammal Protection Act (1972).[8] Collectively these court cases have examined many zoo animal welfare questions, including the following: Do dolphins have legal standing? Can a zoo remove an elephant from its herd because it is dangerous to the others in its group? Can zoo employees euthanize animals if they feel it is necessary to do so? Can an aquarium take a small number of marine mammals from the wild? Is it harassing the marine mammals to take them? Can zoos move animals to other suitable institutions for breeding purposes? Can aquariums remove dolphins from the view of patrons who enjoy seeing them on display? The answer to these questions nearly every time has been "yes."[9] The only completely successful legal challenge to a zoo practice came from a case involving the inhumane treatment of nonhuman primates at the Long Island Game Park (a nonaccredited zoo), and involved the failure of the USDA to implement the enrichment and socialization requirements for nonhuman primates.[10]

So the question is, why have animal welfare groups failed to win legal battles most of the time? The answer is that every one of the major pieces of legislation governing zoo animals—the Animal Welfare Act, the Endangered Species Act, and the Marine Mammal Protection Act—protects zoos' rights to exhibit and acquire wild animals for educational reasons. And second, the courts have consistently ruled that animals are not people and thus they have no legal right of standing in the courts. So, zoo animal advocates who want more legal rights for them need to find another way to help these animals.[11]

This is similar to the central findings about legal rights for animals in other spheres. The fundamental problem well covered by other scholars is that courts have considered animals property and therefore denied them most human rights.[12] According to Steven Wise, an animal legal rights scholar, "generally all domestic animals are regarded as property, and an owner thereof has a property right therein as absolute as that in an inanimate object."[13] Given the American legal perspective that animals are property, judges at the federal level have consistently struck down the illegal right of standing, for example, concluding that this central right is designed only for humans, which makes it extremely difficult to use much of current law to help zoo animals. Legal scholars and advocates such as Steven Wise have argued, however, that animals should be legally entitled to bodily integrity and liberty. By this Wise means the "the general immunity from unconsented touchings" akin to what the US Supreme Court has referred to as "the right of every individual to the possession and control of his own person free from all restraint or interference by others, unless by clear and unquestionable authority of law . . . the right to be let alone." By liberty he means "the right to move about unless one is in danger to oneself and others, which would certainly be the case for chimpanzees or bonobos in the United States, but certainly not the case for, say, Atlantic bottlenose dolphins along America's East and Gulf coasts."[14] Where, then do we place the bonobos and the chimpanzees if they might do themselves or others harm? According to Wise, we should not place them in zoos. Wise was the attorney who represented Kama the dolphin against the New England Aquarium in the failed attempt to gain legal standing. Thus it is perhaps not surprising that he recommends against zoos or aquariums. Instead, he argues they "could be placed in sanctuaries in which they would have some reasonable degree of bodily liberty."[15] Thus, for Wise at least, wild captive animals would still be held in human-controlled communities, but would not be held at zoos or aquariums. However, he acknowledges that his attempt to secure animals these two fundamental rights could take years. We are left then with a central question: Is there any way to speed up the process of gaining legal rights for zoo animals? To answer that question it is helpful to use the ideas of citizenship theorists on companion and sovereign animals and apply them to zoo animals.

CITIZENSHIP THEORY AND ZOO ANIMALS

The illuminating quality of citizenship theory is that it draws from the history, politics, and legal theory of the civil rights and disabled rights movements. Arguably the most helpful parts of this literature for zoo animals involve using the lens of disabled rights advocacy, particularly for people who need collaborative help to function as citizens. Citizenship theorists urge us to rethink the underlying assumptions that all citizens are completely autonomous, highly verbal, self-sufficient, and cognizant of the implications of their political decisions. Imagine here a well-educated, completely verbal citizen going to the voting booth by herself and exercising one of her most important duties as a citizen, which is to vote. Their point is that not all citizens can do any of these things and yet they are represented by our political system. American citizens include a variety of people who cannot vote, sit on juries, run for office, or engage in a public debate even though they are citizens. So what is citizenship for these theorists?

According to citizenship theorists, at a minimum, all people who are born in the United States are citizens, regardless of whether they can participate fully yet in politics or whether they ever do so later in life. The underlying idea is that they are members of our community and as a result they have rights and responsibilities. While many people will engage in the political process in various ways, others will face significant barriers to full participation without outside assistance. People with serious mental disabilities, for example, are citizens, and the law seeks to protect them even though they often do not directly participate. At some point in our lives many of us need help to participate in politics because of, for example, an illness that prevents us from getting to the ballot box. Other people including, for example, the severely mentally disabled have preferences, but struggle to express them and will need help their whole lives participating in American life.

As a result, animal citizen theorists argue that we need new models for civic engagement for "noncommunicating citizens" that we can apply to both humans and nonhumans.[16] Although citizenship theorists ignore zoo animals focusing instead on domesticated, wild, and liminal animals, their ideas are useful for helping us think through how to increase rights for zoo animals. Animal citizenship theorists propose that having "brought such animals into our society, and deprived them of other possible forms of existence (at least in the foreseeable future), we have a duty to include them in our social and political arrangements on fair terms." Citizenship has three components, "residency (this is their home, they belong here), inclusion in the sovereign people (their interests count in determining the public good), agency (they should be able to shape the rules of cooperation)."[17]

When applying these ideas to the disabled, for example, citizenship theorists argue that severely disabled are citizens in that they are residents of a particular country and belong here. Like all people they have interests, but their desires are simply harder to know at first and they need help in expressing them. As a result they propose that we realize that we are interdependent as citizens and sometimes need assistance from another human to help us participate. They point, for example, to the physical assistance that some people need at the ballot box or the broader physical assistance that could be given if we paid more attention to the interests of the severely disabled. And the theorists note that the severely disabled have relational agency in the sense that they rely on collaborators (other people), who they trust to express their ideas of what is good and to help them participate as fully as possible in society. As two prominent animal citizenship theorists Sue Donaldson and Will Kymlicka argue "all of us need the help of others to articulate our subjective good; all of us need the help of supportive social structures to participate in schemes of social cooperation."[18] Applying these ideas to companion animals, they point out that dogs and cats live among us and are not going away anytime soon. We brought them into this world and therefore are responsible for them. The idea that we should simply stop breeding them clashes with their right to engage in reproduction as humans are allowed to, although both sides have the responsibility to not breed to such an extent that we overpopulate the world. We live interdependent lives in which both kinds of animals enrich one another to a great extent. Domesticated animals have clear subjective preferences and the theorists urge us to determine how we can use these desires to create laws that would suit animals better. Cities have created dog parks, for example, out of the clear recognition that many dogs thrive with social interaction of this kind. Humans are the collaborators who make the laws that either increase or decrease animal rights for domestic animals in our communities.

Citizenship theory applied to wild animals is much more limited in its scope. Here wild animal species are likened to sovereign or semi sovereign nations akin to nomadic people. Sovereign animal communities, like human groups, are characterized by their interests in autonomy, modes of self-organization, and self-regulation.[19] "What matters for sovereignty is the ability to respond to the challenges that a community faces, and to provide a social context in which its individual members can grow and flourish."[20] The theorists point to analogous human communities that lack legal institutions and sometimes even clear political boundaries, but instead are sometimes nomadic and indigenous. The general presumption is that we do not capture these people, imprison them, or harm them simply for our pleasure. Whenever possible we should help individuals in these communities flourish even if it means intervening in them as long as we do so in a way that helps that community succeed. We should also act as collaborators in political bodies to make sure that their rights are protected to the extent possible. And we should help refugees who are displaced and need our help.

How then, can we increase zoo animal rights given this model of animal citizenship for both domesticated and sovereign animals? Here again it is useful to separate zoo animals into those who are effectively companion animals and those who will be returned to the wild through reintroductions. Given the more limited nature of responsibilities to wild animals it is easier to start there.

When we apply the ideas of wild animal sovereignty to accredited zoos and aquariums in the United States we find a mixed picture in which these institutions do a fair amount for species preservation *in situ*, but still have the legal the ability to capture wild animals for purposes other than conservation. When it comes to supporting wildlife in their communities, accredited zoos and aquariums are actually doing about as much as they can in the area of wildlife rights. To the extent that they can, given their financial resources, they are working on *in situ* conservation — preserving the species in the wild rather than breeding them at home and then trying to return them to the wild. This is an efficient and humane approach to protecting the sovereign status of wildlife that fits nicely with the wishes of citizenship theory. The Wildlife Conservation Society (NY) with its budget of millions of dollars is working to preserve over 350 species around the world. The Houston Zoo (TX) has worked with conservation groups in Mozambique and increased the number of lions to over 300. And their financial support to gorilla conservation groups in Rwanda has substantially increased the number of those animals. SeaWorld, has a significant conservation record both for funding projects *in situ* and for various kinds of rescue, rehabilitation, and release work.

Zoos with more limited resources like the Boise Zoo (ID) give less for conservation as one would expect given their overall revenue.[21]

While the large zoos devote a significant amount of money to saving species in their natural habitat, they still possess the legal right to capture them for exhibition for educational purposes. Citizenship theory and the current trajectory of the personhood movement for animal rights suggests that this right under the US Animal Welfare Act and the Marine Mammal Protection Act should be amended so that zoos and aquariums are only allowed to capture animals from the wild for the purpose of conservation of the species. And, the animals should have some reasonable chance of being returned to their former home communities if the place from which they were taken is a safe place where they will thrive. Or, they can be captured if they can be relocated to another equally safe environment and will thrive. Currently the ORCA Responsibility and Care Advancement Act introduced by Representative Adam Schiff (D-CA), better known as the ORCA Act, captures this goal of preventing aquariums from collecting killer whales for the purpose of educational display.[22] The problem with this approach, however, is that it focuses on one animal at a time, rather than focusing on the larger goal of ending the capture of all wild animals simply for public display. The goal of zoos and aquariums, according to citizenship theory and the personhood movement, ought to be primarily for the benefit the animals and in that way conservation should be the first priority of *any* captive animal holding facility. That does not necessarily preclude humans visiting the animals who are refugees in those centers. In fact, if they are healthy we can welcome and visit them just as we would welcome any human refugees. It does mean, however, that they should only be captured if it helps them. Sometimes capturing them for breeding purposes for reintroductions is the best way to preserve them.[23]

Reintroductions at zoos are much more limited in number for complicated reasons. Zoos lack the physical might of either a country or a state. It is not an accident that political bodies in the United States such as the Department of Interior and their parallel fish and wildlife regulatory agencies in states are reintroducing apex predators like wolves. Zoos do not have the physical power to stop citizens from hunting animals they perceive as dangerous. They have no legal authority to do so. Federal agencies, in contrast, lack the money to reintroduce all zoo animals into the wild. As a result, in the past, the two organizations have partnered together to reintroduce animals as they did in the case of the red wolf. Because of their limited human enforcement power, zoo employees have primarily reintroduced the types of small animals that citizenship theorists describe as well including, for example, condors, ferrets, mussels, and frogs reintroduced by the San Diego, Smithsonian, Cheyenne, Columbus, and Oregon Zoos.[24] In addition to reintroducing small animals, accredited zoos in the United States capture only a very small number of

wild animals. Like dogs and cats that are bred for human companionship, most animals in zoos are bred at zoos for other zoos or for reintroductions. Thus, preventing zoos from capturing animals in the wild with
the small exception of necessary breeding conservation programs should
not be a hardship.

In rare instances zoos take in animals that are injured and not return-
able to the wild or are exotic pets that have nowhere to go. From the
perspective of citizenship theorists these animal are refugees in the classic sense. Accordingly we have "a duty to welcome them as citizens of
our community." Indeed we need to "shift from seeing them as members
of a separate and autonomous community (or nation) pursuing their own
destiny, to being co-members, or citizens of our community, cooperating
in our new shared destiny."[25] This is exactly what zoos have done in the
past and continue to do today, although they too actively discourage the
exotic pet trade. For example, the Detroit Zoo provides refuge for a lion
used as a "guard dog" for a crack house and the Los Angeles Zoo had
many parrots it rescued from the pet trade at the request of the Los
Angeles police department.[26] Accredited zoos in the United States are
treating wild animals as sovereign citizens and trying to protect their
communities around the world. They are trying to increase their numbers
to sustainable levels in their habitats so that their populations can thrive
because they feel that they have a responsibility as co-citizens of the
world to help these animals. And when they have the space they serve as
a refugee center for wild animals saved from the pet trade.

But what about the many animals who are members of long-term
breeding programs and therefore will never be reintroduced into the
wild in their lifetime? Similarly, what should zoos do with animals who
they may never be able to reintroduce because the political realities are so
difficult for private organizations like zoos? How do we increase the
rights of these animals? What are their rights? The answer is to treat them
as analogous to companion animals and give them the same rights and
responsibilities depending upon their type and our increasing knowledge about their capabilities and needs.[27]

At the highest political level zoo animals deserve representation in
governing bodies like other citizens. This is a frequently discussed suggestion in the field of animal welfare, although it is typically applied
primarily to companion animals.[28] Representation could take the form of
either new political offices that report to local governing bodies like the
Greater Glen Valley neighborhood's Director of Animal Welfare in Los
Angeles. These are individuals who provide a voice for animals in policy-
making bodies. Or it can take the form of political party representation as
it has for small parties in Europe like the Dutch party for animals created
in 2002 that has an explicit platform of placing animal welfare on the
human agenda. Or it could be a federal regulatory agency or quasi-
governmental governing body as it almost did for zoo animals in the

United States when William Whitehurst (R-VA) and Senator Mark Hatfield (R-OR) introduced the "Federal Assistance for Zoos and Aquariums bills (HR 1266 and S 2042) in 1973 that would have created a government corporation controlled by a board with the authority to draft mandatory accrediting standards for all zoos and aquariums. A federal agency like the one proposed by Whitehurst and Hatfield would best represent the interests of our co-citizens in aquariums and should be pushed by both the AZA and animal welfare interest groups.

Because a federal regulatory agency just for zoos was never created, these animals are represented primarily through the private interests of the AZA, zoological societies, or animal welfare groups. Although generally well-meaning, none of these kinds of organizations are completely focused on the animals themselves. Animal welfare organizations come and go, their agendas shift with the interests of their donors, and they often have a broad array of issues that they work on including factory farming and animal research. The AZA represents zoo animals, but they also represent the interests of their human members as they must, given that they are primarily an industry organization. Zoological societies, like other community citizen groups, wax and wane with the particular energy and interests of their current members. At the moment, however, these are the primary groups that represent our co-citizens in zoos and it looks like they will continue to do so in the near future. So what, exactly could they do to maintain and hopefully increase equality, justice, and compassion on the ark for the wild public companion animals at zoos and aquariums who are unlikely to ever return to the wild? Why should zoo animals who are not going to be reintroduced into the wild be allowed to exist at all?

These animals are here and vulnerable because of us. As a result we owe them various rights as co-citizens in our community. It is certainly understandable to feel that exotic captive animals, like companion animals, should never have been brought into our lives. However, that does not tell us what we should do now that they are here. At this point we have an obligation to move forward and ask what is the best for the animals that currently depend on us. We have a moral responsibility to make those animals' lives fulfilling while they reside among us by focusing on their particular type of citizenship.

Citizenship theory suggests that zoo animals have every right to remain in zoos, sanctuaries, sea pens, or any other exotic captive animal home that treats them well rather than being slowly killed off through old age, a refusal to replace them, or by forced reintroductions that might harm them. Just as some anti-slavery advocates wanted to return all blacks to Africa rather than help them move forward in an equal and engaged way in this country, zoo animals deserve the recognition that we placed them in these institutions many years ago and now we have the responsibility to make their lives as meaningful and equal as possible within our current shared community. Saying that zoos in the past captured wild animals does not mean that the animals that they currently have were captured in the wild. In fact, they were bred, much like the companion animals that we own in our home and therefore we have some significant responsibilities for them.

One such responsibility is to keep them safe and this, at a minimum, requires restricting their movement to varying degrees. All of us, human and nonhuman animals, have our movement limited to some extent. People who fail driving tests are legally prohibited from driving, those with extremely communicable tuberculosis are not allowed to leave a small geographic area, pregnant women are strongly discouraged from flying late in pregnancy, most parents allow very limited movement for their children, and most dogs are restricted to yards that are smaller than many wolf exhibits in zoos, even though they share the same ancestors, and if given the chance, many dogs will roam for long distances. Indeed space reduction is increasingly the norm for all humans as we are abandoning the countryside at high rates globally to live in much smaller spaces in cities. What is important for all animals is that we have "enough mobility to be able to lead our lives, make a living, socialize, learn, grow, and have fun—but assuming this scope of mobility is in place we do not have a right to go anywhere were want, or to move anywhere we want."[29]

Although space can be limited it is also true that invisibility and special segregation are signs of inequality. Disabled children in the United States were invisible because schools were not required to provide any services to include them and in this way they lived unequal lives. Racial segregation in the Jim Crow south legalized invisibility in different neighborhoods. In contrast, citizens are reintegrating farm animals into human communities by bringing back animals like chicken and pigs to suburban neighborhoods by fighting against laws that banished them to the countryside. The French bring small dogs to restaurants and yet dogs are banned for health code reasons in the United States, even though there is no real evidence that well-behaved dogs provide any health threats. (In fact, there is some good evidence to the contrary.) Zoo animals deserve the same kind of reintegration into our communities to the extent that this is possible for safety reasons. Simply being present equally within a community is a sign of political participation.

For zoo animals this means that they have a right to have as much interaction with humans as possible. Zoo employees, however, have some thorny issues to deal with if they end the general practice of keeping us all separate from one another. Zoos abandoned lots of human and animal interaction for a couple of reasons. First, they realized that there are some significant transmissible diseases from some zoo animals. Some kinds of monkeys, for example, can transmit tuberculosis. Second, there are some animals who are too dangerous to allow humans unrestricted interaction. Polar bears, for example, should not be around people without some kind of sturdy barrier. And third, a small percentage of people hurt the animals so zoo employees aim to protect them from a violent minority. Protection from people is one of the central responsibilities that we owe these animals. The central question for zoo employees then, is how much can zoos increase contact between their residents and guests? To a limited extent zoos bring animals out into the community through educational outreach programs. But citizenship theory suggests that more zoo animals should be out of their enclosures and cages much more of the time. This would return the zoological world to a much older style of animal welfare in which zookeepers used to walk big cats around the zoo for exercise and human interaction, children were allowed to ride zebras, hippos, and Galapagos turtles, and animal nurseries accessible to visitors stressed the importance of human touch.[30] The animals' space was not as geographically segregated. They built community with humans as they physically interacted with guests. Zoos should consider returning to this previous approach in a modified way by initially undertaking many more human animal interaction studies to determine the extent to which we can interact with one another safely in our shared community. Like any studies, humans should be fully informed of the risks and participate voluntarily in control situations that can be quickly remedied. Although animals are unable to give their verbal consent, zookeepers can tell which animals thrive on interaction with people and which ones prefer to be left alone. As with studies involving children, zookeepers, and curators would act in the interests of these nonhuman animals protecting them from any harm.

As zoo employees would likely respond, however, some human-animal interaction is dangerous for the animals. Given that we live in an interdependent community with zoo animals in which they work and live with us, we have a responsibility to both prevent harm done to them and to also punish injustice to a greater extent than we currently do. Just as there are a disturbing number of humans who physically abuse animals in their homes, a small percentage of zoo visitors do the same there. In the 1950s and 1970s a group of youths at the Detroit Zoo stoned trout to death and harassed a mother polar bear so much that she killed her cub.[31] Because of these kinds of incidents, interactive experiences with zoo animals even in petting zoos are often monitored by zoo employees because of the danger to the animals by the humans. One answer is to close zoos on the argument that because a small percentage of zoo visitors cannot be trusted then we all need to give up on our interdependent relationship with animals, release them all into the wild, or send them all into sanctuaries to die of old age away from people. This is a sad commentary on our promise as humans, and one that is certainly an understandable reaction of researchers who have spent time looking at the vast atrocities committed by humans against animals in other spheres of our lives including meatpacking plants and many animal research institutions. But the reality is that the majority of zoo visitors are not engaging in any kind of violent behavior against zoo animals. Similarly, it would make no sense to say that because some people commit violent crimes in human communities we ought to give up living with one another entirely. The answer is to criminalize violence against zoo animals to the same extent that we criminalize violence against people and increasingly against companion animals. Most states now have felony provisions for aggravated acts of cruelty for companion animals, but the provisions sometimes exclude zoo animals. At a minimum states could follow the lead of California that made it a misdemeanor for any owner or manager of an elephant to engage in abusive behavior toward an elephant.[32] Similarly the AZA and animal welfare groups should push to have punitive economic damages awarded when people intentionally hurt zoo animals. Several states including New York, New Jersey, and Hawaii are considering these awards for companion animals so it seems reasonable to extend them to zoo animals, particularly when they are sometimes literally almost priceless animals in their rarity.[33] In this way we would create justice for the animals at these institutions and foster a sense of equality at the same time. Here again we need lobbying by the AZA, animal rights groups, supportive citizens, and legislators to change the law by increasing the penalties associated with violence against zoo animals.

This includes increasing the penalties for trespassing in animals' homes. Why should a tiger pay a penalty when a trespasser invades his home or harasses him as was the case with the San Francisco tiger who was euthanized for attacking young men who harassed it in San Francisco in December 2005? The Cincinnati Zoo (OH) reacted to the sad case of a child who climbed into a gorilla enclosure by killing the gorilla. Zoos around the United States also immediately spent large sums of money to refortify their barriers, as they should have. The public, however, was significantly less sympathetic to the parents because they recognized that the incident could have been prevented if the child had not trespassed on the gorilla's home. Stronger trespassing laws that penalized parents for the behavior of their children or adults who trespassed on these animals homes should be considered. These kinds of measures should decrease the violence that zoo animals face, free employees to work at other tasks, and allow citizens who are nonviolent to enjoy the rich interdependent world that the companionship of wild captive animals affords.

In addition to increasing safe physical interaction with humans, the citizenship theory approach suggests that zoo animals should be given as much choice as possible in a variety of dimensions of their lives. Do they prefer one kind of food over another? Where do they like to sleep? How do they have fun? Here again, zookeepers, curators, and directors make a point of learning about all of this, but sometimes withhold this information from visitors because of the relentless effort to try and educate guests about the entire species.

Why do they have to focus so much on education? Zoos have to serve as educational institutions because of the US legal precedent from the court case *Guzzi v. New York Zoological Society* (1920). This was a case that tested whether zoos could exhibit dangerous animals. In this case a twelve-year-old girl named Blanche Guzzi played ball near a bear cage at the Bronx Zoo. The ball rolled into the bear's home, Guzzi went to retrieve it and in the process the bear reached over and tore part of her scalp. Guzzi's father sued the Society arguing that the bear was a nuisance. The appellate court disagreed and concluded that the zoo could house the bear because it was a public institution created to educate people about animals.[34] Successive legislation aimed at zoos has protected these institutions based on these two pillars: they are public and educational. Zoo directors and the AZA therefore consistently stress the fundamental educational mission of their institution, while zoo critics accuse them of failing to educate guests as much as a nature show would have done.[35] The whole debate could be put to rest, however, if the fundamental legal purpose of zoos was shifted to conservation, rather than education, and required by the legal statutes that govern them.

Preserving animals through conservation, however, requires breeding programs and these kinds of programs are physically invasive.[36] Citizenship theory then, suggests, that the animals involved should have as much choice as possible. Increasing choice and, and equally importantly, publicizing it better has significant implications for species breeding programs; one of the prized and centrally important parts of the zoological world. Beginning in the 1980s the AZA pushed members to participate in Species Survival Plans (SSPs) to breed animals for zoos and to help preserve animals in the wild. The plans often involve intervening in animal relationships to move them around to the most suitable mate for reproductive reasons. The case of Timmy, a lowland Gorilla from the Cleveland Zoo, illustrates the complexity of this issue.[37] Timmy was isolated cruelly for many years by the Cleveland Zoo before they finally paired him with a female gorilla named Katie. The two gorillas formed a close and loving relationship, but unfortunately Katie turned out to be sterile. In the interest of species preservation, however, Timmy was moved to the Bronx Zoo where he successfully, and happily, mated with several female gorillas and flourished. Katie, however, fared very poorly with her new companion Oscar, biting her foot so badly that one of her toes had to be removed. Dr. Elliot Katz, president of the animal welfare group In Defense of Animals, threatened to sue, prompting the Cleveland Zoo to separate the gorillas. So the question is, how could all of this have been handled better by paying attention to the interests of the animals?[38] The Cleveland Zoo initially consulted Diane Fossey who recommended keeping Timmy and Katie together. This perspective focuses entirely on the happiness of Katie and Timmy and excludes the right of procreation that we give humans. A more encompassing and citizen-based approach might have been to send Timmy to the Bronx Zoo for a short time to reproduce and then reunite Timmy and Katie once that he had successfully conceived. Or a third option would have been to bring both Katie and Timmy to the Bronx Zoo, allow Timmy to conceive and remain with his offspring in a fulfilling family community at the same time that he kept his relationship with Katie. This example illustrates the difficult balance that zoos frequently face in harmonizing the welfare and enjoyment of the individual animals with the good of the species. And it suggests that zoos should place the welfare of the individual animal ahead of the good of the species. Currently zoos try and balance both, but citizenship theory suggests that attention to the individual animal should take precedence given that they are effectively companion animals while in the zoo.

The example of Timothy and Katie illustrates another way to improve justice on the ark and that is in the area of labor rights. An ambassador is an actual occupation that gets paid. If zoo animals are ambassadors then they are on the job. If they are at work, then they ought to be compensated and protected from labor abuses. And all of this should be conveyed to visitors so that they understand that zoos are not just using animals and giving nothing back. Humans use one another all of the time, but we expect reciprocity of some kind. If we have companion animals we expect that our affections are repaid by their affections. The reality is that our dogs are typically not earning money for us unless they have jobs, in which case animal citizenship theory suggests that their labor is sometimes exploited. Here they point to therapy dogs that are trained relentlessly for the benefit of humans. Animal rights critics of zoos are fond of pointing out that many zoos are commercial institutions implying that they are inherently exploitative and they use animals to gain revenue. And zoo supporters, in turn, note that that much of their revenue comes from gift shop and restaurant sales. It is certainly true that zoos rely on gift shop sales and food service revenue to keep their institutions financially sound, but the reality is that the whole place would not exist without the draw of the animals. Zoo designers, zookeepers, curators, and directors recognize that the animals work for them to the extent that they sometimes have places for animals to disappear from view and they close in the evenings allowing animals "time off." The extent to which an animal needs time off sometimes varies by how much it interacts with people and the degree to which it enjoys this process. An animal such as a newt that seems basically unaware of visitors peering into its micro world is probably less impacted by people than say any of the great apes who are clearly aware of visitors and sometimes interact with them. It would be more just to allow them significant time off if interaction with humans caused them any stress at all in their day-to-day job. Employees at several zoos in the United States and elsewhere have studied how and when visitors cause stress to animals when they visit their homes in zoos. But there is currently no legal requirement or even consistent guidelines from the AZA that mandates time off for all animals.[39]

In addition to time off zoo animals should receive financial compensation in the form of animal trusts. Here again we should use the precedent set by companion animals. Until 1990, family pets faced the prospect of sad lives or deaths if their owners died or were incapacitated. Upon the owner's death, animals with nowhere else to go were typically given by the family to the local animal shelter that sometimes sold them to research facilities or euthanized them. For many years people tried to find legally binding ways to protect their pets once they died, but courts dismissed their attempts at helping their pets for a variety of reasons. Sometimes courts held that because pets are classified as property they could not be given direct gifts. Animals were treated here as inanimate property. (For example, we cannot give a car a chair.) Others courts concluded that gifts to animals in general, such as gift to the Humane Society, were legitimate, but gifts to a particular animal were illegitimate. In 1990, the National Conference of Commissioners on Uniform State Laws changed the Uniform Probate Code to permit pet trusts. As amended in 1993 the section states "a trust for a designated domestic pet animal is valid." But it was amended in 2000 and removed the words "domestic pet" to read "A trust may be created to provide for the care of an animal alive during the settlor's lifetime."[40]

Currently forty-six states have animal trust laws that allow owners to take care of animals typically until they die, and trusts can also be set up that allow the offspring of the animal to continue to benefit. The animal rescue world and attorneys refer to these as "pet trusts" largely because they spend most of their time working for companion animal owners rather than exotic animal owners but currently some of the laws are written to protect any animal.[41] Ten of the forty states that have trusts (Colorado, Hawaii, Illinois, Montana, New Jersey, New York, North Carolina, Oklahoma, and Utah) specify that the animals have to be domesticated or pet animals. The rest of the states have language that could be used for captive exotic animals as well. For example, Arizona's so-called pet trust law has language that says a "trust may be created for the care of an animal or animals alive during the settlor's lifetime. The trust terminates upon the death of the animal, or upon the death of the last surviving animal covered by the trust."[42]

These trust laws that cover animals in general could apply to zoos and aquarium animals and the AZA and individual zoos ought to adopt this as a requirement for every animal to reassure the public of their commitment to animal welfare. Each animal that comes into the zoo should have a written animal trust guaranteeing a high quality of lifetime care until the animal dies. The positive work that good animal welfare advocates at zoos do for animals would be highlighted in these documents including lifetime veterinary care, enrichment, high-quality food, the best possible homes within the zoo, and so on. Each zoo animal's trust should be accessible to the public so that they could see exactly where the animal was going to spend the rest of its life and what kinds of provisions are made for its future care should the zoo suddenly face a financial crisis or natural disaster along the lines of Hurricane Katrina. If a zoo ran out of money for the day-to-day care of the animals it could rely on its wild companion animal trust funds to send the animals out in family groups to either other zoos or sanctuaries. These are the kinds of guarantees that would go a long way toward allaying concerns about animal welfare at zoos. It would also completely end the accusations that sometimes zoo animals become "surplus" animals that disappear in the night.[43] The public could trace the animals and follow them, and certainly have a lively debate about when animals should get to retire.

Another possibility that trusts raise is that animals will have their own pool of money and could be sued. Humans have both rights and responsibilities in the legal system. Currently zoo animals have no responsibilities, but they do harm people from time to time. When dogs bite people today and are caught they are often euthanized as a punishment and, if the family is insured, sometimes the victim gets insurance money. The same kind of pool of money could be available for victims of zoo animal attacks that were entirely unprovoked by humans.

Although trusts would take care of many of the financial pitfalls of elderly animals in zoos, they will not cure all problems of old age. Inevitably zoos face end of life decisions for their animals as millions of Americans do with their companion animals. Just like companion animals, zoo and aquarium animals should have the right to die without undue interference by people who do not own or look out for the animals. American zoos have faced this issue in the courts before in the case involving the Detroit Zoo's siberian tigers in the 1980s.[44] In this case a citizen from Detroit, assisted by the Fund for Animals, filed a suit against the Detroit Zoo to stop them from euthanizing three tigers, two of whom where elderly and ill. Kresentia Doppleberger, the person who brought the case argued that she had a right to stop the Detroit Zoo because she was a citizen of Detroit and thus she should have a "say" in that decision. For companion animals in private homes euthanasia is acceptable when animals are so ill that their quality of life is severely diminished or when animals are violent to others in their community, particularly humans. Similarly, when zoo employees make euthanasia decisions for reasons of serious illness they should feel that they have exercised their civic and moral responsibilities to these animals, just as everyday citizens should feel comfortable euthanizing their very ill companion animal or one that poses a danger to others. Euthanizing young healthy animals who are offered other homes, however, is not a morally appropriate act for either companion or zoo animals. Marius' story, from the introduction, clearly illustrates this problem.

Like the situation in Detroit, where citizens asked important questions about the need to euthanize the tigers, the Copehagen Zoo also faced substantial criticism from people about their decision to euthanize Marius. Concerned citizens in Denmark and elsewhere wanted to know why Marius' parents were bred at all given that the zoo did not have a guaranteed place for him? They wanted to know why the zoo did not give him away to those who offered him a place to live? And why the Copenhagen Zoo felt that it had no responsibility to the animal after they used him to bring in money when he was smaller and cuter?[45] Bengt Holst, the zoo's Scientific Director, argued that that they had to kill Marius because he was "part of international breeding program whose bylaws prohibit the inbreeding in an effort to maintain the health of the stock." Because Marius' genes were overrepresented, this meant that they felt that he should be killed. Holst rejected the idea of neutering Marius because oral contraceptives can cause renal failure and neutering would have diminished "his quality of life" because "breeding and parenting are especially important behaviors for a giraffe's well-being."[46]

The series of bad decisions are clear when seen through the lens of citizenship theory. First, the zoo brought Marius into the world so they had a significant responsibility for his health and well-being. They should have allowed his parents to breed only if they had space for another animal or were willing to find space for a family unit elsewhere if breeding is such an important part of this animal's subjective sense of good. They used him to bring in revenue and did not protect him with any of the kinds fundamental bodily integrity laws or labor laws that would apply to humans. They applied a reduced set of legal rights for Marius that would never have been considered for a human or even, increasingly, a companion animal. Can we imagine a zoo bringing a companion animal like a dog into their gates, killing it, and then dissecting it for young visitors? It was, in short, a very sad case study of the ways in which scientific concerns and rhetoric about wild species took precedence over justice for this individual animal.

In an ideal world all exotic animals would have their own large homes in which they choose to engage with us or not, much like the liminal animals such as bird or fish who live among us. But we do not live in that world. We live in a world that our ancestors bequeathed to us and it includes exotic captive animals. Although the legal attempt to give personhood status to nonhuman primates is a fascinating goal, the major advocate and implementer of the strategy, Steven Wise, acknowledges that it could take a long time to find the right judge willing to come to the conclusion that animals deserve personhood status. And even if that happens, there remain questions about which animals will be given this status. Wise may want personhood conferred on all animals, but if legal precedent is any guide, it seems more likely that the courts are likely to confer that status just on the great apes as they have done in Spain for example, rather than all animals. In the meantime, companion animals are already attaining citizenship and representation in the courts while zoo and aquarium animals are losing out on this legal revolution. As a result, the most practical legal strategy for increasing animal welfare for all zoo animals is to afford them the same rights as companion animals and treat them as co-citizens. Although these ideas will likely meet with complaints that they are too expensive and impractical, they would certainly go a long way to ensuring greater justice for these animals.[47]

NOTES

1. For the San Diego Zoo see http://sandiegozoo104.reachlocal.net/content/about-san-diego-zoo. For the Sacramento Zoo see http://www.saczoo.org/Page.aspx?pid=322.

2. Patricia Yollin, Tanya Schevitz, and Kevin Fagan, "S.F. Zoo Visitor Saw Two Victims of Tiger Attack Teasing Lions," *SF Gate*, January 3, 2008. http://www.sfgate.com/news/article/S-F-Zoo-visitor-saw-2-victims-of-tiger-attack-3233323.php. Accessed May 7, 2015.

3. Wildlife Conservation Society Annual Report, 2011, page 17, http://www.wcs.org/files/pdfs/wcs-2011-annual-report.pdf. Accessed July 6, 2016. The Detroit Zoo places their exotic pet warnings in the Humane Education section of their web site, which can be accessed at http://detroitzoo.org/Education/why-is-humane-education-important?highlight=WyJleG90aWMiLCJl>eG90aWNzIiwicGV0cyIsInBldCIsIidwZXRRzJyIsInBldHRlZCIsImV4b3RpYyBwZXRRzIl0.

4. See the AZA for this information at https://www.aza.org/reintroduction-programs/.

5. For a good discussion about the varying opinions on this see Irus Braverman, *Zooland* (Stanford, CA: Stanford University Press, 2013), 57–62.

6. For the story of IndyFeral see David Grimm, *Citizen Canine* (New York: Public Affairs, 2014), 266, 264–68.

7. For an example of a classic full-length examination of animal legal rights see Steven Wise, "Legal Thinghood." *Boston College Environmental Affairs Law Review*, Vol. 23, Issue 3, Article 2 (1996): 471–546.

8. The welfare of zoo animals is minimally covered by the Animal Welfare Act, 7 U.S.C Section 2132 (g). It prescribes minimum standards for "handling, housing, feeding, watering, sanitation, shelter from extremes of weather and temperatures, and adequate veterinary care in section 2143 (a)(2(a). For a brief discussion of the AWA see Bruce A. Wagman, Sonia S. Waisman, and Pamela D. Frash, *Animal Law*, 4th Edition (Durham: Carolina Academic Press, 2010) 534. For a general overview of the laws that currently affect zoos see Kali S. Grech, "Brief Summary of Laws Affecting Zoos." https://www.animallaw.info/intro/laws-affecting-zoos (2004). Or Kali S. Grech, https://www.animallaw.info/article/detailed-discussion-laws-affecting-zoos (2004). Accessed July 18, 2016. The Convention on the International Trade of Flora and Fauna (CITES) also governs US zoos, although to a lesser extent.

9. The court cases that tested these questions are as follows: *Animal Protection Institute of American v. Robert Mosbacher*, 799 F. Supp. 173 (U.S. Dis. 1992); *Citizens to End Animal Suffering and Exploitation, Inc. v. The New England Aquarium*, 836 F. Supp 45 (U.S. Dist. 1993); *In Defense of Animals v. Cleveland Metroparks Zoo*, 785 F. Supp. 100 (U.S. Dist. 1991); *Kresentia M. Doppleberger and Fund for Animals v. City of Detroit, the Detroit Zoological Society and Steve Graham* (Wayne County Circuit Court, no.

82–234592–cz. 1982); *The Humane Society of the United States v. Bruce Babbit*, 310, 228; 46 F.3d 93 (U.S. App. D.C. 1995); *Tim Jones v. William G. Gorden*, 792 F.2d 821 (US App. 1986); *World Wildlife Fund v. Donald P. Hodel*, 1988 (U.S. Dist. 1988);

10. See the *Animal Legal Defense Fund v. Daniel Glickman*, 943 F. Supp. 44 (U.S. Dist. 1996).

11. There are some other internal ways that zoos could help animals as well. See James F. Gesualdi, *Excellence Beyond Compliance: Enhancing Animal Welfare Through the Constructive Use of the Animal Welfare Act* (Anna Maria, FL: Maurice Bassett, 2014).

12. See for example Gary Francione, *Animals, Politics, and the Law* (Philadelphia: Temple University Press, 1995).

13. Steven Wise quoting 3A C.J.S, Animals, at 475 (1973) in Walter B. Rausenbush, *The Law of Personal Property* (Ray Edwards Brown 13 Edition, 1975), in "Legal Thinghood" *Boston College Environmental Affairs Law*, Review Vol. 23, Issue 3, Article 2 (1996): 471–546, 538.

14. Steven Wise, "Rattling the Cage Defended," *Boston College Law Review*, 43, 3 (2002): 623–96, 638–39.

15. Steven Wise, "Rattling the Cage Defended," 639.

16. Sophia Isako Wong, "Duties of Justice to Citizens with Cognitive Disabilities," *Metaphilosophy*, 40/3–4 (2009): 382–401. Quoted in Sue Donaldson and Will Kymlicka, *Zoopolis: A Political Theory of Animal Rights* (Oxford: Oxford University Press, 2011), 59.

17. Sue Donaldson and Will Kymlicka, *Zoopolis: A Political Theory of Animal Rights* (Oxford: Oxford University Press, 2011), 101.

18. Ibid., 107.

19. Ibid., 173.

20. Ibid., 175.

21. For the Wildlife Conservation Society work see http://www.wcs.org/saving-wildlife.aspx. Accessed May 15, 2015. For the Houston Zoo see http://www.houstonzoo.org/protect-animals/global-conservation/. Accessed May 15, 2015. For Sea World see their annual conservation reports at https://swbg-conservationfund.org/en/what-weve-done/annual-reports. Accessed May 16, 2015. The Boise Zoo gave $200,000 in 2014 for 8 projects in 2014. Four of these were for animal restoration and two were for human development needs. For the Boise Zoo see http://www.zooboise.org/zbcfprojects.aspx. Accessed May 16, 2016.

22. William Conway, the former director of the Wildlife Conservation Society suggested that zoos should also buy up large tracts of land to protect animals *in situ*. Unlike with humans we can buy animals' countries. This is an excellent suggestion and one hopes this will happen more frequently than it does. See "Entering the 21st Century," in Alexandra Zimmerman, Matthew Hatchwell, Lesli A. Dicki, and Christ West, eds., *Zoos in the 21st Century: A Catalyst for Conservation* (Cambridge: Cambridge University Press, 2015), 12–21. For a description of the ORCA act see http://schiff.house.gov/news/press-releases/rep-schiff-to-introduce-orca-act-to-phase-out-display-of-captive-killer-whales. Accessed July 13, 2016.

23. For a description of how animals move back and forth between zoos and federal agency breeding facilities and the wild see Irus Braverman's *Zooland* (Stanford, CA: Stanford University Press, 2013).

24. For example, Donaldson and Kymlicka praise the work of Joe Hutto who raises turkeys to live in the wild. This is precisely the kind of smaller animal that zoos reintroduce as well. See Sue Donaldson and Will Kymlicka (2011), 185, for a discussion of turkey reintroduction. For examples of wild animal reintroductions by zoos in partnership with federal agencies see: https://www.aza.org/reintroduction-programs/. Accessed April 5, 2015. For an example of the difficulties of reintroducing animals see Dalia A. Conde, Nate Flesness, Fernando Colchero, Own R. Jones, and Alexander Scheuerlein, "An Emerging Role of to Conserve Biodiversity," *Science* 331, no. 6023 (2011): 1290–91.

25. Donaldson and Kymlicka, 204.

26. For the history of these rescues see Jesse Donahue and Erik Trump, *The Politics of Zoos: Exotic Animals and Their Protectors* (Dekalb: Nothern Illinois University Press, 2006) 58, 85.

27. For a different perspectives on this see Ralph R. Acampora, ed., *Metamorphoses of the Zoo: Animal Encounter After Noah* (Lanham, MD: Lexington Books, 2010).

28. See for example, Kimberly K. Smith, *Governing Animals: Animal Welfare and the Liberal State* (Oxford: Oxford University Press, 2012), 109–14.

29. Donaldson and Kymlicka, 101.

30. For a description of the many ways that people interacted more with zoo animals in the United States in the past see Jesse Donahue and Erik Trump, *Political Animals: Public Art in American Zoos and Aquariums* (Lanham, MD: Lexington Books, 2007), 76–79.

31. William Austin. *The First Fifty Years: An Informal History of the Detroit Zoological Park and the Detroit Zoological Society* (Detroit, MI: Detroit Zoological Society, 1974), 77.

32. See California Penal Code section 596.5 enacted in 1989 and entitled "Abusive Behavior Toward an Elephant." The law prohibits deprivation of food, water or rest, use of electricity, physical punishment resulting in damage, scarring, or breakage of skin; insertion of any instrument into any bodily orifice, use of martingales, use of block and tackles. For a discussion of the abuse at the San Diego Zoo that precipitated this law see Bruce A. Wagman, Sonia S. Waisman, and Pamela D. Frash, *Animal Law*, 4th Edition (Durham, NC: Carolina Academic Press, 2010) 150–51.

33. For an overview of anticruelty statutes see Rebecca F. Wisch, "Brief Summary of State Cruelty Laws" (2005, Updated 2010), at https://www.animallaw.info/intro/state-anti-cruelty-laws. Accessed July 14, 2016. For a discussion of punitive damage awards for companion animals see Rebecca F. Wisch, "Brief Summary of Pet/Companion Animal Damages" (2003), at https://www.animallaw.info/intro/petcompanion-animal-damages. Accessed July 14, 2016.

34. *Blanche Guzzi v. New York Zoological Society*, 192 A.D. 263: 182 N.Y.S 257 (N.Y. App. Div. 1920).

35. Lori Marino, Scott O. Lilienfeld, and Randy Malamud, "Do Zoos and Aquariums Promote Attitude Change in Visitors? A Critical Evaluation of the American Zoo and Aquarium Study," *Society & Animals*, 18, 2 (2010): 126–38.

36. For a good critique of this problem see Matthew Churlew "Managing Love and Death at the Zoo: The Bioethics of Endangered Species." In "Unloved Others: Death of the Disregarded in a Time of Extinction," edited by Deborah Bird Rose and Thom van Dooren, Special Issue, *Australian Humanities Review* 50 (2011): 137–57.

37. *In Defense of Animals v. Cleveland Metroparks Zoo*, 785 F. Supp. 100 (U.S. Distr. 1991).

38. Jesse Donahue and Erik Trump, *The Politics of Zoos*, 140

39. There is quite a bit of literature about animals' need to retreat and get away from human visitors at times for their own sanity. The conclusions vary and there are questions about what constitutes stress. For example, sometimes the researchers find stress hormones from the animals' fecal samples after large numbers of visitors are present. Other times they find the same kind of stress after a feeding that had no visitors. The animals seem to get anxious about the impending arrival of food. Nevertheless, it seems fair to conclude that large numbers of visitors would cause stress to animals that is different from the kind of anticipation they might feel before dinner. Thus, it is worth studying how many human visitors the animals can have without stress and for how long. These studies could then inform laws and regulations that apply to them so that stress levels were minimized or, or preferably, nonexistent. For examples of articles about the importance of retreat space and visitor density problems see: Ursual S. Anderson and Marcie Benne, et al., "Retreat Space and Human Visitor Density Moderate Undesirable Behavior in Petting Zoo Animals," *Journal of Applied Animal Welfare Science*, 5(20), 2002: 125–37. Gareth Davey and Peter Henzi, "Visitor Circulation and Nonhuman Animal Welfare: An Overlooked Variable?" *Journal of Applied Animal Welfare Science*, 7(4), 2004: 243–51; or Rebecca L. Sellinger and

James C. Ha, "The Effects of Visitor Density and Intensity on the Behavior of Two Captive Jaguars (Panthera onca)" 2005, *Journal of Applied Animal Welfare Science*, 8(4), 2005: 233–44.

40. Rachel Hirschfel, "Ensuring Your Pet's Future: Estate Planning for Owners and Their Animal Companions" *Marquette Elder's Advisor*, 9, 155 (2007): 1–25; 6–7.

41. See the ASPA's advice on animal trusts at http://www.aspca.org/pet-care/planning-for-your-pets-future/pet-trust-laws. Accessed December 18, 2014. Or see http://www.humanesociety.org/news/magazines/2013/07-08/backup-plan-planning-for-pets-after-owner-death.html. This is an article on pet estate planning and their best guess about the numbers of animal surrendered to shelters because of death or incapacity of the owner.

42. A.R.S. § 14–10408 (§ 14–2907). Enacted 2008, Amended 2009.

43. For this critique see Alan Green, *Animal Underworld: Inside America's Black Market for Rare and Exotic Species* (New York: Public Affairs, 1999).

44. *Kresentia M. Doppleberger and Fund for Animals vs. City of Detroit, the Detroit Zoological Society, and Steve Graham* (Wayne County Circuit Court, no. 82–234592)-cz, 1982). This case was a complicated one and today the Detroit Zoo likely not have engaged in the study that led to the need to give ill animals anthesia and then had to euthanize them. All zoos, however, have to grapple with end of life decisions for the animals who live within their communities, just as responsible companion animal owners have to as well.

45. Virginia Morell, "The Killing of Marius the Giraffe Exposes Myths about Zoos." February 13, 2012, http://news.nationalgeographic.com/news/2014/02/140212-giraffe-death-denmark-copenhagen-zoo-breeding-europe/. Accessed May 5, 2015.

46. Lisa Abend, "Did Marius the Giraffe Have to Die," at Time.com. February 9, 2014, http://time.com/6097/marius-giraffe-copenhagen-zoo/. Accessed May 6, 2015.

47. For an idealized world for current captive exotic animals see Helena Pedersen and Natalie Dian, "Earth Trusts: A Quality Vision for Animals," 171–92, in Ralph R. Acampora, ed., *Metamorphoses of the Zoo*.

BIBLIOGRAPHY

Abend, Lisa. "Did Marius the Giraffe Have to Die," at Time.com. February 9, 2014, http://time.com/6097/marius-giraffe-copenhagen-zoo/. Accessed May 6, 2015.

Acampora, Ralph R., ed. *Metamorphoses of the Zoo: Animal Encounter After Noah* (Lanham, MD: Lexington Books, 2010).

Anderson, Ursual S., and Marcie Benne, et al. "Retreat Space and Human Visitor Density Moderate Undesirable Behavior in Petting Zoo Animals," *Journal of Applied Animal Welfare Science*, 5(20), 2002: 125–37.

Austin, William. *The First Fifty Years: An Informal History of the Detroit Zoological Park and the Detroit Zoological Society* (Detroit, MI: Detroit Zoological Society, 1974).

Braverman, Irus. *Zooland* (Stanford, CA: Stanford University Press, 2013), 57–62.

Churlew, Matthew. "Managing Love and Death at the Zoo: The Bioethics of Endangered Species." In *Unloved Others: Death of the Disregarded in a Time of Extinction*, Deborah Bird Rose and Thom van Dooren, eds. Special Issue, *Australian Humanities Review* 50 (2011): 137–57.

Davey, Gareth and Peter Henzi. "Visitor Circulation and Nonhuman Animal Welfare: An Overlooked Variable?" *Journal of Applied Animal Welfare Science*, 7(4), 2004: 243–51.

Donahue, Jesse and Erik Trump. *The Politics of Zoos: Exotic Animals and Their Protectors* (Dekalb: Nothern Illinois University Press, 2006).

———. *Political Animals: Public Art in American Zoos and Aquariums* (Lanham, MD: Lexington Books, 2007).

Donaldson, Sue and Will Kymlicka. *Zoopolis: A Political Theory of Animal Rights* (Oxford: Oxford University Press, 2011).

Conde, Dalia A., Nate Flesness, Fernando Colchero, Own R. Jones, and Alexander Scheuerlein. "An Emerging Role of to Conserve Biodiversity," *Science* 331, no. 6023 (2011): 1290–91.

Gesualdi, James F. *Excellence Beyond Compliance: Enhancing Animal Welfare Through the Constructive Use of the Animal Welfare Act* (Anna Maria, FL: Maurice Bassett, 2014).

Green, Alan. *Animal Underworld: Inside America's Black Market for Rare and Exotic Species* (New York: Public Affairs, 1999).

Francione, Gary. *Animals, Politics, and the Law* (Philadelphia: Temple University Press, 1995).

Grech, Kali S., "Brief Summary of Laws Affecting Zoos." Michigan State University Animal Legal and Historical Center, 2004. https://www.animallaw.info/intro/laws-affecting-zoos.

———. "Detailed Discussion of Laws Affecting Zoos." Michigan State University Animal Legal and Historical Center, 2004. https://www.animallaw.info/article/detailed-discussion-laws-affecting-zoos.

Grimm, David. *Citizen Canine* (New York: Public Affairs, 2014), 266, 264–68.

Hirschfel, Rachel. "Ensuring Your Pet's Future: Estate Planning for Owners and Their Animal Companions," *Marquette Elder's Advisor*, 9, 155 (2007): 1–25.

Marino, Lori, Scott O. Lilienfeld, and Randy Malamud. "Do Zoos and Aquariums Promote Attitude Change in Visitors? A Critical Evaluation of the American Zoo and Aquarium Study," *Society & Animals*, 18, 2 (2010): 126–38.

Morell, Virginia. "The Killing of Marius the Giraffe Exposes Myths about Zoos." February 13, 2012, http://news.nationalgeographic.com/news/2014/02/140212-giraffe-death-denmark-copenhagen-zoo-breeding-europe/. Accessed May 5, 2015.

Pedersen, Helena, and Natalie Dian. "Earth Trusts: A Quality Vision for Animals," 171–92, in Ralph R. Acampora, ed., *Metamorphoses of the Zoo: Animal Encounter After Noah* (Lanham, MD: Lexington Books, 2010).

Sellinger, Rebecca L. and James C. Ha. "The Effects of Visitor Density and Intensity on the Behavior of Two Captive Jaguars (Panthera onca)" 2005, *Journal of Applied Animal Welfare Science*, 8(4), 2005: 233–44.

Smith, Kimberly K. *Governing Animals: Animal Welfare and the Liberal State* (Oxford: Oxford University Press, 2012).

Wagman, Bruce A., Sonia S. Waisman, and Pamela D. Frash. *Animal Law*, 4th Edition (Durham, NC: Carolina Academic Press, 2010).

Wise, Steven. "Legal Thinghood." *Boston College Environmental Affairs Law Review*, Vol. 23, Issue 3, Article 2 (1996): 471–546.

———. "Rattling the Cage Defended." *Boston College Law Review*, 43, 3 (2002): 623–96.

Zimmerman, Alexandra, Matthew Hatchwell, Lesli A. Dicki, and Christ West, eds. *Zoos in the 21st Century: A Catalyst for Conservation* (Cambridge: Cambridge University Press, 2015).

TWO

Reintroductions and Animal Welfare

Laws and Regulations

Donald E. Moore III

Humanity is in one of the most massive extinction events known on Planet Earth.[1] At the same time, scientists have suggested that some species extinctions may be reversible during the Anthropocene, the time when humans are dominating the planet.[2] Labeled "de-extinction," these reintroduction activities can apply to any species which are still extant somewhere on the planet or for which DNA can be recovered, from extinct-in-the-wild, scimitar-horned oryx (Oryx dammah) to long-extinct woolly mammoths, or even thylacines and passenger pigeons that went extinct at the hands of humans during the twentieth century but were not maintained in captivity as scimitar-horned oryx were.

Recent developments in de-extinction were showcased in 2013 at a daylong conference called "TEDx DeExtinction," held in Washington, DC, demonstrating through TEDx selection of the topic that de-extinction has wide public interest.[3] Zoo and aquarium scientists based in modern zoos play a leading role in many of these reintroductions of zoo-born animals to their historic habitats, and helped to start the field of restoration science with early reintroductions of golden lion tamarins in Brazil, red wolves and whooping cranes in the United States, and with restorations of other species that are among the most endangered animals in the world. Critics of de-extinction in the popular science media have indicated potential negative impacts of these de-extinction programs. From an ethical perspective, these critics have suggested potential violations of animal welfare standards for the animals involved, as well as the potential drain on resources that could be used in the conservation of still-existing species.[4] For example, reintroduced animals could be killed by individuals of similar species in the same habitat, by human hunters or habitat users, or by the stress of handling pre-release (even professional handling, in which the professionals are well-trained in welfare-based handling, can cause wild animals to overly stress during nonroutine handling). Animal welfare and rights activists have raised welfare concerns about reintroductions as well.[5]

Some animal welfare and animal rights critics do not support reintroductions (they apparently mean translocations as well, possibly even head-starting; the term *reintroduction* is not defined on their websites). Some website language suggests that a particular group does not support predators (e.g., red wolves?) reintroduction because of "nuisance" predators being "poisoned, hit by cars, or shot. In failed attempts to escape, they might be entangled in barbed wire or shocked by electric fences." There are a lot of possibilities mentioned, with very little scientific data (in either direction) behind the negative welfare outcomes suggested by the critics. This is neither a fair nor is it a useful critique during the massive extinction event that our planet is now suffering. Indeed, the USFWS ESA 10-j rule (nonessential, experimental population) would mitigate most negative welfare outcomes suggested by these critics, because this clause allows for the recovery of reintroduced animals that experience conflict or negative welfare at the human-animal interface, as discussed above. In addition, professional ethical standards for modern zoos collaborating on science-based species restoration are governed by regional associations like AZA and by the World Association of Zoos and Aquariums (WAZA), which includes the welfare-based ethics statement "No release-to-the-wild programme shall be undertaken without the animals having undergone a thorough veterinary examination to assess their fitness for such release and that their welfare post-release is reasonably safeguarded. Following release, a thorough monitoring programme should be established and maintained."[6]

Critics raise some important concerns that suggest that members of the zoological profession need to do a better job of communicating with the public about reintroductions. In this chapter, I show the challenges of successfully reintroducing animals by drawing upon my own experiences in working on reintroductions, using notes from interviews with other scientists who have worked on them, and using some of the primary and secondary literature on the animals and reintroduction sciences. The goal of this chapter is to bridge the communication gap and describe how reintroductions are done, the many external barriers the conservation biology profession faces in implementing them, and the ways that some laws could be changed to help us accomplish these programs to save animals from extinction. Through case studies of the red wolf, condors, whooping crane, Wyoming toad, and vole, I show that reintroductions are complex and that members of the zoological profession face many difficult questions and sometimes legal barriers when trying to implement them.

Jorgensen suggests that well-established standards for species restoration projects provide a solid foundation on which de-extinction can be built. Species restoration includes "reintroduction," "translocation," and "head-starting" as defined by different stakeholders, and all types of reintroduction are increasingly common as species conservation and restoration tools.[7] However, little attention has been given to some of the welfare needs of animals during the restoration process, nor to the laws around welfare of animals involved in reintroductions, nor to some different methods for monitoring the stress encountered by reintroduced individuals.[8] Optimal, or even minimal, data collection pre- and post-reintroduction,[9] and during the process of the active reintroduction, could have implications for reintroductions within the legal framework of animal welfare regulations and laws that can be applied to these programs.

The term *reintroduction* as used here will include captive-to-nature transfers of animals born in captivity and then restored to their natural habitat ("reintroduction" sensu stricto), nature-to-nature introductions of wild animals from one home range to another ("translocation" as it has been defined by others and in Moore and Smith 1991) and captive growth of wild animals in protective captive conditions until reintroduction to their natural habitat is safe ("head-starting").[10] Reintroduction science has been accepted as a valid niche within conservation sciences and has been institutionalized by the International Union for Conservation of Nature and Natural Resources (IUCN) via its Species Survival Commission Reintroduction Specialist Group (IUCN SSC-RSG), founded in 1988 (note: this author has been a member of the IUCN-SSC-RSG). IUCN developed guidelines for reintroduction,[11] which have recently been under revision,[12] and these guidelines have been adopted by the Association of Zoos and Aquariums in North America as well as other zoo associations with strong animal welfare-based conservation missions. Current IUCN Reintroduction Guidelines suggest background studies to allow identification of a species' habitat requirements, review and identification of strengths and opportunities known from previous reintroduction projects of similar species, critical evaluation of potential sites within the historical range of the species, as well as assessment of historic threats to species survival to ensure they are mitigated, all to maximize the welfare and ultimate survival of reintroduced animals. Even with close attention, sometimes reintroductions fail, and many reintroductions need multiple introductions of large groups of animals before they succeed.[13]

A recent World Association of Zoos and Aquariums report[14] suggests that any breed-for-reintroduction programs might undertake pre-release conditioning that may then lead to a temporary reduction in animal welfare. Preconditioning should involve, for example: manipulating an individual's diet to mimic more closely the species' natural diet in nature, which might include limiting food resources (for instance with a feast-and-famine diet); introduction of live prey items (which, as I indicate in the red wolf species section below, can raise concerns for the welfare of the prey animal); or even introducing predator conditioning that initiates a flight response from a predator (black footed ferret fleeing from a badger) or prey animal (quail fleeing from raptorial bird). The World Association of Zoos and Aquariums suggests that, prior to committing to a reintroduction program, zoos and aquariums should assess whether long-term survival risks to individual animals, and current and future survival of the species, outweigh the temporary compromise(s) to individual animal welfare during the pre-release conditioning stage. Input of other stakeholders in addition to the input of conservation authorities, potentially via an animal welfare committee, can assist in assessment of costs and benefits. In some jurisdictions, such a committee is required by law.[15]

Watters and Meehan[16] emphasized that reintroduction programs for endangered animals operate under the assumption that protected habitats can sustain viable populations without much human management. The goal of modern zoo captive breeding and reintroduction programs is to ensure that animals will have the skills and even resources they need to succeed in the modern version of nature (not wild as nature would have been hundreds of years ago, but "wild" as perceived and managed by humans). Watters and Meehan point out however, that predicting the set of skills necessary to respond to unpredictable life events is difficult and that zoo professionals' efforts sometimes fail as animals respond inappropriately post-release to environmental variation, because these animals lack behavioral flexibility due to their different life experience in captivity. Population resilience in the face of environmental change may be enhanced if members of a population exhibit different responses when selection pressures change, as is occurring quickly in this time of rapid climate change and human alteration of habitats in nature. In many species, individual animals express behavioral diversity that allows individual behavioral "types" to exhibit alternative responses to the same stimuli. However, Watters and Meehan are of the opinion that, when animals are prepared for release to the wild by wildlife professionals (and I would add, even with veterinary oversight), there is not often a consideration of this desirable behavioral variation between individuals as individuals are assessed pre-release to be within norms of the species but are not assessed for their behavioral variation against the norm. That is, individual behavioral types at the extremes of the normal curve might have better survival in a changing world. Since the experiences of individual animals influence both the behavioral and physiological responses to varied environmental stimuli and can shape the future behavioral type of animals within a species, pre-release environmental enrichment in zoos or other pre-release facilities may be successful in facilitating the expression of varied behavioral types in animals designated for release. It is important that professionals acknowledge this need at the individual and population level. As Watters and Meehan suggest, a modern approach to zoo-based environmental enrichment requires a departure from a "one-size-fits-all" enrichment diversity strategy and should involve exposure to increased challenge and competition that addresses the diverse behavioral needs and capabilities of individuals across the assurance populations. Watters and Meehan indicate that the intense management aspects of the zoo environment allow for an excellent investigative environment for examining the development and expression of behavioral types within a population and across individuals, and for taking a novel approach to environmental enrichment and pre- and post-reintroduction research that may prove to be very important to reintroduction efforts.

Animal care involves these inputs of daily care and enrichment, while animal welfare considerations are quantitative and qualitative reflections on an animal's internal state. Therefore, we need to pay attention to individual animals and their unique physiology and behavior, to the captive habitat and behavioral opportunities these animals are offered, to the outcomes on animal welfare and longevity, and to the outcomes of reintroductions. Ultimately, we need to pay attention to survival of reintroduced animals and survival and welfare of their offspring. Some of these needs have been recognized by the World Association of Zoos and Aquariums Animal Welfare strategy that recommends actively balancing individual positive animal welfare in the zoo/aquarium environment, that is to balance the cost/benefit for programs in which animals are provided with natural breeding opportunities, for all animals including those in release programs, against replenishing animal populations in nature and the survival of those animals that are reintroduced.[17]

RED WOLF

The red wolf is one of the world's most endangered wild canids, and USFWS determined that it was imperative for the United States to create a recovery program in the 1970s. The red wolf population was decimated as early as the 1960s due to loss of habitat and intensive predator control programs. A remnant population of a small number of red wolves was found along the Gulf Coast of Louisiana and Texas, and in 1973 red wolves were declared an endangered species. Then, USFWS initiated efforts to locate and capture the remaining wild wolves found in the Gulf Coast area.

Fourteen of seventeen remaining wolves captured by USFWS biologists became the founders of a successful off-public-display captive breeding program lead by Point Defiance Zoo and Aquarium, then joined by other AZA zoo facilities including the zoo in which I worked at the time in Syracuse, New York, in collaboration with the federal government. The founding red wolves were considered a genetically pure species, despite modern research that suggests otherwise for red wolves and "eastern timber wolves."[18] In 1980, USFWS declared red wolves extinct in the wild and they remained only in the captive population. Captive wolf care and husbandry is regulated by the USDA Animal Welfare Act. The Animal Welfare Act,[19] first passed by the US Congress in 1966, is intended to ensure the humane treatment of animals that are exhibited to the public, intended for research, bred for commercial sale, or commercially transported. So, all accredited zoos and roadside menageries (these roadside menageries are also called "zoos" by the public and media) are covered by the AWA. Under the AWA, businesses and others with mammals covered by the law must be licensed by or registered with USDA, and they must adhere to minimum standards of husbandry and veterinary care. Birds and farm animals are among the animals not covered by the act, which nonetheless provides a broad set of statutory protections for red wolves and other animals in species restoration programs for which there is a public exhibition component. This Act provides minimum standards for AZA-accredited zoos and aquariums and roadside menageries, but not for sanctuaries and other nonexhibit facilities, which means that those facilities do not need to meet the minimum animal care standards for animal husbandry, and veterinary care established in regulation by the Act (even if they mean well).

For zoos that dedicate resources to endangered species reintroduction programs, the level of care established by the Animal Welfare Act is bolstered by AZA's Accreditation Standards, which establish dozens of additional modern-practice standards for safe and complex physical facilities, zookeeper training and husbandry, and veterinary care, animal behavior and nutritional needs. These and other AZA accreditation standards are far above the level of minimal animal care and welfare standards established by USDA/AWA, and are constantly evolving with increases in knowledge about science-based husbandry, behavioral opportunities to stimulate captive animals, and veterinary care. The AZA also oversees over 450 Species Survival Plans, many of which have accompanying Animal Care Manuals that are written by experts in the biology, management, and veterinary care of each species, and which establish optimal species-specific veterinary and husbandry standards for diverse species, from invertebrates to mammals.[20] As these standards continually evolve, and zoo biologists provide ever-improving homes, diets and opportunities to enhance the positive welfare of animals in their care, the natural behavioral abilities of captive animals in assurance populations whose individuals are destined for release also continue to improve.

By 1987, enough red wolves had been bred in captivity by AZA zoos to begin a restoration program in northeastern North Carolina at Alligator River National Wildlife Refuge.[21] These wolves were ready for release: while they were often fed coarsely-chopped meat diets supplemented by whole bones in zoos, the zoos' large, natural habitats—native woodland wolf habitats that had been developed by that time—were perfect for wolves to develop critical physical and behavioral abilities. These physical and behavioral abilities included some level of prey capture, and even tree climbing. External prey animals like woodchucks and pheasant could choose to enter into the habitats, and zoo biologists were concerned with the welfare of these animals, so we had a moral responsibility to make a good-faith attempt to keep these wild animals out of the wolf habitats. We also had a competing moral responsibility to the wolves to give them the opportunity to capture live prey before they were released into nature where they would need to feed themselves through prey finding and capture. So while we kept most wild animals outside the wolf habitat, woodchucks, pheasants, and even wild turkeys that breached the barrier were ultimately captured, killed, and consumed by the wolves as they would have been in nature. This breaks a legal requirement by Animal Welfare Act that restricts wild animal ingress and contact with captive animals in the facility: even the facility's perimeter fence

> must be constructed so that it protects the animals in the facility by restricting animals and unauthorized persons from going through it or under it and having contact with the animals in the facility, and so that it can function as a secondary containment system for the animals in the facility. It must be of sufficient distance from the outside of the primary enclosure to prevent physical contact between animals inside the enclosure and animals or persons outside the perimeter fence.[22]

This section of the law goes on to state that all outdoor housing facilities need to restrict access by wild and feral animals outside the facility to animals inside the facility. This helps to illustrate the legal complexities that zoo biologists face when trying to accomplish conservation tasks.

Our moral obligation to ensure best possible survival after reintroduction led zoo biologists and federal biologists to mimic the circumstances of the best-known reintroductions from history—those of raptorial birds like falcons and eagles, in which a halfway-house situation called a "hacking tower" was used to provide extra protection from the elements and to provision the animals post-release. The wolves at Alligator River National Wildlife Refuge were placed in fence-surrounded homes in their historic habitat, with trained technicians delivering roadkill and other natural foods over the top of an opaque wall. And, animals of other species could infrequently enter from the outside if they were motivated to climb the perimeter fence of the wolf release habitat. The Red Wolf

Species Survival Plan coordinator and curator from Point Defiance Zoo, made assessments of the wolves' behavior in conjunction with federal biologists, per the multidisciplinary reintroduction team's protocol. And in one case, a captive-born female wolf with a compromised leg was able to climb a tree in her habitat, to capture and kill a raccoon that had entered the space from the outside. Smith, the program's attending veterinarian and others determined that her physical and behavioral abilities made her ready for reintroduction despite her compromised leg, and that her welfare in nature would be appropriate.

The other key part of this was a "soft-release" reintroduction program that was well-planned, and needs to be a key part of future reintroduction programs if appropriate for the species. A "soft-release" in this program meant: first, acclimation of the wolves from zoos in other parts of the country to the local area of North Carolina, which let them become accustomed to local day length, star orientation, temperatures, etc; second, this acclimation happened in a relatively large naturalistic habitat so the wolves could become accustomed to that kind of habitat (frequently wet, which is unlike zoo conditions in which that kind of wetness is not allowed under the Animal Welfare Act, due to veterinary concerns for paw health and potential disease conditions); third, once acclimated and released, the enclosure doors remained open and carcass provisioning continued to allow the wolves time to learn to hunt on their own (and if they do not learn, then they can return to their "home" enclosure where food is assured). This kind of soft release assures positive welfare for the reintroduced animals in terms of offering weather-protected shelter in a familiar habitat that the animals can consider their "territory," while offering "free food" on an ongoing basis so the wolves do not lose condition while transitioning back to a "wild" state.

To achieve public support for this red wolf reintroduction, the USFWS developed the legal notion of an "experimental, nonessential" population. The US Endangered Species Act recognizes that fish, wildlife, and plant species have aesthetic, ecological, and scientific value, and provides a means to conserve species and the ecosystems upon which endangered or threatened species depend. Section 10 of the Act, entitled "Exceptions," provides an avenue to authorize activities that would otherwise be prohibited under the Act. Under section 10(j), the Secretary of the US Department of the Interior can designate reintroduced populations established outside the species' current range, and within its historical range, as "experimental." The agency can also designate certain populations as "nonessential": while Section 10(j) provides for the designation of specific reintroduced populations of endangered species as "experimental populations," using the best available information the USFWS can determine whether an experimental population is "essential" or "nonessential" to the continued existence of the species. A "nonessential" designation for a 10(j) experimental population means that (on the basis of best available information) the experimental population is not genetically or demographically essential for the continued existence of the species. Restrictions about "taking," and other regulations are considerably reduced under a Nonessential Experimental Population (NEP) designation (USFWS 2016), which may allow individuals of these populations to be recaptured to be protected back in human care, or to be treated for health issues in captivity, and for the benefit of the restoration effort.

Despite intense preconditioning prior to reintroduction, reintroduced wolves that got into trouble post-reintroduction could be removed from the wild and placed back in captive habitat as part of the captive assurance population because of the 10-j designation. This conferred a certain potential "refugee" status to these wolves that needed intense management in human care to assure their own individual welfare or the survival of the species. In the case of livestock or domestic pet depredations by red wolves, relaxed regulations were passed in 1995, which allow landowners to "take" (kill) red wolves while depredation is occurring, provided that freshly wounded livestock or pets are evidence for USFWS officials. On the positive side for wolf welfare, there were also mechanisms for landowners to be monetarily compensated if they chose to become involved with red wolf recovery. This meant that the landowners could choose to help protect individual wolves while at the same time choosing to be compensated for potential livestock losses. Since 1987, the total experimental population area for red wolves has expanded to include Alligator River plus two more national wildlife refuges, a Department of Defense bombing range, state-owned lands, and private property, for a total of 1.7 million acres for the red wolves.[23] Currently, around 60 percent of the red wolf population can be found on private lands within the recovery area. Conservation of the species is regulated for the benefit of future generations of humans, and taking via harassment, killing, etc., is restricted under the Endangered Species Act for the benefit of future generations of wolves. This represents a substantial animal welfare protection for red wolves, since taking even of red wolves from the "experimental, nonessential" population is somewhat restricted through the ESA and related regulations. Although the ESA is intended to protect full populations of species for recovery purposes, the taking of individual animals should not be trivialized by courts and non-Federal governmental jurisdictions simply because the taken animals are individual members of an entire protected class.[24] That is, there is a balance between "taking" for livestock depredation etc., and "taking" from the wild to increase individual wolf welfare, as might be accomplished by professionals on a species survival team. If all endangered animals including red wolves were to receive full protection from "taking," including full prevention from any and all harassment from humans, red wolves would be as comfortable in wildlife refuge areas as in zoo habitats, and so would have positive natural welfare and would have the full potential to contribute to growth and stability of their conspecific populations.

There were red wolves that were born and paired in zoos and then released so that they were able to both help rebuild the population and return to nature. This is the reality of a "nonessential" population (the animals are not essential to the future genetics and demographics of the assurance population). The wolves were protected in terms of their individual welfare. No matter how long the wolves were in the new home environment in nature, the "experimental" designation allows biologists to remove the wolves from nature if necessary (for either physical or behavioral reasons, to allow these individuals to live a life that continues to benefit the species in some way).

The red wolf population continued to grow until 2013. In 2013, there were thirty-four pups born among seven litters in the wild population, plus one fostered pup. In the captive population, there were five pups born within one litter, showing good welfare if our metric is healthy individual adult wolves that are behaviorally comfortable enough to rear an average-sized litter of pups. The wild population was estimated at over 125 red wolves by 2012, but declined precipitously following the US Fish and Wildlife Service's actions to cut back the species' recovery program. The USFWS eliminated the program's recovery coordinator position in 2014, and stopped introducing new red wolves into nature in July 2015. Interestingly, this federal agency also stopped law enforcement investigations of red wolf deaths and stopped offering rewards to the public to help identify and investigate poachers.[25] Currently, 50–75 red wolves live in their current range, and around 175–200 survive in the 40 participant facilities in AZA's Species Survival Plan captive insurance population, although some introgression with coyotes might threaten this.[26] Adaptive management techniques by wildlife officials are augmented by data from wild animals using capture methods that include padded leghold traps and frequent ongoing monitoring to ensure good animal welfare during the management activities. Scientific analysis at detailed, individual animal levels is providing a treasure trove of discoveries that we can use to improve individual animal welfare. Lincoln Park Zoo (Chicago, IL) scientists have created models to evaluate the health of red wolf populations in zoos and in the wild, providing reintroduction teams with the facts they need to make good decisions to ensure population stability,[27] and this population stability is dependent on the health and welfare of individual animals.

Despite the successes of historic captive breeding and reintroductions, coyote hunting under permits and hunting licenses is allowed in North Carolina, on both private and state-owned game lands and is another continuing threat to the red wolf. All coyotes must be reported within twenty-four hours of the taking. Red wolves, of course, can be mistaken for coyotes (especially at midnight, in a 24-hour-per-day coyote hunting area!), and their deaths must also be reported to USFWS. Death is the absence of welfare, because the animal feels nothing after death. The USFWS has currently suspended reintroductions via the 10-j experimental nonessential population designation for the area as it reviews the goals and results of this program in conjunction with state administrators and scientists in North Carolina; during this time, wolves will continue to be removed from private lands if requested by the landowner. Death will continue to be the absence of welfare, for all individuals, but each individual death represents decreased welfare for the population of wolves. Wolves in the zoo population will continue to be the assurance population for this species as persecution in nature continues. Of course, zoo biologists will continue to be concerned for the welfare of red wolves returned to captivity, and will provide the daily and regular care by zookeepers and veterinarians that wolves in nature do not receive.

The survival of wolves in nature depends critically on acceptance by humans. Lack of acceptance of wolves by people is strongly rooted in the history of human wars followed by wolves depredating on injured people on the battlefields, in stories like "Little Red Riding Hood," "The Three Little Pigs," and other big bad wolf stories, and in human reactions following recent depredations on livestock. Any law or regulation that helps preserve wolf welfare in nature would be helpful for the survival of individual wolves and wolf populations. Meanwhile, red wolves in the AZA Species Survival Plan population will continue to be survival insurance for the species in nature, and will be used to leverage awareness of the plight of red wolves throughout the United States since this species is a unique US endemic wild canid. They will be genetic and demographic insurance against extinction of the species, as is required by the Endangered Species Act. And they will have individual welfare protections via the Animal Welfare Act and from AZA's Accreditation Standards for animal care and welfare, as well as for veterinary care.

Can we do more to safeguard the species, and the individual animal welfare that is integral to the species' survival? It is difficult to conceive of additional laws and regulations in the face of the ongoing level of human persecution of wolves across our country and even our world. However, we could link stronger individual protections under the Endangered Species Act. The ESA's "Harassment" provision is a strong one, but we may not be able to invoke it in conjunction with the 10(j) provision. Under the ESA, we can sometimes invoke species' protections via "similarity of appearance" to achieve increased individual and species protections. We have not been successful in achieving these protections for red wolves in the face of coyote persecution and hunting by humans, while using the 10(j) provision for red wolf reintroduction. Could we establish similarity-of-species protections in the context of 10(j), with the acknowledgement that individual coyotes also suffer pain and suffering if trapped in leghold traps or wounded by hunters? Such protections for similar-appearing coyotes might help to protect the welfare of red wolves themselves. And if agency behaviors seem to run contrary to existing laws, nongovernmental agencies can act to balance agency behavior as the Center for Biological Diversity has with lawsuits and emergency petitions to increase protections for red wolves.[28] It will be this kind of deep consideration of individual red wolf welfare, that makes a real difference to the lives and welfare of animals of the endangered species plus to individual animals from species that are similar appearance, that will make a difference via laws and regulations in the future.

WHOOPING CRANES

The whooping crane (Grus americana) is the tallest bird in North America, and is a majestic icon of wetlands. There were an estimated 15,000 to 22,000 birds in nature in the 1800s and early 1900s. There were only 15 whooping cranes remaining in nature in 1941, having been pushed to the brink of extinction by habitat loss and uncontrolled hunting. The species was declared endangered in the United States in 1967. By the end of 2015 there were approximately 145 birds in reintroduced populations and 161 birds held in captivity due to intense conservation efforts. These birds can live twenty to thirty years in the wild and up to eighty years in captivity.[29]

Following years of captive breeding and other reintroduction attempts, USFWS proposed establishment of a nonessential, experimental population in the eastern United States. The Final Rule designates a whooping crane Nonessential Experimental Population within a twenty-state area in the eastern United States.[30] USFWS biologists believe the Nonessential Experimental Population status will adequately enhance and protect this eastern whooping crane population, while still allowing presence of these rare cranes to be compatible with routine human activities in the proposed reintroduction area. The USFWS made it very clear that the cranes would be behaviorally and physiologically conditioned prior to release, so providing a proactive way of enhancing animal welfare post-release. That is, they will know how to eat and fly well, on their own, prior to release, so should achieve welfare comparable to their wild relatives after release back into the reintroduction area.

What are the welfare challenges with these cranes? Reintroduced whooping cranes have integrated with sandhill cranes, and there is a hunting season on the sandhill cranes. Whooping cranes have been killed illegally by people hunting the other species of cranes, and a wild population of just over 400 birds will decline in the face of unnecessary deaths. As indicated above for red wolves, species that are similar in appearance should be protected so that reintroduced individuals of an endangered species are also protected against death and other adverse impacts on welfare. At the very least, there should be a temporary ban on hunting while the reintroduced species is established to levels considered fully "recovered."

CONDORS

The California condor (Gymnogyps californianus) is North America's largest bird, known to some indigenous peoples as the "Thunderbird." This large vulture plays a critical role in ecosystems by disposing of dead, sometimes diseased, animals and by recycling the nutrients from these animals. These huge birds have long been revered by humans, but the human pressures of habitat change and human-caused declines of condor food sources of large animal carcasses drove their populations down during the nineteenth and twentieth centuries. The California condor was the first species listed under the Endangered Species Act in 1973.

California condors were depleted to only 22 birds in the wild in 1987, when the last individuals were removed from the wild to be bred in captivity by several AZA-accredited zoos and the Peregrine Fund for species restoration. This was done in collaboration with USFWS and state wildlife agencies at a cost of millions of dollars per year borne by the zoos, and millions more borne by the agencies. The birds thrived in captivity and the first birds were restored back to their native habitat in 1992. Today, there are still about 200 California condors in the AZA Species Survival Plan captive-breeding program, and over 200 flying again in the wild. They are protected by the federal Endangered Species Act, as well as by state endangered species acts, which protect against harassment and "taking." As birds, they are not protected by the USDA Animal Welfare Act, but Endangered Species Act "taking" provisions protect them from certain harmful activities.

Lead poisoning is the single greatest threat to the survival of condors today. Condors feed on carrion, mostly on carcasses or gut piles left by hunters who leave resources that are key to condor survival over time. However, as hunters shoot lead slugs or shot into an animal, the projectile explodes into micropieces of toxic lead spread throughout the meat of the game animal. Hunters' families unknowingly eat this lead-laden meat, unless the animal is wounded, dies later in nature, and is then eaten by condors. Lead toxicity is well known in people, which is why we no longer use lead paints in houses and lead additives in gasoline (which would then enter the air we breathe). When condors and other scavengers feed on the remains of animals shot with lead ammunition, lead can enter their bloodstream, adversely affecting individual scavenger's welfare by attacking the central nervous system and leading to starvation or predation by other animals while the sick condors are in their weakened state. Using lead-free ammunition spares scavengers a slow death and provides a vital and lead-free seasonal food source (e.g., gut piles) for many animals.

Death by lead poisoning is certainly bad welfare, and bad for recovery of condors, and in June 2013 the California State Assembly voted in favor of CA bill AB711, a law requiring the use of nonlead ammunition throughout the state.[31] In September 2013, the entire California State Legislature voted to pass this significant nonlead ammunition law, and Governor Jerry Brown then signed the historic legislation into law in October 2013. The California Fish and Game Commission subsequently adopted final regulations that begin phase-in of implementation of AB711, thus requiring the use of nonlead ammunition for all taking of wildlife in the state. This nonlead ammo phase-in will be complete by 2019, at which time California will officially be lead-free for hunting everywhere in the state. Other states (e.g., Oregon) have educational efforts by hunters and for hunters to show how lead ammunition distributes through game meat when it explodes, and have decided (for now) to not adopt legislation mandating nonlead ammo,[32] so are instead dependent on the good conservation actions of ethical hunters to reduce their lead use to keep the environment clean and ensure the good welfare of condors.

In the meantime, lead poisoning can still cause agonizing death for condors, and condors that are sickened can be recaptured by condor managers to be removed to captivity where experienced zoo veterinarians can treat the birds via chelation. This is true whether the condors have complete protection as they do in California, or whether they are released under the ESA 10(J) provision as is true in Arizona.[33] Chelation therapy involves administration of chelating chemicals to remove excessive heavy metals from the bloodstream. The chelation agent attaches itself to lead circulating in the blood, which allows the kidneys to filter and remove the lead from the blood. The welfare of every individual in the captive and wild populations is now monitored constantly throughout their lives, especially because of lead and even microtrash in the environment. The recovery goal for this program is self-sustaining populations of healthy condors in captivity and in the wild.

A question for the future might be whether any of the 200 condors in zoos will ever be released into nature. The answer will depend on a series of other questions, as we had for bald eagles after they were brought back from the brink of extinction through federal (Patuxent wildlife research center) and zoo-based breeding programs. Are the animals able to be released back into nature, or are they nonreleasable because of physical or behavioral deficiencies? Will the animals in nature be dependent on continuing expert veterinary care, for instance for chelation treatment of ongoing lead poisoning, and if so what are the costs and benefits of having a population of captive birds so that zoo veterinarians and veterinary students located close to urban centers can have appropriate training and experience in working with these unique birds, so these professionals can be more effective when they need to capture, handle, and treat birds that experience health difficulties in nature? Is there a continuing reason for urban-based "animal ambassadors" to educate the millions of zoo-going public about the needs of these animals in nature so the birds who are returned to nature can experience lives worth living in a healthy and productive way? For instance, can captive birds be used as leverage to have a neutral, honest conversation about nonlead ammunition? Or can zoo-based birds be ambassadors to engage and inspire the public as urban advocates for the species argue for endangered or non-game species funding for state or federal agencies? Answers to these questions might suggest that condors should, or should not, be released back in nature.

Meanwhile, there are founder condors, the birds originally removed from the wild, which have "native knowledge" because they were wild-born, learned from their parents in nature until the birds were removed for the captive species survival program, and have now been in zoo-based breeding programs for over twenty-five years. If these birds are no longer needed in the program for genetic and demographic reasons, and because the population has successfully increased to 400 birds in the global population, then is it timely to entertain the above questions. Will founders who are reintroduced into human-dominated nature be able to use their native knowledge to help other condors survive better, or might they return to original range where life for condors is now more dangerous? These are important questions for the possibility of returning founders back to nature after their assistance in species survival is no longer needed by species managers, a possibility which is now being considered for some founder birds.[34]

One of the additional important considerations for this possibility of return to nature will be median longevity of the species, and length of a recovery program for the species. If a species is endangered due to habitat alteration and other human activities, and recovery takes thirty to fifty years, we could imagine that no wild-born frogs would ever be returned to nature (for example) because their lifespans are so short at only several years for median lifespan. Even wolves, with their relatively short lifespans, would not be able to live from the date of removal from the wild to a beyond-lifespan date of restoration. Condors, on the other hand, with a median life expectancy of forty-seven years, have now survived to the point in the species survival effort during which we can consider returning founders to native range.

WYOMING TOAD

One might think that recovery programs would have adequate scientific data, public support, and funding.[35] Such is not always the case, as Gelling and colleagues indicate,[36] and AZA-accredited zoos help substantially to get muddy boots in the field, to gather biological data, and to fund meetings for endangered species programs like the Wyoming toad program. The Wyoming toad (Bufo baxteri) is a Pleistocene relic, related to the Canadian toad, and was listed as endangered in 1984 following rapid declines from the 1970s through 1980s. A single population was discovered in Lake Mortensen, WY, in 1987, and individuals were removed in 1993 from the last remnant population for a captive breeding program.[37]

Chytrid fungus is a major killer of this toad and other amphibians, and insecticides have been implicated in declines due to their presence in insects and in the environment. The toad's rediscovery in 1987 stimulated the formation of an ad hoc recovery group by USFWS and the Wyoming Game and Fish Department, which also included participants from the University of Wyoming, The Nature Conservancy, and various AZA-accredited zoos.[38] A recovery plan was subsequently adopted,[39] which outlined basic goals but did not include specific objectives or methods to meet those goals.[40] In 1992, a Wyoming Toad Task Force was convened as requested by the governor of Wyoming, with the support of the Environmental Protection Agency. The task force objective was to resolve conflicts between a local mosquito control program and protection measures for the Wyoming toad; this group was active only between 1993 and 1995.[41] Captive breeding was initiated in 1993, and the American Zoo and Aquarium Association (AZA) approved a Species Survival Plan in 1996. Although amphibians are not covered by the USDA/AWA, AZA Species Survival Plans require population management and animal care manuals as "best practice," and these address population and individual-level welfare by defining state-of-the-science husbandry and veterinary care for captive as well as wild-released individuals as necessary.

AZA's Amphibian TAG helps to keep husbandry workers abreast of new developments in caring for Wyoming toads in the captive insurance population. There is a thin margin of error for recovery programs, especially in amphibians where (by definition) the individuals within the species inhabit at least two very different habitats—land and water—throughout their life cycle; in fact, there can be a third habitat for this toad and that is the hibernaculum.

Research undertaken on the Wyoming toad has included field studies and population monitoring, captive husbandry, and breeding studies, and disease identification efforts. The most positive and numerous research activities have been in the zoo veterinary and curatorial communities, where endocrinologists and pathologists have worked successfully to identify diseases and physiological processes that govern breeding in

Wyoming toads. Disease needs to be consistently controlled through modern biological control techniques, and husbandry practices need to be consistent across institutions for best-possible individual animal welfare.

According to Dreitz,[42] field research on Wyoming toads has missed the mark. The few studies conducted have been hampered by the scarcity of animals and by flawed methods. Research and monitoring have both been constrained by the reluctance of regulatory agencies (USFWS, WGFD) to allow methods that involve more than minimal handling of individual animals of this endangered species. Our biological heritage cannot afford minimization of management for a species that needs intensive management of individuals, rather than populations, to survive as a species.

The reintroductions of these toads illustrates the learning curve of complex of reintroductions. Although we might like to reintroduce all animals, we have to figure out how to do it safely first and that requires a tremendous amount of research, time, and effort. Sometimes captive population husbandry workers had guessed at preferred abiotic parameters based on the Wyoming toad's last refuge in Lake Mortensen, but in the late 1990s curatorial staff from WCS' Central Park Zoo (NY) placed data loggers in shallow areas of the lake and in known hibernacula in order to study the toad's preferences for abiotic conditions; this work changed the location the USFWS preferred to use for toad releases in the lake, based on the toad's own habitat preferences.[43] This kind of work most likely improved the welfare of individual toads in captivity as well as in the wild post-release, but despite increased data available since the inception of the successful captive breeding effort for this recovery program, toads in captivity still do not survive as long as we might expect, and SSP husbandry experts continue to work on this program to increase age-related survivorship and health and well-being, that includes disease prevention, nutrition, and abiotic and biotic husbandry practices, in order to support the continuous reintroductions this toad needs. Assessment of needs of each life history stage—water-dependent egg, tadpole, juvenile "metamorph, " and adult toad—is critical for this program moving forward, and currently there is a recognized need for post-release data on postmetamorph survivorship. "Head-starting" with this species, growing toads from eggs to morphing tadpoles, to a lifestage that is relatively less predated, is accomplished by zoos collaborating with agencies on toad restoration. If survivorship of the released adults is subsequently lower than expected, this suggests that animal welfare post-release may also be low (although we recognize that naive animals could also experience positive welfare right up to the time of their predation and death!). And sometimes, reintroduction is chosen without understanding all of the original threats to the species. For animals like toads, this may include introduced species like brown trout, and these threats need to be mitigated before reintroduction success can be achieved because the additional threats also have potential negative impacts on individual animal well-being and survival. Program leadership, in zoos and wildlife agencies, need to have continuing education to keep abreast of these issues and research results.[44] This is all partly dictated by legal and regulatory frameworks for restorations, but we have much to do with minimal resources and conservation biologists have a steep learning curve for husbandry and welfare since our profession is so young.

VOLE REINTRODUCTIONS AND ANIMAL WELFARE RESEARCH

If animal welfare of conservation species can be regulated by laws, agency rules, and professional ethics, how might we assess that welfare? Gelling and colleagues[45] recently compared ten potential measures of stress within four different categories (neuroendocrine, cell function, immune system function, and body condition) as proxies for animal welfare in small rodents (water voles) being reintroduced to the Upper Thames region, in Oxfordshire (UK). The team assessed captive-bred vole health pre-release, and each month post-release for up to five months. Wild-born voles were also captured in the field and then similarly assessed from two months post-release. Body condition and immunocompetence measures were significantly different for captive-bred voles post-release between a short-term and long-term recapture. Captive-bred animals had lower fat reserves, higher weight/length ratios and better immunocompetence, and also had higher ectoparasite burdens compared to wild-born animals. As reintroduction site quality decreased, the captive-bred voles became less hydrated, which also negatively impacts welfare. Gelling and colleagues suggested that these measures from different physiological systems indicate that some methods can identify changes in reintroduced individuals over time, highlighting areas of welfare risk in a reintroduction program. This kind of science is needed to address welfare-oriented laws and regulations that impact compassionate conservation efforts, and should perhaps be considered for promulgation by regulatory agencies.

In summary, zoo-based biologists and agency biologists pay close attention to animal welfare in species restoration programs partly because they want the animals to succeed and partly because current laws, regulations, or professional ethics and standards require them to do so. However, there is a general recognition that we can do better, especially to diversify behavior, and we are identifying appropriate metrics to measure welfare over the lifetime of a diversity of animals during different life stages in captivity and in the wild. Intensive management and observation of captive animals pre-release allows us better access to gather physiological data and assess behavioral types/diversity, and to ground-truth these individual animal assessment methods for released animals and their wild relatives. It is important to have effective animal welfare assessment techniques, and peer-reviewed reporting of these, for the survival of critically endangered species that will benefit from reintroductions during the near future in the Anthropocene

There is an argument that wild animals are like nomadic sovereign people, that they have the right to be generally left alone in their own home in the wild, unless they are in trouble and need our help. The weakness in this argument is that there is no "wild" left on this planet.[46] We humans have imprinted every inch of this planet, either directly or indirectly. There is a spectrum of quality and quantity of animal habitats and homes. Our approach to management of animal habitats and homes and the sustainability of wild populations is along the same spectrum — from an ability that is almost primitive and naïve from centuries ago, that allows us to have "hands-off" management and expect a species to survive, to one that is like a patient in intensive care that needs 24/7 doctor and nursing care simply to survive until the next day.

In the case of a species in trouble that needs our help in intensive care, we have both a moral obligation and a legal responsibility to help them survive and thrive. We can give them a home in zoos, perhaps as we would give refugees homes in our countries, to protect them, to rebuild their populations, and ideally to send as many as possible of them back home (i.e., reintroductions). There is a spectrum of intensive management that we can offer, from small and intense to large and minimal. Zoos, with their large animal populations that receive daily care by experienced keepers and veterinarians, are uniquely positioned to provide such critical care for endangered species, and do so. Less regulated spaces like sanctuaries and state or national parks allow animals to roam in a slightly freer way, and perhaps with supplemental feeding, but without intense daily observation and care from experienced keepers and veterinarians. And larger legally designated "wilderness" areas or wildlife corridors may only have habitat management and some level of animal protection by legal authorities who provide protection against poaching or habitat destruction for instance. The last example in this spectrum is perhaps the weakest link for animal welfare, and is the link that is often the cause of current species declines due to illegal activities that leave animals in pain and suffering as they are shot and wounded by poachers or as their habitat is altered for humans.

How then can we increase or improve animal welfare laws for zoo animal reintroductions given what we have learned in these cases. To begin, our cases suggest the importance of listening to the input of stakeholders particularly those with science-based expertise, potentially through an Animal Welfare Committee that is found in some laws,[47] to maximize animal welfare and success. Both the red wolf and the whooping crane illustrate that "similarity of appearance" rules could be enacted to establish protection for local coyotes as well as the wolves, giving both species better individual and population welfare. It is also worth thinking about how we might use the Endangered Species Act 10-j (experimental, nonessential population) designation, which can establish different rules for a geographically isolated population of an endangered species. Since this type of animal is considered "nonessential" the population can have special rules that reduce protection under the Act and may allow better welfare through more intensive human management of the reintroduced animals. Changes to this part of the designation might allow us to protect more of them who get into trouble during reintroductions. Banning lead-based ammunition to reduce welfare impacts on scavenger animals could also be a way to help reintroduced scavenger animals who are reintroduced. Creating state environmental programs that pay landowners not to kill endangered wolves or other species in reintroduction programs, and perhaps even moving the authority to issue hunting licenses out of wildlife agencies and to agencies that are dedicating to protecting endangered species are all additional ways to minimize welfare impacts on reintroduced animals and wild counterparts. Finally we could incorporate stress research results from longitudinal studies into regulations on animal reintroductions as a way to foster their long-term success in their new homes. These studies could highlight areas of welfare success and welfare risk for the reintroduced population.

Reintroductions need to continue with healthy animals, with due attention paid to animal welfare, for the survival of critically endangered species like giant panda bears, Amur tigers, California condors, red wolves and other critically endangered species, whose presence will benefit the ecological web of life and future generations of humans. So, why is it that zoos should continue these reintroductions? Why not turn the task over to federal agencies? Zoos continue to hold endangered animals in their zoo-based habitats and continue to work on daily animal care and welfare, and subsequent reintroductions, as well as funding for those activities. Modern zoos and aquariums are the only conservation organizations that use the results of leisure dollar spending for family activities on these conservation activities, and these monies are then leveraged with donor dollars and agency resources to achieve ongoing conservation of endangered species. I have suggested some potential advances that would both increase animal welfare potential for animals destined for reintroductions and would increase their abilities to survive post-reintroduction. The two may not be compatible and equitable for all animals, because in nature predators like wolves are not equal to their prey and in fact kill prey with little attention to prey animal welfare. The legal and regulatory reforms I call for in this chapter may be difficult, but this presents an opportunity to examine the best potential legislation to achieve compassionate conservation through focusing on animal welfare during conservation activities

NOTES

1. Elizabeth Kolbert, *The Sixth Extinction: An Unnatural History* (New York: Picador/Henry Holt 2014), 319.

2. Dolly Jorgensen, "Reintroduction and de-extinction," *BioScience*, 63, 9 (2013): 719–20 (doi: 10.1093/bioscience/63.9.719).

3. See "TEDX Dextinction, x=independently organized TED Event," Friday, March 15, 2013, Washington, DC. http://tedxdeextinction.org. Accessed January 3, 2017.

4. Dolly Jorgensen, "Reintroduction and de-extinction," *BioScience*, 63, 9 (2013): 719–20 (doi: 10.1093/bioscience/63.9.719).

5. PETA, 2016, http://www.peta.org/about-peta/why-peta/predator-reintroduction-programs/.

6. See www.waza.org. http://www.waza.org/files/webcontent/1.public_site/5.conservation/code_of_ethics_and_animal_welfare/Code%20of%20Ethics_EN.pdf. Accessed September 3, 2016.

7. Donald E. Moore and Roland Smith, "The red wolf as a model for carnivore reintroductions," *Symposium of the Zological Society London*, 62 (1991): 263–78.

8. Meryl Gelling, Paul J. Johnson, Tom P. Moorhouse, and David W. Macdonald, "Measuring Animal Welfare within a Reintroduction: An Assessment of Different Indices of Stress in Water Voles Arvicola amphibius," *PLoS ONE*, 7, 7 (2012): e41081 (doi:10.1371/journal.pone.0041081).

9. Meryl Gelling, Paul J. Johnson, Tom P. Moorhouse, David W. Macdonald, 2012, "Measuring Animal Welfare within a Reintroduction: An Assessment of Different Indices of Stress in Water Voles Arvicola amphibius," *PLoS ONE*, 7, 7 (2012): e41081 (doi:10.1371/journal.pone.0041081).

10. Donald Moore and Roland Smith, 1991, and unpublished data on head-starting of western pond turtles at Oregon Zoo and elsewhere.

11. International Union for Conservation of Nature (IUCN), *IUCN Guidelines for Reintroductions*, IUCN, 1998.

12. S. E. Dalrymple and A. Moehrenschlager, "'Words matter.' A response to Jørgensen's treatment of historic range and definitions of reintroduction," *Restoration Ecology*, 21 (2013): 156–58.

13. Donald E. Moore and Roland Smith, "The red wolf as a model for carnivore reintroductions," *Symposium Zolological Society London*, 62 (1991): 263–78.

14. David Mellor, Susan Hun, and Markus Gusset, eds., 2015, "Caring for Wildlife: The World Zoo and Aquarium Animal Welfare Strategy," *Gland: WAZA Executive Office publication*, 87. http://www.waza.org/files/webcontent/1.public_site/5.conservation/animal_welfare/WAZA%20Animal%20Welfare%20Strategy%202015_Portrait.pdf. Accessed September 12, 2016.

15. See www.waza.org. http://www.waza.org/files/webcontent/1.public_site/5.conservation/animal_welfare/WAZA%20Animal%20Welfare%20Strategy%202015_Portrait.pdf. Accessed November 2015.

16. Jason Watters and Cheryl Meehan, "Different strokes: Can managing behavioral types increase post-release success?" *Applied Animal Behaviour Science*, 102 (2007): 364–79.

17. David Mellor, Susan Hun, and Marcus Gusset, eds., 2015, "Caring for Wildlife: The World Zoo and Aquarium Animal Welfare Strategy," *Gland: WAZA Executive Office publication*, 87. http://www.waza.org/files/webcontent/1.public_site/5.conservation/animal_welfare/WAZA%20Animal%20Welfare%20Strategy%202015_Portrait.pdf. Accessed September 12, 2016.

18. Bridgit M. VonHoldt, Jason A. Cahill, Zhenxin Fan, Ilan Gronau, Jaqueline Robinson, John P. Pollinger, Beth Shapiro, Jeff Wall, and Robert K. Wayne, "Whole-genome sequence analysis shows that two endemic species of North American wolf are admixtures of the coyote and gray wolf," *Science Advances*, 2, 7 (2016): e1501714. DOI: 10.1126/sciadv.1501714

19. Animal Welfare Act, 36 FR 24925, Dec. 24, 1971, unless otherwise noted. Re-designated at 44 FR 36874, July 22, 1979, Section 3.127: Facilities, Outdoor.

20. See "Species Survival Plans," www.aza.org. Accessed December 13, 2015.

21. D. E. Moore and Robert Smith, "The red wolf as a model for carnivore reintro-ductions," *Symp Zol Soc London* 62 (1991): 263–78.

22. Taken from the *AZA Accreditation Standards and Related Policies* 2017 Edition, no author, page 30, https://www.aza.org/assets/2332/aza-accreditation-standards.pdf. Accessed August 4, 2016.

23. See fws.gov/red wolf. Accessed July 2015.

24. Eric Pearson, *Environmental and Natural Resources Law*, 4th edition (Conklin, NY: Lexis-Nexis, 2012).

25. Anonymous, "Center Steps Up Fight to Protect America's Last 45 Red Wolves," *Endangered Earth Summer* (2016): 9 (Tucson, AZ: Center for Biological Diversity).

26. Eric M. Gese, Fred K. Knowlton, Jennifer R Adams, Karen Beck, Todd K. Fuller, Dennis L. Murray, Todd D. Steury, Michael K Stokopf, Will T. Waddell, and Lisette P. Waits, "Managing hybridization of a recovering endangered species: The red wolf *Canis rufus* as a case study," *Current Zoology*, 61, 1 (2015): 191–205. (See also http://wildlife.org/supposed-wolf-species-may-actually-be-hybrids/. Red wolf and eastern wolf genetic data and commentary about pure genetics being outdated as a conserva-tion management tool.)

27. Lincoln Park *Zoo Magazine* and *Annual report*, 2016.

28. Anonymous, "Center Steps Up Fight to Protect America's Last 45 Red Wolves," *Endangered Earth Summer* (2016): 9 (Tucson, AZ: Center for Biological Diversity).

29. See "Whooping Crane" National Wildlife Federation, https://www.nwf.org/wildlife/wildlife-library/Birds/whooping-Crane.aspx. And see Wade Harell and Mark Bidwell, "Annual Whopping Crane Recover Activities," October 2016, fws.gov/midwest/whoopingcrane/. Accessed January 3, 2017.

30. See "Establishment of a Nonessential Experimental Population of Whooping Cranes in the Eastern United States," Final Rule, Federal Register, Vol. 66, N. 123/Tuesday, June 26, 2001: 33903–17. fws.gov/midwest/whoopingcrane/pdf/FinalRuleFR.pdf. Accessed January 4, 2017. fws.gov/red wolf.

31. See "Nonlead Ammunition in California," Wildlife Branch Game Management, wildlife.ca.gov/hunting/nonlead-ammunition. Accessed January 4, 2017.

32. Personal communication with Oregon Deptartment Fish and Wildlife and Ore-gon Zoo Nonlead educator.

33. Mike Mace personal communication August 2016.

34. Mike Mace personal communication August 2016.

35. Victoria Drietz, "Issues in species recovery: an example based on the Wyoming toad," *Bioscience*, 56, 9 (2006): 765–71.

36. Meryl Gelling, Paul J. Johnson, Tom P. Moorhouse, and David W. Macdonald, "Measuring Animal Welfare within a Reintroduction: An Assessment of Different Indices of Stress in Water Voles, Arvicola amphibius," *PLoS ONE*, 7, 7 (2012): e41081 (doi:10.1371/journal.pone.0041081).

37. R. Andrew Odum and Paul S. Corn, *Bufo baxteri* Porter, 1968, "Wyoming toad," 390–92, in Michael J. Lannoo, ed., *Amphibian Declines: The Conservation Status of United States Species* (Berkeley: University of California Press, 2005).

38. Victoria Drietz, "Issues in species recovery: an example based on the Wyoming toad," *Bioscience*, 56, 9 (2006): 765–71.

39. USFWS 1991.

40. Victoria Drietz, "Issues in species recovery: an example based on the Wyoming toad," *Bioscience*, 56, 9 (2006): 765–71.

41. Drietz, 2006.

42. Drietz, 2006.

43. Mark Halvorsen, personal communication.

44. Victoria Drietz, "Issues in species recovery: an example based on the Wyoming toad," *Bioscience*, 56, 9 (2006): 765–71.

45. Meryl Gelling, Paul J. Johnson, Tom P. Moorhouse, and David W. Macdonald, "Measuring Animal Welfare within a Reintroduction: An Assessment of Different Indices of Stress in Water Voles Arvicola amphibius," *PLoS ONE*, 7, 7 (2012): e41081 (doi:10.1371/journal.pone.0041081).

46. Irus Braverman, *Wild Life: The Institution of Nature* (Stanford, CA: Stanford University Press, 2015).

47. See WAZA.org for examples of these committees.

BIBLIOGRAPHY

Braverman, Irus. *Wild Life: The Institution of Nature*. Stanford, CA: Stanford University Press, 2015.

Drietz, Victoria. "Issues in species recovery: an example based on the Wyoming toad." *Bioscience*, 56, 9 (2006): 765–71.

"Establishment of a Nonessential Experimental Population of Whooping Cranes in the Eastern United States," Final Rule, Federal Register, Vol. 66, N. 123/Tuesday, June 26, 2001: 33903–33917. fws.gov/midwest/whoopingcrane/pdf/FinalRuleFR.pdf. Accessed January 4, 2017. fws.gov/red wolf.

Gelling, Meryl, Paul Johnson, Tom Moorhouse, David Macdonald. "Measuring Animal Welfare within a Reintroduction: An Assessment of Different Indices of Stress in Water Voles Arvicola amphibius." *PLoS ONE*, 7, 7 (2012): e41081.

Gese, Eric M., Fred F. Knowlton, Jennifer R. Adams, Karen Beck, Todd K. Fuller, Dennis L. Murray, Todd D. Steury, Michael K. Stokopf, Will T. Waddell, and Lisette P. Waits. "Managing hybridization of a recovering endangered species: The red wolf *Canis rufus* as a case study." *Current Zoology*, 61, 1 (2015): 191–205.

Harell, Wade and Mark Bidwell. "Annual Whopping Crane Recover Activities," October 2016. fws.gov/midwest/whoopingcrane/. Accessed January 3, 2017.

International Union for Conservation of Nature (IUCN). *IUCN Guidelines for Re-introductions*. IUCN, 1998.

Jorgensen, Dolly. "Reintroduction and de-extinction." *BioScience*, 63, 9 (2013): 719–20.

Kolbert, Elizabeth. *The sixth Extinction: An Unnatural History*. New York: Picador/Henry Holt, 2014.

Mellor, David, Susan Hunt, and Markus Gusset, eds. "Caring for Wildlife: The World Zoo and Aquarium Animal Welfare Strategy." *Gland: WAZA Executive Office publication* 2015.

Moore, Donald E. and Roland Smith. "The red wolf as a model for carnivore reintroductions." *Symposium Zolological Society London*, 62 (1991): 263–78.

"Nonlead Ammunition in California." Wildlife Branch=Game Management, wildlife.ca.gov/hunting/nonlead-ammunition. Accessed January 4, 2017.

Odum, R. Andrew and Paul S. Corn. *Bufo baxteri* Porter, 1968, "Wyoming toad," 390–392. In Michael J. Lannoo, ed. *Amphibian Declines: The Conservation Status of United States Species*. Berkeley: University of California Press, 2005.

Pearson, Eric. *Environmental and Natural Resources Law*, 4th edition. Conklin, NY: LexisNexis, 2012.

"Species Survival Plans." www.waza.org. Accessed January 4, 2017.

"TEDX Dextinction, x=independently organized TED Event." Friday, March 15, 2013, Washington, DC. tedxdeextinction.org.

VonHoldt, Bridgit M., James A. Cahill, Zhenxin Fan, Ilan Gronau, Jaqueline Robinson, John P. Pollinger, Beth Shapiro, Jeff Wall, and Robert K. Wayne. "Whole-genome sequence analysis shows that two endemic species of North American wolf are admixtures of the coyote and gray wolf." *Science Advances*, 2, 7 (2016): e1501714.

Watters, Jason and Cheryl Meehan. "Different strokes: Can managing behavioral types increase post-release success?" *Applied Animal Behaviour Science* 102 (2007): 364–79.

"Whooping Crane." National Wildlife Federation, https://www.nwf.org/wildlife/wildlife-library/Birds/whooping-Crane.aspx.

"The World Zoo and Aquarium Animal Welfare Strategy." *Gland: WAZA Executive Office publication*, 87. http://www.waza.org/files/webcontent/1.public_site/5.conservation/animal_welfare/WAZA%20Animal%20Welfare%20Strategy%202015_Portrait.pdf.

THREE

Zoos as Venues for Research

Changes in Focus, Changes in Perception

Susan Margulis

At least once a week, I am at my local zoo doing research. I position myself at the gorilla exhibit, home to a troop of six western lowland gorillas, smartphone in hand, ready to record patterns of behavior, space use, and interindividual interactions among the troop members. I feel fortunate to have the chance to study such a rare species, and am grateful for the opportunity afforded to me and other researchers like me who are able to capitalize on the unique venue that zoos offer to the researcher. The zoo also provides a valuable training environment for students to learn skills that will be critical for their development as scientists. Each year, I train fifteen to twenty students to collect behavioral data, to use these data to answer questions, and to develop an understanding of how behavioral research is conducted.

During my hours observing gorillas, I also informally observe zoo visitors which can sometimes be rather frustrating. It is hard to count the number of times I have seen zoo visitors point to the gorillas and say "look at the monkeys." But, despite all of this, observing the zoo visitors can also be very enlightening. Most zoo visitors find observing nonhuman animals up close to be a humbling experience and one that can motivate them to be stewards of nature. Indeed, it is often the children who initiate such conversations that hopefully lead to changes in the behavior of their families. For the vast majority of people, a zoo is the closest they will ever come to seeing the diverse species with whom they share this planet. While some may question the existence of zoos and express great concern over the welfare of the animals that live there, in my opinion the benefits of zoos—the educational opportunities they offer to visitors, and the support of conservation programs to save remnant wild populations—outweigh any perceived costs.

One often overlooked benefit of zoos is the contributions made to science via research. This benefit is largely unnoticed because no zoo exists today specifically *for the purpose of* research. While many of the nineteenth-century European zoos were established in close association with museums as zoological research entities, and were often run by zoologists (for example, the Jardin des Plantes in Paris was established in 1793 in association with the Muséum d'Histoire Naturelle with Etienne Geoffroy Saint-Hilaire as its first director; the Zoological Society of London was formed in 1826 with the aim of establishing a research facility— Regents Park—which opened two years later),[1] the public remained largely unaware of these research goals. In their early days in fact, zoos were places of entertainment, with little regard for education, research, conservation, or even the welfare of the nonhuman animals exhibited.[2] This is no longer the case, and zoos now have as their mandate and mission a focus on education, research, and conservation.[3] Furthermore, the welfare of the individual animals housed in zoos is of paramount importance. Research is often viewed by the general public as something that is, by definition, antiwelfare. How can one subject an individual to unwanted procedures and still claim positive welfare?

Zoo research is unique in several respects. First, research conducted in zoos is (for the most part), opportunistic, taking advantage of the presence of zoo animals. These animals are not maintained in captivity in order for research to be done; rather, animals are housed in zoos for other reasons, including species conservation and public education. Capitalizing on this fact, and conducting research, becomes not just a benefit, but a responsibility for zoos. Second, most zoo research is noninvasive. Animals are rarely subjected to alterations in their management expressly for research. I for example, observe the gorillas but rarely do I interfere with their management; if I do interfere, it is for anticipated enhancement of their lives. Finally, zoo research is generally voluntary. That is, just as for research on humans, if an individual animal opts not to participate in a particular research study, he or she simply does not. These three features—opportunistic, noninvasive, and voluntary—mark zoo research as distinctly different from the stereotypical view of experimental research.

While there are features of zoo research that make it unique and distinctly different from the general perception of "animal research," research conducted in a zoological setting must still adhere to all guidelines, regulations, and requirements established for other types of research involving nonhuman animals. Guidelines generally provide minimum standards: minimum standards of care, minimum husbandry requirements, and so on. The zoo community in the United States at accredited zoos strives for optimum levels of care, and must adhere not only to federal regulations regarding animal research, but to the higher standards imposed by accrediting agencies and by public opinion.

It should be clear at the outset that this chapter is not about the ethics of maintaining animals in zoos. Suffice it to say that this author is decidedly in favor of the existence of good zoos and the maintenance of sustainable zoo populations. That is not a question for this chapter (or for this volume), though. The questions that this chapter aims to answer are in relation to research. Given that we have such diverse collections in zoos, what are the limitations, requirements, and ethical dilemmas associated with the conduct of research in zoos?

To explore the issue of research in zoos and the impacts and implications for the subjects of such research, I will first review the evolution of zoos and the societal, ecological, and economic milieu in which they evolved. Next, the definition of research in general and specifically in the context of the zoo will be fully explored. There tends to be much confusion regarding the distinction between "research" and "experiment," and "invasive" versus "noninvasive" research. Third, I will review the difference between laboratory animals maintained explicitly for research and opportunistic research conducted on zoo populations. Fourth, the benefits of research for conservation will be articulated. Next, I will address the issue of informed consent, and how this might apply to nonhuman animals in the zoo setting. Finally, I will offer recommendations to facilitate the conduct of zoo research in a manner that is appropriate for zoo inhabitants and demonstrates strict adherence to guidelines, optimum care of subjects, and broad applicability.

HISTORY OF RESEARCH IN ZOOS

In 1874, the Philadelphia Zoo opened its gates to the public. While there continues to be much debate regarding which zoo can claim to be the first zoo in the United States—besides the Philadelphia Zoo, the Central Park Zoo in New York City, the Lincoln Park Zoo in Chicago, IL, the Buffalo Zoo in Buffalo, NY, and many others may be able to claim this title—the first zoos in the United States date back to the late 1800s. Their rise followed a similar pattern in Europe, and for similar reasons. In an increasingly urban environment, many people craved an afternoon in nature, and an opportunity for family fun.[4] Indeed, the primary function of the nation's first zoos was entertainment. Little attention was paid to animal welfare, conservation, education, or research. It would take nearly one hundred years before the mission statements of the nation's zoos would expand beyond pure entertainment and encompass the components that are fundamental to "modern zoos": education, conservation, and research.

With the growing number and popularity of zoos, the development of an organization to facilitate professional development, high-quality care, and standardization of practice was not far behind. The American Association of Zoological Parks and Aquariums (AAZPA) was established in 1924 as a subgroup of the American Institute of Park Executives (AIPE), and later as a branch of the National Recreation and Park Association (NRPA). Ultimately, AAZPA became an independent organization in 1972.[5] Two years later, the Oregon Zoo and the Philadelphia Zoo became the first two zoos to be accredited by AAZPA, followed shortly thereafter by many other institutions. While accreditation was viewed as an optional component of membership, this changed in 1985 and for a time, the number of accredited institutions declined as a result of the added cost and effort of accreditation, but it has since rebounded. In 1994, AAZPA changed its name to the Association of Zoos and Aquariums (AZA), which today accredits 233 zoos, nearly all of which (227) are in North America.[6]

The AZA mandates that all member zoos demonstrate clear, specific, and substantial investment in conservation, education and research. Zoos have made amazing strides in the areas of education and conservation, and in fact the role that zoos play in both *in situ* and *ex situ* conservation is becoming increasingly important.[7] Yet the incorporation of research into zoo operations continues to lag behind the other pillars on which zoos stand. The 104 pages of AZA's accreditation standards are explicit about expectations regarding conservation, education, and research. The details however, are relatively brief and nonspecific, especially in comparison to animal care standards. For example, the standards for elephant care cover thirty-three pages, while conservation, education, and research combined encompass only five pages. Nevertheless, the guidelines do point out that the conduct of research is a fundamental endeavor for zoos.

The accreditation guidelines stipulate the following in regards to conservation: "Conservation efforts have been identified as a priority for AZA-accredited institutions. These include interpretive materials and programs, participation in AZA animal management programs, *in situ* conservation efforts, and resource support for cooperative conservation programs. Participation in conservation programs, to the extent appropriate, must be demonstrated."[8] With respect to education, the guidelines indicate "Education must be a key component of the institution's mission. Education is an important component in the conservation mission of each institution. Effective educational programming is a proven method of increasing awareness and participation in stewardship of the natural world."[9] The mandate for research is a bit more vague: "Research activities must be under the direction of a person qualified to make informed decisions regarding research."[10] This section does suggest the importance of research in zoos in its general considerations:

Contemporary animal management, husbandry, veterinary care and conservation practices should be based in science. A commitment to scientific research, both basic and applied, is a trademark of the modern zoological park and aquarium. An AZA accredited institution must have a demonstrated commitment to scientific research that is in proportion to the size and scope of its facilities, staff and animals. There must be a formal written research policy including a process for the evaluation and approval of scientific research project proposals. [11]

The nuances in the wording of the guidelines are subtle, but nonetheless telling. The sections on "Conservation" and "Education" explicitly have a mission statement, suggesting that these are fundamental and necessary for any modern zoo. The wording for the "Research" section is not organized in the same way, does not include a mission statement, and is less than 175 words in length. In contrast, "Education" comprises over 500 words, and "Conservation" includes over 550 words. From this, we may conclude that while research is recognized as being an important component of what zoos must do, it clearly does not garner the same level of attention, expectation, or clarity that conservation, education, and entertainment receive.

Despite the advances and the recognition that research is important and relevant in zoos, research has continued to generally lag behind in its integration into zoo mission. If for example, one searches the websites of some of the nation's oldest zoos, research is rarely mentioned. The Philadelphia Zoo mission statement claims "By connecting people with wildlife, the Philadelphia Zoo creates joyful discovery and inspires action for animals and habitats." [12] The Chicago Zoological Society, the first zoo in the country to create the position of curator of research, does not include research in its mission statement: "The mission of the Chicago Zoological Society is to inspire conservation leadership by connecting people with wildlife and nature." [13] The Wildlife Conservation Society, which currently oversees five zoos and aquariums in New York City, explicitly include science in its mission statement: "WCS saves wildlife and wild places worldwide through science, conservation action, education, and inspiring people to value nature." [14] Lincoln Park Zoo similarly includes science in its mission statement: "Lincoln Park Zoo is dedicated to connecting people with nature by providing a free, family-oriented wildlife experience in the heart of Chicago and by advancing the highest quality of animal care, education, science and conservation." [15] But while *science* has begun to find its way into the mission and goal of zoos, the term *research* has not.

DEFINING "RESEARCH"

Why has zoo research failed to be included in changes to the zoo mission? Is this lack of inclusion warranted? Zoos always walk a fine line in justifying the maintenance of their collections, and the suggestion of "research collections" may lead to some misinterpretation. First, the definition of "research" may cause misconceptions about the ways in which zoo facilities, and in particular the nonhuman animals that reside there, are used. Second, the specific goals of research may not have been clearly articulated. Third, funding of research in zoo settings has fallen behind funding for research in other venues (including the field, the lab, and semi-free-ranging facilities). Fourth, research has generally been viewed as the "last piece" of the fundamental operating principles of zoos (that is, education, conservation, and recreation are considered to be more mission-critical to zoos; research may be an optional piece added if time and resources permit, and the extent to which it is included in accreditation standards supports this conclusion).

1956 marked the hiring of the first curator of research by a zoo, and one of the first (and perhaps the first) zoo researchers with a PhD. The Chicago Zoological Society hired Dr. George Rabb as its first curator of research, in an effort to support and facilitate research with its animal collection. Rabb endorsed and encouraged a range of research studies with the animal collection, ranging from cognitive research to reproductive biology to behavioral studies. Rabb conducted many of his own research studies, but also recruited outside researchers. His continued and expanding role in research and conservation led to his eventual appointment as zoo director in 1976; a position he held until his retirement in 2003.[16] Devra Kleiman, another of the earliest PhD-level zoo researchers, headed the department of zoological research at the National Zoo for many years. She lamented that the emphasis on conservation and applied research, while critical, happened at the expense of basic scientific research, and urged that

> zoos must continue to provide opportunities for the conduct of basic research while simultaneously pursuing applied work in conservation and animal management; only through a combined approach can we hope to achieve some of the scientific breakthroughs that are required, if zoo biologists hope to contribute to the preservation of this planet's biodiversity.[17]

Geoffrey Hosey found a similar lack of basic behavioral research in a survey of studies published in the journal *Zoo Biology* and urged expanded collaboration between zoos and academic researchers.[18]

The definition of *research* may seem clear and obvious, but this is often not the case. To lay people, the terms *research* and *experiment* may be synonymous. "Experiment" carries with it the connation of invasive, manipulative research, often to the detriment of nonhuman subjects utilized in such programs. This misinterpretation, and misrepresentation, of what constitutes research, may be at the heart of some misunderstandings about the nature of research. Broadly, research may be defined as the "diligent and systematic inquiry or investigation into a subject in order to discover or revise facts, theories, applications, etc."[19] Research may be observational or experimental. Observational research involves collecting information without altering or interfering with subjects. This is often the method of choice in field behavioral ecology as well as zoo-based studies, and its methods were codified in 1974 in a seminal paper by Jeanne Altmann.[20] While developed to systematically explore patterns of behavior, observational research can be used in a range of scientific disciplines including nutrition, endocrinology, and population biology. Experimental research involves controlling and manipulating key variables and measuring their impact on an outcome variable (behavior, health, and so on). This latter type of research is often what the public interprets all research to be, yet this comprises only a subset of research, and is arguably the least common form of research to be conducted in the zoo setting.

LEGAL PROTECTION FOR ZOO ANIMALS

All zoos in the United States must meet the minimum welfare standards as set out by the Animal Welfare Act (AWA), and enforced by the Animal and Plant Health Inspection Service (APHIS) of the US Department of Agriculture (USDA). The scope and coverage of the AWA is limited, its requirements represent minimum standards, its omissions are conspicuous, and the requirements for licensure are far less demanding than the AZA requirements for professional accreditation. USDA does not, for example, inspect exhibits that do not house mammals. The USDA also excludes numerous mammalian species in specific contexts, such as laboratory rats and laboratory mice.[21] The AZA, on the other hand, inspects all institutions seeking accreditation, regardless of the taxonomic makeup of the collection. Similarly, USDA inspections are aimed entirely at the physical facilities and practices regarding the nonhuman animals in the facility, and do not address such areas as education, visitor experience, financial stability, and governance, all of which are essential components of an AZA accreditation inspection. It is important to note that AZA standards are invariably more stringent than those imposed locally or nationally.

While all zoos housing mammals must be inspected and licensed by the USDA, AZA membership is not mandatory, but it nevertheless serves as a label that indicates that the institution meets or exceeds a very rigorous set of standards. As of March 2016, there were 233 accredited zoos in the United States.[22] A search of the APHIS database yields 2,588 licensed exhibitors in the United States.[23] Licensed exhibitors are defined as "Individuals or businesses with warm-blooded animals that are on display, perform for the public, or are used in educational presentations," and include circuses, zoos, educational displays, animal acts, petting farms/zoos, wildlife parks, marine mammal parks, and some sanctuaries. Thus, less than 10 percent of licensed animal exhibitors have met AZA accreditation standards.

The term *research facility* is defined in the Animal Welfare Act as

> any school (except an elementary or secondary school), institution, organization, or person that uses or intends to use live animals in research, tests, or experiments, and that (1) purchases or transports live animals in commerce, or (2) receives funds under a grant, award, loan, or contract from a department, agency, or instrumentality of the United States for the purpose of carrying out research, tests, or experiments: *Provided,* That the Secretary may exempt, by regulation, any such school, institution, organization, or person that does not use or intend to use live dogs or cats, except those schools, institutions, organizations, or persons, which use substantial numbers (as determined by the Secretary) of live animals the principal function of which schools, institutions, organizations, or persons, is biomedical research or testing, when in the judgment of the Secretary, any such exemption does not vitiate the purpose of this chapter.[24]

This definition is somewhat vague and unclear, however it should be noted that only three zoos currently have "active" research facility licenses, suggesting zoos are generally not categorized as research facilities. One might thus conclude that if research is opportunistic, noninvasive, and voluntary, then an institution does not need to be licensed as a research facility. This may not be the case if, for example, federal funding is used for research or if animals are obtained specifically for a research project.

The requirements of the Animal Welfare Act are sufficiently vague and general that painful procedures, while requiring justification, are not prohibited.[25, 26] The omissions in the Animal Welfare Act—in terms of species coverage, and the nature of research which may be undertaken if it is deemed justifiable—often subject animals to levels of pain and suffering that would never be considered acceptable in a zoo setting.[27] Zoo research committees would be loath to approve procedures that would lead to pain and suffering among the animals that reside in their zoos as this runs counter to the aims of zoo-based research: the enhancement of the lives of zoo animals and the conservation of remnant wild populations. In contrast, laboratory research generally has as its goal outcomes that benefit humans: medical advances, safety, and so on. To consider "animal research" in the laboratory setting and the zoo setting as similar undermines the nature of zoo research, and highlights some of the limitations of the Animal Welfare Act.

The self-regulation that zoos have imposed on themselves could be more firmly established and specifically mandated with changes to the Animal Welfare Act. The challenge to this of course would come from the laboratory community; from a welfare perspective, the research policies that zoos adhere to should be in place in any research venue (including laboratories), but the likely obstacles could be immense. As already noted, research in zoos almost invariably is directed specifically toward the welfare of the animals, or the conservation of the species. Invasive research, or research that might involve pain, is *almost never* supported in a zoo context, despite the AWA loopholes that permit "justifiable" pain in procedures. A stronger Animal Welfare Act would likely have no negative impact on zoo research, as it already adheres to the most stringent animal welfare guidelines, but such a change (despite likely opposition) would have positive impacts on animals used in other types of research. The opportunistic approach used by zoo researchers—collecting samples when an animal is sedated for other reasons, for example—should be a requirement. Sedation or manual restraint solely for the purpose of research does not have a place in the zoo world. Zoos must view the opportunistic collection of data and samples as a responsibility and should make every effort to collect information during routine physicals that can be used for research.

Although the Animal Welfare Act suffers from loopholes and simply not going far enough in terms of putting animal welfare at the forefront, it does nevertheless provide some protections and regulation and sets minimum standards of care. Zoos however, voluntarily adhere to far stricter standards, and as a result, would easily meet any more stringent regulations, should the Animal Welfare Act ever be modified to strengthen its requirements.

In addition to the protection afforded under the Animal Welfare Act, zoo animals may also garner legal protection based on the stipulations of other pieces of legislation, including the Endangered Species Act and the Lacey Act. Both of these acts were designed to protect wildlife *in situ* and to prevent sale or illegal transport of wildlife. The implications of such legislation for zoos, while problematic, have been addressed via exceptions made by the USFWS and/or the USDA. For example, zoos may be exempt from the provisions of the Endangered Species Act in the context of veterinary care, transfer for breeding, or exhibition. Similarly, transfer of animals for breeding purposes does not violate the Lacey Act.[28]

AZA AND ZOO RESEARCH

The Animal Welfare Act does not clearly distinguish between "research" and "experiment." This is troubling, given the unstated but generally accepted notion that these terms are synonymous, and that "experiment" implies invasiveness. Research, however, may be conducted in noninvasive ways without an experimental manipulation of variables. The German Animal Welfare Act section specifically defines an experiment as "procedures or treatments of animals, if these may be linked to pain, suffering or damage to these animals, or on the hereditary material, if these may be linked to pain, suffering or damage to the animals with modified hereditary material or the animals which bear these."[29] Establishing such a clear and specific definition for "experiment," and distinguishing it from the broader category of "research," is a critical step in the pursuit of zoo research and distinguishing zoo research from harmful or invasive experiments.

Arguably, zoos may participate in observational research, but they rarely (if ever) engage in experiments. While it may be the case that some observational studies do indeed involve changing or manipulating variables (for example, diet content or timing, provision of enrichment, or social grouping), and while it is possible that such manipulations may have adverse consequences (a new diet may prove to be inadequate or unpalatable; a new enrichment item may be stressful; aggression and possible injury may result from the establishment of new social groupings), these manipulations are done with the expectation that the welfare of subjects will be enhanced, not degraded, by the manipulation. But is this acceptable? What protections do nonhuman animals have in the context of research? Do the same protocols, regulations, and procedures apply to animals housed in zoos as to animals housed in laboratories?

AZA recognizes the importance of clearly defined guidelines and principles with respect to the conduct of research, and continues to make efforts to support, clarify and operationalize research in zoos. As an accrediting body, AZA manages a number of committees and advisory groups to facilitate many aspects of zoo operations, including research. As early as 1991, AZA began to establish Scientific Advisory Groups (SAGs) "to facilitate, support, collaborate on, communicate about, and coordinate relevant science-based activities."[30] Thus even in its early years, AZA recognized the importance of taking a scientific approach to the management of zoo populations. Each SAG reports to a Board-level AZA *Committee* for oversight (Table 1). Committees provide guidance, direction, and goals for each SAG. The SAGs in turn, serve as scientific advisors to lower-level AZA programs, including Taxon Advisory Groups (TAGs) and Species Survival Plans (SSPs). The aim is for consistency across all AZA programs, and application of scientific methods and approaches to all aspects of zoo operations.

Research plays a significant role in every SAG, and the overseeing Committees serve to formalize the input that SAGs have within AZA. The Research and Technology Committee indicates that "research priorities are focused on the animals in our care, in situ conservation, and public education."[31] This Committee provides a clear description of what constitutes "mission-focused research" in the zoological setting:

> Mission-Focused Research includes any project undertaken by a AZA-accredited institution or certified related facility that: Involves application of the scientific method: is hypothesis-driven (or question-driven), involves systematic data collection and analysis of those data, and draws conclusions from the research process; Is primarily focused on studying questions relevant to the conservation, animal care and welfare, science, or education missions of institutions.[32]

Thus mission-focused research encompasses a broad array of topics, ranging from applied research for management purposes, to basic research on species behavior and biology, to research applicable to field conservation. The commonality is that a quantitative, scientific approach is used to address a clearly defined hypothesis or question. The Committee's charge goes beyond the applied aspects of research to encompass theoretical areas with broad interest to scientists, conservation research that can have substantial impacts on wild populations, and educational research that can support zoos' mission to educate the public. To fulfill the AZA's mission, it is vitally important to fully embrace ongoing scientific inquiry and integrate research in strategic program areas. By building upon a sound base of scientific knowledge and pursuing the prior-

Table 3.1. Relationship between AZA board-level committees and Scientific Advisory Groups (SAGs)

Committee	SAG
Animal Health Committee	Veterinary
Animal Welfare Committee	Behavior
Conservation Education Committee	Ambassador Animal
Field Conservation Committee	Green
Research and Technology Committee	Reproduction and Endocrinology
Wildlife Conservation and Management Committee	Avian
	Biomaterials Banking
	Institutional Data Management
	Molecular Data for Population Management
	Nutrition
	Small Population Management

ities identified in this document, stronger practices will be developed and increased conservation impacts will be achieved.

In addition to the Research and Technology Committee and its associated SAGs, the Animal Welfare Committee is particularly involved in questions concerning research and the impact of research on animal welfare. The mission statement of the Animal Welfare Committee states, "The AZA Animal Welfare Committee promotes good welfare for animals in AZA-accredited zoos and aquariums, by assisting member institutions in identifying and applying best practices in animal welfare and through promoting advances in *animal welfare science*." [33] (emphasis added). Thus there is clear recognition that a scientific approach to the study of animal welfare is essential in order to maximize said welfare. Furthermore, this mandate is noted as being a responsibility of AZA-accredited institutions, both scientifically and ethically. Facilitating research is one of the key mandates of the Committee. Overseeing both the Behavior and Endocrinology Scientific Advisory Groups, the Animal Welfare Committee operates at the forefront of zoo research, given the extent to which zoo research is so heavily biased toward behavior. Behavioral research and more recently endocrinological research, share a common approach and a common goal: both utilize noninvasive approaches to the collection of scientific data, and both have as one of their goals collecting information that can inform animal management and welfare decisions.

NONINVASIVE, OPPORTUNISTIC, VOLUNTARY

The conduct of research that is noninvasive is a key aspect of the most common types of scientific investigations conducted in zoos. In the case of behavioral research, data are routinely collected without interfering with the subjects of the study in any way. A researcher may observe zoo animals in much the same way as a visitor might observe. Oftentimes, behavioral research is conducted with a very specific management goal in mind. Thus while there may be some manipulation of subjects, it is a manipulation that is going to take place regardless of the research. For example, moving a group to a new home may occur as part of normal zoo improvements or renovations. Researchers may capitalize on this opportunity to scientifically assess whether behavior changes following this move. Changes in husbandry, diet, or enrichment may be implemented for management purposes in hopes of eventually leading to enhancements in animal welfare. Without concomitant research, it becomes impossible to assess the efficacy of any such changes. Such studies may not be without risk. An enhancement may not have the anticipated positive effect or, perhaps, it may even have a negative one. But, without the carefully and systematically gathered data, it becomes impossible to draw conclusions, and we risk repeating mistakes.

The development of noninvasive methods of measuring hormones has had a tremendous impact on research in both zoo and field settings. Whereas assessment of hormone concentrations—stress hormones, for example—previously required physical restraint or anesthesia and blood draws (ironically leading to elevations in stress), modern techniques allow for noninvasive measurement of some hormones using urine or fecal samples. In some cases, hair or saliva may also be used. In any case, these methods not only allow researchers to monitor hormones noninvasively, but support research that can directly and specifically lead to enhanced welfare via reductions in stressful stimuli. Shepherdson et al., for instance, describe three case studies in which noninvasive hormone monitoring was instrumental in assessing well-being in three diverse species: polar bears, clouded leopards, and Hawaiian honeycreepers. In all three cases, information gained from fecal glucocorticoid (stress hormone) analyses facilitated management changes to enhance welfare of highlighted environmental factors that could negatively impact welfare.[34]

In addition to *noninvasive* methods of research, much zoo research is *opportunistic*. As noted in the mission statement of the Animal Welfare Committee of the AZA, "AZA-accredited institutions have a scientific responsibility to gain a greater understanding of the well-being of the animals in their care,"[35] thus it is the responsibility of zoos to learn as much as they possibly can from the animals in their care. This includes capitalizing on occasional routine physicals, and ultimately gaining as much knowledge and information postmortem as possible. Researchers who require a blood sample from the animal (for genetic analysis, or for veterinary medical research) could request that an animal be restrained and a sample collected, but under most circumstances, this will be viewed as too invasive. However, if the researcher is willing to wait, such a sample is likely obtainable within a year, given that most accredited zoos conduct routine annual physicals on animals in the collection. In this context, zoos represent an incredibly valuable, unique and often untapped resource for scientists. Similarly, zoos routinely conduct necropsies, or postmortem examinations of all individuals at the time of death. This too can provide a wealth of information, and acquiring such information once again is the responsibility of every zoo.

Finally, participation in research by zoo animals is typically *voluntary*. In the case of observational studies (which are often conducted from public areas, subjects may choose to be visible/on-exhibit or not. In studies that require more direct participation, such participation is not mandated. As discussed in more detail later, cognitive research involving computer touchscreens and other interactive devices generally involves the subject entering a specified area to engage with the device. Animals are not forced to participate, nor are they punished for not participating. They may choose to participate or not, and may be rewarded for their participation. This use of a positive reinforcement approach is standard procedure in zoos for both management and research.

Research in zoos thus rarely involves invasive or manipulative experimentation. Herein lies a key misconception among the general public that is reflected by the occasional reluctance of zoos to fully capitalize on their research potential. If the public considers "research" and "experiment" to be synonymous, then this can raise a red flag about "zoo research." Zoos do not experiment on their collections, but they are engaged in research. How can we disentangle this confusion and clarify this distinction?

UNIQUE ASPECTS OF ZOO-BASED RESEARCH

What is the nature of zoo research, and in what ways does it impact the nonhuman animals on which it is conducted? The emphasis of zoo research is invariably applied: research that serves to enhance well-being, reproductive success, and public awareness. This is somewhat of a tautology in the sense that it implies that research on zoo animals is justified because it improves or enhances the lives of zoo animals. Those who question the existence of zoos would surely not be swayed by this argument, however a growing body of zoo research has as its main goal to enhance conservation of remnant wild populations; this is arguably a laudable goal, to put conservation of rare species as its aim. It is thus important to recognize that conservation-related research, both *in situ* and *ex situ*, contributes to conservation efforts directed at wild populations.[36]

During the past thirty years, a number of surveys and meta-analyses have endeavored to summarize the types of research conducted in zoos, the rationale for the research, and the outcomes. The very fact that this effort has been undertaken more than once suggests that there is considerable emphasis on zoo-based research, that it is expanding in scope, and that the nature of such research has changed, and continues to change. Brambell described the changes in zoo research trends in historical perspective. He highlights the 1950s as a time when scientists first took notice of zoos, often in an unfavorable light: "they were purposeless, net consumers, badly run, badly designed."[37] This began to change as zoos began to change, first in Europe, under the guidance of visionaries such as Heini Hediger, Bernhard Grzimek, and Gerald Durrell, whose emphasis on barless exhibits, conservation, and scientific investigation did not take hold in the United States until some years later. During the next twemty-five years, scientific approaches to animal nutrition, genetics and population management, and conservation began to advance.

Finlay and Maple first surveyed zoos about research in 1986, early in the development of the "modern zoo" in North America. This survey followed shortly after the requirement of accreditation for membership in

AAZPA. The findings suggested that research was being conducted at 70 percent of institutions that responded to the survey, but only 59 percent of institutions indicated that it was a part of the institution's objectives. Behavior and reproduction were the most common areas of research, but applied areas, including husbandry and exhibit design, were also prominently featured. Interestingly, only 21 percent of respondents had written guidelines that researchers must adhere to.[38] This suggests that most research was done on the fly, without a clear motivation or overarching goal. While nearly all respondents reported that research was either stable or expanding, several reported that it was declining, in part as a result of public perceptions: "Because of the public nature of zoos, some types of research are inappropriate and politically inopportune."[39]

Maple and colleagues repeated the survey to evaluate changes in the nature and extent of zoo research over an approximately ten-year period. While patterns generally remained consistent with the 1986 survey, only 10 percent of institutions at this time reported that they did not have a committee or other means of research oversight, and 64 percent had specific written guidelines that researchers were asked to adhere to.[40] This represents a noticeable and meaningful change in the nature of zoo research. Research efforts continued to develop and become more clearly delineated and codified, with more substantial oversight and expectation of follow-up. In terms of the role of research in zoos, the proportion of zoos that included "research" as one of their formal objectives increased as well, from 59 percent in 1986 to 83 percent in 1998. However, a disconnect still remained in the topics of research, and the extent to which research findings were published. For example, while the current study suggested that over 40 percent of zoo research may be related to animal well-being (for example, enrichment effectiveness and exhibit design), less than 4 percent of published articles listed in AZA's Annual Report on Conservation and Science (ARCS) by zoos related to these areas.[41] Thus at this point in time, a substantial amount of zoo research was not being published in peer-reviewed journals. Most likely, the information was used for internal decision-making and scientific assessment of animal well-being. In 2008, Lukas reviewed ARCS reports from 2002 to 2006, and concluded that on average, reporting institutions published one to two journal articles a year, however this was not evenly distributed across reporting institutions. For example in 2006, 75 percent of institutions reported no journal publications, while 4 percent of institutions report ten or more publications.[42] Thus while many zoos were able to report research involvement, the vast majority of research occurred at a noticeable minority of institutions.

Maple and colleagues conducted another follow-up survey several years later and continued to track changes in zoo research, this time focusing on individual, rather than institutional, responses.[43] The factors that appeared to be most significant in facilitating the conduct of research included support from the director, staff with dedicated research effort, clear institutional research objectives, and research included in the institution's strategic plan. Anderson et al. argued that lack of dedicated research personnel, and a relatively limited number of highly trained (PhD level) research staff hindered the advancement of zoo research,[44] a sentiment noted nearly twenty years earlier by Devra Kleiman. Furthermore, they cited a continued misunderstanding between researchers and animal care staff about the importance of research, and the extent to which it might interfere with basic animal care and husbandry.[45] This troubling finding may relate to Finlay and Maple's earlier comment about the perception of research by the public. It is important to note that although this study was published in 2010, the survey was conducted in 2001, so it does not really reflect changes in the ensuing ten years. Additionally, the respondent pool for the 2010 publication was likely different from the previous surveys, in that it was individual-based and not institution-based, and reflects the opinions and perceptions of individual researchers, rather than institutional research objectives. The role of research in zoos continues to expand in some areas while simultaneously contracting in others, as evidenced in the composite graph shown in figure 3.1, which summarizes the results of these three surveys. Furthermore, scientifically based decision making is now incorporated into management decisions at many zoos, and the value of such data is increasingly being recognized.

If zoos wish to position themselves as institutions of research, they face a unique set of challenges, and a considerable amount of public misperception to overcome. Any facility conducting research on vertebrate animals is expected to have an Institutional Animal Care and Use Committee (IACUC) to review the potential impact of research on the well-being of nonhuman animal research subjects. Review is recommended, though not required, unless the research is invasive, or expected to cause pain or discomfort to subjects. In 2003, Goodrowe surveyed zoos involved in research, and reported that 54 percent of the 147 institutions that responded to the survey have an established IACUC.[46] While this may seem like a relatively small percentage, Goodrowe pointed out that this represents a substantial increase: twenty-five years earlier, only a single institution reported having an IACUC. The definition of "invasive" is critical to whether or not an IACUC is required. In the laboratory world, "invasive" implies surgical or physical manipulation of the subject. In the zoo context, research may be considered invasive if it falls into one of several categories:

> (1) very broadly, from anything that alters the daily husbandry/ management practices for an animal or group (e.g., collection of fecal samples, changes in temperature, lighting, diet, housing, and exhibit composition; (2) more restrictively, to include procedures that can cause

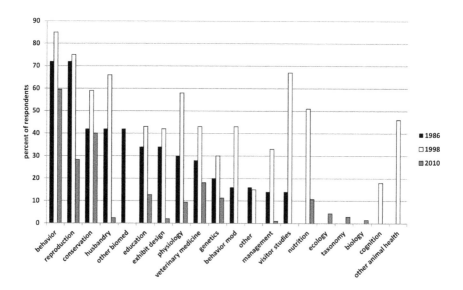

Figure 3.1. Types of research conducted in zoos based on survey data. Behavioral research is consistently the most prominent type of research conducted in zoos. *Source*: Results from Finlay and Maple (1986), Stoinski et al. (1998), and Anderson et al. (2010). Figure created by the author.

> stress or distress (e.g., increased human presence, remote biopsy, introduction of objects or scents not part of the exhibit furniture, and voluntary semen collection or venipuncture (blood-draw)); or (3) specifically, to include those procedures that require animal manipulation/restraint or anesthesia (e.g., manual restraint for administration of drugs/edication, venipuncture, or ultrasonography; anesthesia for elective procedures including tissue biopsy, surgical manipulation, artificial insemination, and semen collection).[47]

Most zoos err on the side of caution, and review all research proposals that fall into any of these three categories. However, to place these types of research studies in the same category as surgically invasive procedures is misleading. From the perspective of animal welfare, and research protocols, opportunistic collection of data—whether it is hormonal information obtained from fecal samples, or analysis of blood collected during a routine physical exam that was being conducted anyway—does not subject individuals to additional, unwarranted, invasive procedures. A zoo's IACUC or research committee considers the impact on zoo animals, staff time, and visitor experience in evaluating a research proposal. Research that has a clear and obvious application to zoo management or conservation is typically prioritized over "pure research," however any research that is deemed to be noninvasive, opportunistic, and with limited impact on staff time is likely to be approved. Unlike laboratories,

where nonhuman animals are present specifically for the purpose of research (both invasive and noninvasive), the IACUC at a zoo serves as a
proxy for nonhuman animal consent to participate voluntarily in research. We trust that the representatives of the IACUC consider all possible negative impacts that research may have on the nonhuman subjects
and approve only those studies that are not believed to have any negative
impacts on the subjects. Might the change in diet lead to nutritional defi-
cits, weight loss, or competition? Does the use of scent enrichment cause
stress? Regarding the specific conduct of the research, the IACUC examines the extent to which management changes are required and the potential impact this may have on subjects. Does an individual animal need
to be isolated from the group for the study? Are changes in routine husbandry practices required, and what might the impact of such changes
be? Regarding isolation of an individual, this may be permitted for some
studies, particularly if short-term separation is part of the normal routine.
Animals may be separated from the group for short periods of time for
provision of specific dietary items or medications, or as part of routine
husbandry training. In such cases, short-term separation or isolation
would not represent a change in husbandry. Changes in routine may be
considered if the proposed change is part of a study that aims to evaluate
improvements to welfare (increasing frequency of feedings or enrichment provisioning, for example) or to evaluate planned changes that are
occurring with or without the research (transfer to a new home or addition of an individual to a group).

As an example of research that spans both the applied and theoretical
realm, from aiding management to providing baseline norms to addressing questions of human evolution, consider a study conducted by researchers at Lincoln Park Zoo and the University of Chicago.[48, 49] Motivated by the need to provide a blood transfusion to a gorilla, and lacking
any information on blood types to facilitate a donor match, keepers, veterinarians and researchers set out to catalog blood types of zoo-housed
great apes by asking zoos to opportunistically use a simple human-based
blood-typing procedure during annual physical exams. Because the research was opportunistic, and had clear and obvious benefits to the zoo-
housed population, participation was high. The research was supported
by the Ape Taxon Advisory Group and its associated Species Survival
Plans. Based on preliminary results, and successful funding, the group
expanded the study in two ways: first, samples were obtained from great
apes in European zoos and in sanctuaries in range countries to further
expand the sample size; and second, researchers at the University of
Chicago began to do more systematic genetic analyses of the samples in
order to explore the evolution of blood types in great apes. The research
proved valuable to zoos for veterinary care—a database of blood types of
all individuals could readily be developed—and provided important
theoretical insights into human evolution. Samples were collected oppor-

tunistically and thus did not require any additional manipulations of subjects; results provided practical and theoretical information that contributed to the current body of knowledge, and supported enhanced care of zoo-housed populations. This is the essence of zoo research, and represents what can be accomplished when research is integrated into the objectives and mission of zoos and strong collaborative ties are established.

In addition to maintaining an IACUC or some other unit for reviewing research applications, accredited zoos must also demonstrate that they have a process in place to address issues of animal welfare. Accreditation standards state that "The institution must develop a clear process for identifying, communicating, and addressing animal welfare concerns within the institution in a timely manner, and without retribution."[50] In academic settings, the IACUC maintains this responsibility, and a zoo may opt to charge its IACUC with this duty as well. Alternatively, a zoo may establish its own animal welfare committee to provide a mechanism whereby staff may lodge a complaint that relates to animal welfare. This may be in the context of husbandry, or in the context of research, or may relate to any other situation that calls into question the welfare of animals in the collection. In traditional laboratory settings, concerns about animal welfare may be more prevalent due to the sometimes invasive nature of research. Given the generally noninvasive, opportunistic, and voluntary nature of zoo-based research, such concerns are rare in the research context.

ACCEPTABLE TYPES OF RESEARCH IN ZOOS

Invasive Research

Within the scope of zoo-based research, "invasive" is more likely to imply an alteration in routine husbandry than an intrusive and almost certainly stressful procedure. Research deemed "invasive" in the traditional sense may occur in rare circumstances where the presumed benefit to the population (captive or wild) is thought to outweigh the potential costs to the individual. Research involving assisted reproductive technology may fall into this category. In this example, animals may need to be separated from their group, given hormone injections to prepare them for insemination, sperm may need to be collected, and depending on the specific method, the animal may need to be sedated for the procedure. In the case of critically endangered species, or individuals who are genetically valuable to the population, the assessment of the IACUC or Animal Welfare Committee may warrant invasive procedures of this kind. In this case, the benefit to the species or population may outweigh the anticipated stress on the individual. In some situations, operant conditioning and positive reinforcement training may be used to facilitate procedures, minimize stress, and effectively allow the animal to participate voluntarily in procedures.

Another example in which research that may be perceived as invasive has been approved and conducted with zoo populations relates to surveillance for West Nile Disease. In a unique collaboration among the New York State Animal Health Diagnostic Center at Cornell University, AZA, the Centers for Disease Control and Prevention (CDC), and the US Department of Agriculture (USDA), zoos were asked to closely monitor birds and mammals that were maintained in outdoor enclosures and collect samples from healthy, sick, and deceased animals.[51] While samples from sick or deceased animals may be considered opportunistically collected (that is, a sick animal would be expected to undergo a veterinary exam permitting sample collection), sample collection from a healthy animal may be interpreted as being invasive. Again, the potential benefit—to human and nonhuman animal health—was interpreted as outweighing the cost of the stress imposed by brief restraint for blood collection.

Noninvasive Sampling

It should be clear that research approaches that are noninvasive are vastly preferred in the zoo setting. Such procedures, by definition, do not impact the nonhuman animal subjects involved. For biological samples, feces would be the simplest sample type to collect. It is produced in quantity; keepers remove it from the exhibit regularly, and it can provide information on reproductive status, stress hormones, nutrition, parasite load, and genetics. While fecal samples present a set of challenges for the researcher, they are the least intrusive for the animals as well as the animal care staff, and thus are preferred. Urine samples require less postcollection processing, but may require training and/or separation of individual animals to facilitate collection.

Observational Research

Behavioral data collected from a public area of a zoo also constitutes a form of noninvasive research. As noted, it is the most common form of research conducted in zoos, may involve students, zoo staff, and outside researchers, and generally emphasizes applied research to enhance well-being. Behavioral observations may be done to evaluate the impacts of a planned change, and while the change itself might be interpreted as being invasive, in the sense that it might require a change in management or husbandry, the change itself is occurring for management reasons, not for research reasons. Behavioral monitoring (regular observation and assessment of behavior so that deviations can be detected) does not necessarily assume any planned change in management but can be used to evaluate the impacts of unplanned events on behavior: the birth or death of an individual, for example and how this influences other group members.[52] In some situations, a change in management or husbandry may be requested by the researcher. The timing or form of food presentation may be varied, a new enrichment protocol implemented, or an ongoing enrichment device removed in order to monitor its impact. By the precise, IACUC definition of invasive, such alterations in management do constitute a change that warrants evaluation before implementation. And while it is possible that the best-intentioned alteration may have unforeseen negative consequences, it is the intent of such research efforts to enhance welfare and reduce stress, even if the outcome is occasionally antithetical to this aim.

Opportunistic Sampling

One of the largest untapped research resources that zoos have to offer is the ability to capitalize on unique collections and routine procedures to facilitate research. If a researcher needs a sample immediately, this may constitute a degree of invasiveness that is unacceptable. However, with careful planning, a researcher may be able to compile all necessary samples over the course of twelve to eighteen months. Additionally, zoos must consider it to be their responsibility to learn as much as possible from the nonhuman animals in their collections postmortem. Thus, zoos should reach out to scientists who might benefit from access to tissue, skeletal, or other biological samples that can only be collected after death. Such opportunities serve to enhance basic scientific knowledge, while also providing insights to better manage the living collections in zoos.

Applied Research

While admittedly tautological to some degree, research that serves to enhance captive management can and should be carried out at zoos. From the perspective of the institution, research that can lead to enhancements in animal care, animal reproduction, and animal welfare should be supported and encouraged. Applied research includes such aspects as assessment of enrichment effectiveness, strategies for maintaining social and mixed-species groups, modifications to diet (quantity, quality, and timing), changes in the physical environment and post-occupancy evaluation in new spaces, and reduction in stress via management changes.

In sum, there are a wide range of research topics that are amenable to implementation in the zoo. These are largely noninvasive, opportunistic, voluntary studies that have the potential to improve management and welfare of zoo populations and contribute to the body of scientific knowledge about species that we often know little about.

INFORMED CONSENT

A critical ethical conundrum in zoo-based research involves the extent to which zoo animals are voluntary and willing participants in research. When human subjects are recruited, they are, by definition, participating in research voluntarily, are informed about the likely outcomes and potential risks, and may choose to participate or not. International guidelines for the use of human subjects stipulate that participation is voluntary, with rare exceptions:

> For all biomedical research involving humans the investigator must obtain the voluntary informed consent of the prospective subject or, in the case of an individual who is not capable of giving informed consent, the permission of a legally authorized representative in accordance with applicable law. Waiver of informed consent is to be regarded as uncommon and exceptional, and must in all cases be approved by an ethical review committee. [53]

How can the concept of informed consent be applied to nonhuman animals? In the laboratory setting, this is not yet considered an issue of concern. Laboratories using nonhuman animal subjects are required to justify the number of subjects used, to ensure that pain and suffering are minimized, (if it is not a pain study), and in some cases are required to ensure appropriate psychological well-being of subjects. [54] From a legal perspective, nonhuman animals are considered to be property—"things." Legal personhood is limited to member of our own species only. Only legal "persons" are guaranteed legal rights. Human beings who are not capable of making decisions or consenting to procedures (infants, for example) are still persons under the law, and thus possess the same rights as all other humans. Despite extensive debate as to whether certain nonhuman species should be granted legal personhood, from the perspective of animal welfare, and use of animals in research, the issue becomes not one of legal personhood, but of basic natural rights that all sentient organisms are entitled to. While this does not represent legal status in court, it does nonetheless provide a framework for identifying the natural rights of nonhuman animals in any context: laboratory, farm, zoo, or companion animals.

In the zoo setting, the overarching aim is, and always will be, that the nonhuman animals are maintained in species-appropriate social groups in a manner that facilitates the performance of natural behaviors and minimizes any stressors. In 1979, the UK Farm Animal Welfare Council established what has come to be known as the "Five Freedoms." Developed with farm animals in mind, the intent was to provide guidance for the care of animals that minimized pain and suffering. The Five Freedoms were: (1) Freedom from hunger and thirst; (2) Freedom from discomfort; (3) Freedom from pain, injury, or disease; (4) Freedom to express normal behavior; (5) Freedom from fear and distress. Building upon the idea of the Five Freedoms, Marian Stamp Dawkins articulated criteria for recognizing pain and suffering in animals. She suggests that to ensure positive welfare, we must utilize the following criteria: (1) Evidence of injury or sickness; (2) Behavioral evidence of distress; (3) Physiological evidence of stress; (4) Comparison with natural life; (5) Free choice of animals; (6) Putting oneself in the animal's place.[55] While we may not be able to ask nonhuman animals about their welfare, the developing field of animal welfare science provides mechanisms to assess welfare based on behavior, physical state, and noninvasive physiological measures. Although this is perhaps a somewhat reactive approach, these tools allow us to assess after the fact whether a particular intervention or procedure had a positive or negative effect on welfare.

Human subjects participate voluntarily in research, and oftentimes are rewarded for their participation (typically via financial remuneration). Voluntary participation has become a key component of zoo-based research as well. In some cases, an animal may need to move to a particular location for research participation, but the individual has the option of participating, or not participating. If the individual chooses to participate, he or she is typically reinforced via a food reward, and may terminate the session at any time. Thus research participation is voluntary and, alluding to Stamp Dawkins' criteria, the individual has freedom of choice to participate. For example, the use of computer touchscreens has become increasingly common for investigation of cognitive abilities in great apes.[56] In such studies, apes may choose to engage with the touchscreen or not with no coercion or forced participation. Positive reinforcement training has become a fundamental strategy for zoo animal management, and establishment of a training program is part of the AZA accreditation requirement. Training is used in zoos to facilitate voluntary husbandry behavior (voluntary injection or veterinary monitoring, for example), to provide enrichment, and to increase the cognitive complexity of the environment. Procedures are well-established, generally use positive reinforcement (as opposed to negative reinforcement or punishment), and enhance the keeper-animal relationship.[57, 58] Voluntary participation in research has been particularly useful in cognitive studies. Some institutions, such as the National Zoo, provide opportunities for great apes to engage in cognitive tests in the "Think Tank" exhibit, in which orangutans are able to travel from their home area via a series of elevated platforms and cables to the Think Tank exhibit itself, where they may engage in a variety of cognitive tests. Visitors are able to observe the process.[59]

A second mechanism that may serve as a proxy for informed consent to participate in research is the oversight provided by the IACUC or Animal Welfare Committee. The charge of an IACUC (or other zoo research committee) is threefold: first, to evaluate the potential impact of the proposed research on the nonhuman animals proposed as subjects;

second, to assess the impact on staff and management procedures; finally, to consider the overall value of the research with respect to conservation and animal management. It is the first of these considerations that bears directly on animal welfare and informed consent. Any research that is deemed to have negative consequences for the subjects has little chance of approval. While there may be situations in which such a study may be deemed acceptable, this would be the rare exception. The responsibility of the IACUC is thus a substantial one, as this body makes decisions on behalf of the research subjects that are not able to make such decisions for themselves.

There is no simple, obvious way to facilitate informed consent in research participation by nonhuman animals housed in zoos. However, the caretakers, managers, and research directors of zoos can ensure that the needs of the zoo inhabitants are prioritized. If we adhere to the intent of the Five Freedoms, and Stamp Dawkins method for assessing welfare; if we ensure that noninvasive methods are routinely employed; if we take advantage of the myriad opportunities afforded with zoo populations; if we develop strategies to encourage voluntary and not mandatory participation in research by providing freedom of choice to zoo residents, then we can be confident that we have addressed the welfare needs of our population. Unlike laboratories, zoos do not maintain nonhuman animals expressly for the purpose of doing research; zoos do however retain the responsibility for ensuring that research is conducted, and that it is done so in such a manner that it addresses the needs, rights, and welfare of the subjects as the primary focus of its decision making and approval process.

GUIDELINES FOR THE FUTURE

Zoo research faces a number of challenges, both practical and ethical. From a practical perspective, the conduct of research in zoos is fraught with many challenges to success: researchers often deal with small sample sizes that limit the ability to draw valid conclusions; because the environment does not include the tight controls inherent in a laboratory, there may be confounding and uncontrollable variables that may influence results. Some, but not all, zoos incorporate research into their mission and support it with staff, funding, and resources. Nevertheless, the advances in zoo research in the past thirty-five years have been remarkable. The first publication dedicated to zoo research, *International Zoo Yearbook*, has been published annually since 1960. The journal *Zoo Biology* debuted in 1982, and is a well-established, peer-reviewed publication with a specialized target audience. The papers published in *Zoo Biology* represent the entirety of the scope and types of research published in zoos. *Applied Animal Behaviour Science* (1981) covers a diverse range of articles with relevance to zoo, wild, farm, and companion animal research. More recently, journals such as the *Journal of Applied Animal Welfare Science* (1998), and the *Journal of Zoo and Aquarium Research* (2013) have joined the field of peer-reviewed publications that strive to highlight research carried out in zoos. This represents a critical change in the nature of zoo research: from informal, in-house studies conducted to address specific questions, to formal, peer-reviewed research carried out by staff researchers and academic collaborators.

Foreshadowing the changes to come in the zoo world, George Rabb described the evolution of zoos from their humble beginnings as menageries that displayed postage-stamp collections of exotic beasts to centers of research and conservation.[60] While we have come a long way, we still have far to go. Not only must zoos strive to enhance and expand their research efforts, but they must publicize these efforts and clarify to the general public the nature and value of such research. This involves clearly describing, defining, and explaining the rationale for zoo research, and emphasizing the differences between the observational, noninvasive, opportunistic, voluntary research conducted in zoos, and the sometimes invasive experimental studies that are often assumed to be the essence of any animal-based research. Zoos do not exist in order to support research, but they exist and therefore must support research in context. The information that can be gleaned from zoo studies can support conservation, enhance zoo animal management, clarify assessments of welfare, and contribute basic biological knowledge. In the absence of a clear methodology for obtaining informed consent from research subjects, zoos must continue to capitalize on emerging research methodologies that allow voluntary participation, free choice, and provide open information on the nature and scope of research efforts to the public. Only by publicizing the important research conducted at zoos can we hope to garner the understanding and support of a public that may conflate "research" with "experiment."

NOTES

1. G. Hosey, V. Melfi, and S. Pankhurst, *Zoo Animals: Behaviour, Management, and Welfare* (Oxford, UK: Oxford University Press, 2009), 21–25, Print.

2. W. Conway, "The conservation mission in the wild: zoos as conservation NGOs?," *Zoos in the 21st Century: Catalysts for Conservation*, A. Zimmerman, M. Hatchwell, L. A. Dickie, and C. West, eds. (Cambridge, UK: Cambridge University Press, 2007), 12–21, Print.

3. Association of Zoos and Aquariums, *AZA Strategic Plan 2015–17*, *Association of Zoos and Aquariums*, Silver Spring, MD, 2015, Web.

4. I. Braverman, *Zooland: The Institution of Captivity* (Stanford, CA: Stanford University Press, 2013), Print.

5. J. Donahue and E. Trump, *The Politics of Zoos: Exotic Animals and their Protectors* (Dekalb: Northern Illinois University Press, 2006), Print.

6. Association of Zoos and Aquariums, "Institutional Status," Web, May 15, 2016. https://www.aza.org/inst-status.

7. See for example A. Zimmermann, R. Wilkinson, M. Hatchwell, L. A. Dickie, and C. West, "The conservation mission in the wild: zoos as conservation NGOs?," *Zoos in the 21st Century: Catalysts for Conservation*, A. Zimmerman, M. Hatchwell, L. A. Dickie, and C. West, eds. (Cambridge, UK: Cambridge University Press, 2007), 303–21, Print.

8. Association of Zoos and Aquariums, "The Accreditation Standards and Related Policies, 2016 edition," *Association of Zoos and Aquariums*, Silver Spring, MD, 2016, Web, p. 13. https://www.aza.org/searchresults.aspx?s=%u201CThe%20Accreditation %20Standards%20and%20Related%20Policies%2C%202016%20edition%2C. Accessed March 4, 2016.

9. Ibid., 15.

10. Ibid., 17.

11. Ibid., 16.

12. "About The Philadelphia Zoo," Philadelphiazoo.org, Web, July 25, 2016.

13. "About Chicago Zoological Society," Czs.org, Web, July 25, 2016.

14. "About Us: WCS.org," Wcs.org, Web, July 25, 2016.

15. "About Lincoln Park Zoo," Lpzoo.org, Web, July 25, 2016.

16. A. F. Ross, *Let the Lions Roar! The Evolution of Brookfield Zoo* (Brookfield, IL: Chicago Zoological Society, 1997), Print.

17. D. G. Kleiman, "Behavior Research in Zoos: Past, Present, and Future," *Zoo Biology* 11 (1992): 304, Print.

18. G. R. Hosey, "Behavioural Research in Zoos: Academic Perspectives," *Applied Animal Behaviour Science* 51 (1997): 199–207, Print.

19. *Merriam-Webster Dictionary*, Merriam-webster.com, Web, July 25, 2016.

20. J. Altmann, "Observational Study of Behavior: Sampling Methods," *Behaviour* 49 (1974): 227–67, Print.

21. United States Department of Agriculture, *Animal Welfare Act and Animal Welfare Regulations* (Washington, DC: GPO, 2013), Print.

22. Association of Zoos and Aquariums, "Institutional Status," Web, May 15, 2016. https://www.aza.org/inst-status.

23. Animal and Plant Health Inspection Service (APHIS), "Customer Search," Web, May 15, 2016. https://usdasearch.usda.gov/search?utf8=%3F&affiliate=usda-aphis& query=customer+search&commit=Search.

24. United States Department of Agriculture, *Animal Welfare Act and Animal Welfare Regulations* (Washington, DC: GPO, 2013), 1, Print.

25. L. Carbone, "Pain in Laboratory Animals: The Ethical and Regulatory Impera- tives," *PLoS ONE* 6.9 (2011): e21578, doi:10.1371/journal.pone.0021578, Web. Accessed July 15, 2016.

26. United States Department of Agriculture, *Animal Welfare Act and Animal Welfare Regulations* (Washington, DC: GPO, 2013), Print.

27. For a case study, see for example A. Pacheco and A. Francione, "The Silver Spring Monkeys," *In Defense of Animals*, P. Singer, ed. (New York: Basil Blackwell, 1985), 135–47, Print.

28. K. S. Grech, "Detailed Discussion of the Laws Affecting Zoos," *Animal Legal & Historical Center*, Michigan State University College of Law, 2004, Web. https://www. animallaw.info/article/ detailed-discussion-laws-affecting-zoos. Accessed May 4, 2016.

29. Senate Commission on Animal Protection and Experimentation, *Animal Experi- ments in Research*, Bonn, Germany, 2007, Print, p. 6.

30. AZA Scientific Advisory Group, "AZA Scientific Advisory Group Handbook," *Association of Zoos and Aquariums*, Silver Spring, MD, 2013, Web. https://www.aza.org/ assets/2332/scientific_advisory_group_handbook_june_2016.pdf.

31. AZA Research and Technology Committee, "AZA Research Priorities," *Associa- tion of Zoos and Aquariums*, Silver Spring, MD, 2012, Web. https://www.aza.org/assets/ 2332/rtc_white_paper_on_aza_research_priorities_-_board_approved_29_mar_12.pdf.

32. AZA Research and Technology Committee, "Defining Mission-Focused Research for the AZA Community," *Association of Zoos and Aquariums*, Silver Spring, MD, 2013, Web. https://www.aza.org/assets/2332/definingresearchfortheazacommunity-rtc2013.pdf.

33. Association of Zoos and Aquariums, "Animal Welfare Committee," *Association of Zoos and Aquariums*, Silver Spring, MD, Web, July 26, 2016. https://www.aza.org/animal_welfare_committee.

34. D. J. Shepherdson, K. C. Carlstead, and N. Wielebnowski, "Cross-Sectional Assessment of Stress Responses in Zoo Animals Using Longitudinal Monitoring of Faecal Corticoids and Behavior," *Animal Welfare* 23 (2004): S105–13, Print.

35. Association of Zoos and Aquariums, "Animal Welfare Committee," *Association of Zoos and Aquariums*, Silver Spring, MD, Web, July 26, 2016. https://www.aza.org/animal_welfare_committee.

36. B. A. Minteer, and J. P. Collins, "Ecological Ethics in Captivity: Balancing Values and Responsibilities in Zoo and Aquarium Research Under Rapid Global Change," *ILAR Journal*, 54 (2013): 41–51, Print.

37. M. Brambell, "The Evolution of the Modern Zoo," *International Zoo News* 40 (1993): 29, Print.

38. T. W. Finlay and T. L. Maple, "A Survey of Research in American Zoos and Aquariums," *Zoo Biology* 5 (1986): 261–68, Print.

39. Ibid., 266.

40. T. S. Stoinski, K. E. Lukas, and T. L. Maple, "A Survey of Research in North American Zoos and Aquariums," *Zoo Biology* 17 (1998): 167–80, Print.

41. Ibid., 178.

42. K. E. Lukas, "The Status of Research in AZA Zoos and Aquariums," *The Well-Being of Animals in Zoo and Aquarium-Sponsored Research: Putting Best Practices Forward*, T. L. Bettinger and J. T. Bielitzki, eds. (Greenbelt, MD: Scientists Center for Animal Welfare, 2008), 7–24, Print.

43. U. S. Anderson, T. L. Maple, and M. A. Bloomsmith, "Factors Facilitating Research: A Survey of Zoo and Aquarium Professionals," *Zoo Biology* 29 (2010): 1–13, Print.

44. Ibid., 5.

45. Ibid., 6.

46. K. L. Goodrowe, "Programs for Invasive Research in North American Zoos and Aquariums," *ILAR Journal* 44 (2003): 317–23, Print.

47. Ibid., 320.

48. K. C. Gamble, J. A. Moyse, J. N. Lovstad, C. B. Ober, and E. Thompson, "Blood Groups in the Species Survival Plan, European Endangered Species Program, and Managed in situ Populations of Bonobo (Pan paniscus), Common Chimpanzee (Pan troglodytes), Gorilla (Gorilla ssp), and Orangutan (Pongo pygmaeus ssp)," *Zoo Biology* 30 (2011): 427–44, Print.

49. L. Seguerel, E. E. Thompson, R. Flutre, J. Lovstad, A. Venkat, S. W. Margulis, J. Moyse, S. Ross, K. Gamble, G. Sella, C. Ober, and M. Przeworski, "The ABO Blood Group is a Trans-Species Polymorphism in Primates," *PNAS*, 109 (2012): 18493–98, Print.

50. Association of Zoos and Aquariums, The Accreditation Standards and Related Policies, 2016 edition," *Association of Zoos and Aquariums*, Silver Spring, MD, 2016, Web. https://www.aza.org/accreditation. Accessed March 1, 2016.

51. E. Pultorak, Y. Nadler, D. Travis, A. Glaser, T. McNamara, and S. D. Mehta, "Zoological Institution Participation in a West Nile Virus Surveillance System: Implications for Public Health," *Public Health* 125 (2011): 592–99, Print.

52. J. V. Watters, S. W. Margulis, and S. Atsalis, "Behavioral Monitoring in Zoos and Aquariums: A Tool for Guiding Husbandry and Directing Research," *Zoo Biology* 28 (2009): 35–48.

53. Council for International Organizations of Medical Sciences and World Health Organization, *International Ethical Guidelines for Biomedical Research Involving Human Subjects* (Geneva: CIOMS, 2002), 21, Print.

54. United States Office of Laboratory Animal Welfare, *Institutional Animal Care and Use Committee Guidebook, 2nd ed.* (Washington, DC: GPO, 2002), Print.

55. M. Stamp Dawkins, "A User's Guide to Animal Welfare Science," *Trends in Ecology and Evolution* 21 (2006): 77–82, Print.

56. See for example K. E. Wagner, L. M. Hopper, and S. R. Ross, "Asymmetries in the Production of Self-Directed Behavior by Chimpanzees and Gorillas During a Computerized Cognitive Test," *Animal Cognition* 19 (2016): 343–50, Print.

57. G. E. Laule, M. A. Bloomsmith, and S. J. Shapiro, "The Use of Positive Reinforcement Training Techniques to Enhance the Care, Management, and Welfare of Primates in the Laboratory," *Journal of Applied Animal Welfare Science*, 6 (2003): 163–73, Print.

58. G. R. Hosey, "A Preliminary Model of Human-Animal Relationships in the Zoo," *Applied Animal Behaviour Science* 109 (2008): 105–27, Print.

59. Smithsonian Institution, "About Think Tank," Nationazoo.si.edu, Web, July 25, 2016. https://nationalzoo.si.edu/animals/exhibits/primates.

60. G. B. Rabb, "The Changing Roles of Zoological Parks in Conserving Biological Diversity," *American Zoologist* 34 (1994): 159–64.

BIBLIOGRAPHY

"About Chicago Zoological Society." Czs.org. Web. July 25, 2016.

"About Lincoln Park Zoo." Lpzoo.org. Web. July 25, 2016

"About The Philadelphia Zoo." Philadelphiazoo.org. Web. July 25, 2016.

"About Us: WCS.org." Wcs.org. Web. July 25, 2016.

Altmann, J. "Observational Study of Behavior: Sampling Methods." *Behaviour* 49 (1974): 227–67. Print.

Anderson, U. S., T. L. Maple, and M. A. Bloomsmith. "Factors Facilitating Research: A Survey of Zoo and Aquarium Professionals." *Zoo Biology* 29 (2010): 1–13. Print.

Animal and Plant Health Inspection Service (APHIS). "Customer Search." Web. May 15, 2016. https://usdasearch.usda.gov/search?utf8=%3F&affiliate=usda-aphis&query=customer+search&commit=Search.

Association of Zoos and Aquariums. AZA Strategic Plan 2015–17. *Association of Zoos and Aquariums*, Silver Spring, MD. 2015. Web. https://www.aza.org/strategic-plan.

———. "The Accreditation Standards and Related Policies, 2016 edition." *Association of Zoos and Aquariums*, Silver Spring, MD. 2016. Web. https://www.aza.org/accreditation.

———. "Animal Welfare Committee." *Association of Zoos and Aquariums*, Silver Spring, MD. Web. July 26, 2016. https://www.aza.org/animal_welfare_committee.

———. "Institutional Status." Web. May 15, 2016. https://www.aza.org/inst-status.

———. "Membership." Web. May 15, 2016. https://www.aza.org/organization-membership.

AZA Research and Technology Committee. "AZA Research Priorities." *Association of Zoos and Aquariums*, Silver Spring, MD. 2012. Web. https://www.aza.org/assets/2332/rtc_white_paper_on_aza_research_priorities_-_board_approved_29_mar_12.pdf.

———. "Defining Mission-Focused Research for the AZA Community." *Association of Zoos and Aquariums*, Silver Spring, MD. 2013. Web. https://www.aza.org/assets/2332/definingresearchfortheazacommunity-rtc2013.pdf.

AZA Scientific Advisory Group. "AZA Scientific Advisory Group Handbook." *Association of Zoos and Aquariums*, Silver Spring, MD. 2013. Web. https://www.aza.org/assets/2332/scientific_advisory_group_handbook_june_2016.pdf.

Brambell, M. "The Evolution of the Modern Zoo." *International Zoo News* 40 (1993): 27–34. Print.

Braverman, I. *Zooland: The Institution of Captivity*. Stanford, CA: Stanford University Press, 2013. Print.

Carbone, L. "Pain in Laboratory Animals: The Ethical and Regulatory Imperatives." *PLoS ONE* 6.9 (2011): e21578. doi:10.1371/journal.pone.0021578. Web. Accessed January 13, 2016.

Council for International Organizations of Medical Sciences and World Health Organization. *International Ethical Guidelines for Biomedical Research Involving Human Subjects*. Geneva: CIOMS, 2002. Print.

Conway, W. "The conservation mission in the wild: Zoos as conservation NGOs?." *Zoos in the 21st Century: Catalysts for Conservation*. A. Zimmerman, M. Hatchwell, L. A. Dickie, and C. West, eds. Cambridge, UK: Cambridge University Press, 2007. 12–21. Print.

Dawkins, M. Stamp. "A User's Guide to Animal Welfare Science." *Trends in Ecology and Evolution* 21 (2006): 77–82. Print.

Donahue, J., and E. Trump. *The Politics of Zoos: Exotic Animals and their Protectors*. Dekalb: Northern Illinois University Press, 2006. Print.

Finlay, T. W. and T. L. Maple. "A Survey of Research in American Zoos and Aquariums." *Zoo Biology* 5 (1986): 261–68. Print.

Gamble, K. C., J. A. Moyse, J. N. Lovstad, C. B. Ober, and E. Thompson. "Blood Groups in the Species Survival Plan, European Endangered Species Program, and Managed in situ Populations of Bonobo (Pan paniscus), Common Chimpanzee (Pan troglodytes), Gorilla (Gorilla ssp), and Orangutan (Pongo pygmaeus ssp)." *Zoo Biology* 30 (2011): 427–44. Print.

Goodrowe, K. L. "Programs for Invasive Research in North American Zoos and Aquariums." *ILAR Journal* 44 (2003): 317–23. Print.

Grech, K. S. "Detailed Discussion of the Laws Affecting Zoos." *Animal Legal & Historical Center*. Michigan State University College of Law. 2004. Web. https://www.animallaw.info/article/detailed-discussion-laws-affecting-zoos. Accessed May 4, 2016.

Hosey, G. R. "Behavioural Research in Zoos: Academic Perspectives." *Applied Animal Behaviour Science* 51 (1997): 199–207. Print.

———. "A Preliminary Model of Human-Animal Relationships in the Zoo." *Applied Animal Behaviour Science* 109 (2008): 105–27. Print.

Hosey, G., V. Melfi, and S. Pankhurst. *Zoo Animals: Behaviour, Management, and Welfare*. Oxford, UK: Oxford University Press, 2009. Print.

Kleiman, D.G. "Behavior Research in Zoos: Past, Present, and Future." *Zoo Biology* 11 (1992): 301–12. Print.

Laule, G. E., M. A. Bloomsmith, and S. J. Shapiro. "The Use of Positive Reinforcement Training Techniques to Enhance the Care, Management, and Welfare of Primates in the Laboratory." *Journal of Applied Animal Welfare Science*, 6 (2003): 163–73. Print.

Lukas, K. E. "The Status of Research in AZA Zoos and Aquariums. *The Well-Being of Animals in Zoo and Aquarium-Sponsored Research: Putting Best Practices Forward*. T. L. Bettinger and J. T. Bielitzki, eds. Greenbelt, MD: Scientists Center for Animal Welfare. 2008. 7–24. Print.

Merriam-Webster Dictionary. Merriam-webster.com. Web. July 25, 2016.

Minteer, B. A., and J. P. Collins. "Ecological Ethics in Captivity: Balancing Values and Responsibilities in Zoo and Aquarium Research Under Rapid Global Change." *ILAR Journal*, 54 (2013): 41–51. Print.

Pacheco, A, and A. Francione. "The Silver Spring Monkeys." *In Defense of Animals*. P. Singer, ed. New York: Basil Blackwell, 1985. 135–47. Print.

Pultorak, E., Y. Nadler, D. Travis, A. Glaser, T. McNamara, and S. D. Mehta. "Zoological Institution Participation in a West Nile Virus Surveillance System: Implications for Public Health." *Public Health* 125 (2011): 592–99. Print.

Rabb, G. B. "The Changing Roles of Zoological Parks in Conserving Biological Diversity. *American Zoologist* 34 (1994): 159–64.

Ross, A. F. *Let the Lions Roar! The Evolution of Brookfield Zoo.* Brookfield, IL: Chicago Zoological Society, 1997. Print.

Seguerel, L., E. E. Thompson, R. Flutre, J. Lovstad, A. Venkat, S. W. Margulis, J. Moyse, S. Ross, K. Gamble, G. Sella, C. Ober, and M. Przeworski. "The ABO Blood Group is a Trans-Species Polymorphism in Primates." *PNAS*, 109 (2012): 18493–98. Print.

Senate Commission on Animal Protection and Experimentation. *Animal Experiments in Research.* Bonn, Germany. 2007. Print.

Shepherdson, D. J., K. C. Carlstead, and N. Wielebnowski. "Cross-Sectional Assessment of Stress Responses in Zoo Animals Using Longitudinal Monitoring of Faecal Corticoids and Behavior." *Animal Welfare* 23 (2004): S105–13. Print.

Smithsonian Institution. "About Think Tank." Nationazoo.si.edu. Web. July 25, 2016.

Stoinski, T. S., K. E. Lukas, and T. L. Maple. "A Survey of Research in North American Zoos and Aquariums." *Zoo Biology* 17 (1998): 167–80. Print.

United States Department of Agriculture, *Animal Welfare Act and Animal Welfare Regulations.* Washington, DC: GPO, 2013. Print.

United States Department of Agriculture, Animal and Plant Health Inspection Service. *Licensing and Registration Under the Animal Welfare Act: Guidelines for Dealers, Exhibitors, Transporters, and Researchers.* Washington, GPO, 2005. Web. https://www.aphis. usda.gov/animal_welfare/downloads/aw/awlicreg.pdf.

United States Office of Laboratory Animal Welfare. *Institutional Animal Care and Use Committee Guidebook, 2nd ed.* Washington, DC: GPO, 2002. Print.

Wagner, K. E., L. M. Hopper, and S. R. Ross. "Asymmetries in the Production of Self-Directed Behavior by Chimpanzees and Gorillas During a Computerized Cognitive Test." *Animal Cognition* 19 (2016): 343–50. Print.

Watters, J. V., S. W. Margulis, and S. Atsalis, S. "Behavioral Monitoring in Zoos and Aquariums: A Tool for Guiding Husbandry and Directing Research." *Zoo Biology* 28 (2009): 35–48.

Zimmermann, A. R. Wilkinson, M. Hatchwell, L. Dickie, and C. West. "The conservation mission in the wild: zoos as conservation NGOs?." *Zoos in the 21st Century: Catalysts for Conservation.* A. Zimmerman, M. Hatchwell, L. A. Dickie, and C. West, eds. Cambridge, UK: Cambridge University Press, 2007. 303–21. Print.

FOUR

Animal Welfare Legislation in New Zealand and Its Application to Zoos and Aquaria

Michael Morris and Mary Murray

In this chapter, we explore the central question of the book—ways in which rights for animals in zoos can be furthered—through consideration of animal welfare legislation in New Zealand, and the application of that legislation to zoos and aquaria. In so doing, we discuss limits and possibilities of legislative change with respect to the development of rights for animals in aquaria and zoos.[1]

New Zealand has an extensive system of legislation and administrative oversight of animal welfare, the cornerstone of which is the Animal Welfare Act (2000). This act replaced the Animals Act and has been praised by industry officials[2] for changing the emphasis on animal welfare to a more preventative approach, instead of setting out crimes against animals.

The Animal Welfare Act expands the obligations of animal caregivers to correspond to the Five Freedoms recommended by the Farm Animal Welfare council in the United Kingdom. The impetus for the adoption of these Freedoms was a government report, which in turn was prompted by public outrage following the publication of Ruth Harrison's book *Animal Machines*,[3] an expose of horrific-seeming husbandry techniques such as keeping hens and pigs in severely confined conditions.[4]

The first four of the Five Freedoms determined by the Farm Animal Welfare Council have been codified in Section 4 of the New Zealand Animal Welfare Act as freedoms from hunger and thirst, cold and heat, pain and distress, and injury and disease.

The fifth freedom is a positive one, and is the "opportunity to display normal patterns of behaviour" (Section 4c). This obligation was not present in the Animals Act, and its inclusion in the Animal Welfare Act represents a shifting of awareness of the needs of animals. Animals are no longer simply seen in terms of having only physical needs, but are now considered to be complex beings with emotions and awareness, that require mental stimulation as well as looking after physical wants.

The field of animal behavior in general has changed its emphasis from simple observation of behavior to recognition that subjective animal feelings are a legitimate subject for scientific study.[5] As an indicator of how far this awareness has become part of mainstream thinking, the title of the Animal Welfare Act was amended in May 2015 to include the purpose to recognize that animals are sentient.

THE APPLICATION OF THE ANIMAL WELFARE ACT TO ANIMALS IN ZOOS

The requirement that animals be able to display normal patterns of behavior is of particular relevance to animals kept in zoos, given that behavioral deprivation through constriction of natural home ranges is inherent in the system of zookeeping, and in many cases cannot be mitigated by better management. Evidence that animal suffer psychologically as a result of this curtailment of freedom for this can be seen in many ways.

The most obvious manifestation of boredom is "stereotypical" behavior, defined as repetitive behavior with no obvious function.[6] Examples of these are swaying in elephants[7] repetitive pacing in big cats, bears, foxes[8] and ungulates[9] and continuous spiral swimming in fish.[10]

Colin Spedding of the Farm Animal Welfare Council considered that stereotypies are an indication that animals are being driven "insane."[11] This view is confirmed by later studies showing associations between stereotypes and abnormal brain function in humans[12] and companion animals.[13]

Mason and Latham[14] considered that stereotypes are not functionless, but that they may act as a coping mechanism, and therefore they question whether they are a reliable indicator for animal welfare. However, this then prompts a further question as to why animals are in such stressed conditions that they require repetitive behavior to cope with their predicament. In the conclusion to their later review on stereotypies, Mason[15] re-evaluates more recent research on stereotypes and concludes that while in some cases stereotypes may have a beneficial function in coping, in many others they represent "pathological" cases of maladaptation, leading to a malfunction of the central nervous system.

Another example of empirical measurements indicating poor welfare is the presence of behavior indicating stress, such as increased vigilance and aggressive behavior of zoo animals toward zoo visitors or to each other. In this regard it is interesting to note that background noise from zoo visitors can be a stressor. The interaction between visitors and zoo animals can lead to a vicious circle. Visitors like to see animals that are "lively," often an indication that animals are stressed. Visitors seeing such behavior are likely to become more animated themselves, leading to more stress in the animals, and more "lively" behavior.[16]

Behavior indicating stress or boredom such as stereotypes and aggression can be mitigated to some extent by enrichment, which includes increasing the complexity of the environment, improving sensory stimulation, and providing more space. A meta-analysis on the benefits of these types of enrichment[17] indicated that enrichment led to a 50 to 60 percent reduction of abnormal behavior in many captive animals, though stereotypical behavior did not disappear totally. Carnivores are particularly prone to stereotypical behavior. Another meta-analysis revealed that in spite of the increasing prevalence of enrichment programs, captive tigers can spend up to 16 percent of their time in stereotype pacing, lions up to 48 percent, cheetahs up to 24 percent, and some bears up to 52 percent.[18] The overall frequency of stereotypical pacing behavior was correlated with the home range of the species in its natural environment. Species with larger home ranges spent more time pacing.

For some species such as elephants, behavioral deprivations can be exacerbated by conditions that compromise other Freedoms, such as unsuitable climates and hard and wet floors. The RSPCA commissioned a study on elephant captivity,[19] and based on this study recommended that elephants should not be kept in confinement at all.

The sense of this recommendation was tragically borne out in New Zealand in 2012, when Mila, a rescued circus elephant being rehabilitated at Franklin Zoo prior to being shipped to a sanctuary, killed her keeper. This is believed to have come about because Mila suffered from mental illness brought about by her long confinement in the circus.[20]

DELEGATED LEGISLATION UNDER
THE ANIMAL WELFARE ACT IN NEW ZEALAND

The requirements for all animals to be provided with all the Five Freedoms, and in particular the Freedom to express normal patterns of behavior, would preclude most animal interactions, especially animals used in farming, if it were rigorously enforced. However, the provisions of part 4 of the Animal Welfare Act have conditions in place to protect agricultural production and other entrenched traditions of animal use, which can mean that practices such as factory farming of pigs and layer hens are exempt from most of the provisions of the Act.[21]

The law allows *Codes of Welfare* to be promulgated as deemed regulations (a type of delegated legislation under the principle Act), to protect the interests of those keeping animals. It is a defense under the Act if a farmer or other person in charge of animals was complying with allowed treatment under the relevant *Code*. The latest amendments of the Animal Welfare Act (2015) allow actual regulations to be promulgated instead of a *Code*.

Codes of Welfare have been promulgated for commercial agriculture (pigs, layer hens, broilers etc.), certain treatments of animals (transport, painful procedures), companion animals (cats, dogs), and—relevant for this discussion, animals used in entertainment (zoos and aquaria, rodeos).

There are strict conditions under which codes may violate the wider protections of the Animal Welfare Act. These include a provision that submissions from the public must be taken into account, that animals must be looked after according to scientific practice and "good practice," and that egregious breaches of the Five freedoms can only occur in "exceptional circumstances."[22]

Codes of Welfare are administered by the National Animal Welfare Advisory Council (NAWAC), which is appointed by the Minister of Primary Industries, through the Minister's advisers at the Ministry of Primary Industries (MPI). Codes have to be signed off by the Minister of Primary Industries. This shows the dominance of the farming industry in regulating animal welfare. Agriculture represents the biggest share of animal use and abuse in New Zealand, and those who use animals for education, science, and entertainment are placed under the same regulatory protocol.

LEGAL PROTECTION OF ANIMALS IN ZOOS AND AQUARIA

Zoos, aquaria, and circuses are subject to the same laws as operators of other businesses and organizations that use animals, and as such they are required to comply with the principle act and with the relevant code of welfare. In the case of zoos, this is the *Animal Welfare (Zoos) Code of Welfare*, which was promulgated in 2005. Under the original terms of the Animal Welfare Act in 2000, codes of welfare were required to be reviewed every ten years, to reflect changing understanding of good animal welfare practice and public perceptions and beliefs, though this requirement has since been amended. In addition to the Animal Welfare Act and associated regulations, there are other statutory instruments regulating zoo and aquarium animals, some of which have a bearing on animal welfare. Zoos in New Zealand that import animals deemed to be "New Organisms" under the Hazardous Substances and New Organisms (HSNO) Act of 1996 are required to be registered with the MPI as containment facilities. A "New Organism" is defined under the HSNO Act as an organism that was not present in New Zealand outside confinement in 1998.

Zoos importing and confining New Organisms, including species such as big cats, elephants, and tarantulas, have to gain approval from the Environmental Protection Authority (EPA), and must comply with the Standard on *Containment Facilities for Zoo Animals*, administered by the MPI. The MPI audits these containment facilities annually to ensure compliance. The standard on containment facilities is mainly designed to ensure that new organisms, which may have disastrous social or environmental consequences if they escape into the environment, are securely contained. Animal welfare is not its purpose, though there are some behavioral requirements, which can incidentally give rise to better treatment of animals. These include stipulations that social animals have their social needs met and solitary animals are not forced into unwelcome contact with others; and that animals are provided with natural cover and sufficient space to provide for their "instinctive behaviors." In addition to these general provisions, sections for each type of animal provide specific requirements on how behavioral needs should be met, to ensure the animals are not induced to flight/fight responses, and therefore to escape confinement.

The MPI audits containment facilities registered under the HSNO Act annually to ensure compliance with the standard. The MPI guidelines for zoos state that although the HSNO inspectors are not warranted to investigate possible instances of poor welfare other than those stipulated under the behavioral requirements of the standard, if they observe suspected poor welfare, they may notify the MPI animal welfare inspectors to follow up their concerns.

Zoos and aquaria displaying marine mammals have to comply with the Marine Mammals Protection Act (1978), which requires a permit issued by the Department of Conservation before any marine mammal is allowed to be placed in captivity. The Marine Mammals Protection Act is administered by the Department of Conservation, and includes other provisions such as setting up marine mammal protection areas, so its main purpose is conservation, not animal welfare.

However, as with the HSNO Act, the extra layer of regulation does provide some further protection for marine mammals, defined in the Act as seals, dolphins, porpoises, whales, dugongs, and manatees, as well as any other mammal that is "morphologically adapted to, or which primarily inhabits, any marine environment." It was the requirements of the Marine Mammals Protection Act, not the Animal Welfare Act, that caused the controversial Marineland dolphinarium in Napier to close down in 2009. Marineland's permits to capture dolphins were not renewed in 1983, and an application was declined by the Department of

Conservation in 1991. The dolphin park closed to the public after the death of its last dolphin in 2008.[23]

The register for marine mammal permits contained 149 entries in May 2015. Most of these were for tourism (e.g., "whale watching" and "swim with dolphins" operations), observation and research, and the taking or displaying of dead material. Only three permits related to capture. The Southern Ocean Salmon company has a permit to capture and relocate seals attempting to take salmon from their farms, and Otago University has a permit for capture and release for research purposes. The only permit for capturing and holding marine mammals was for Auckland Zoo, which has a permit to rescue and hold pinnepids (seals and sea lions) that cannot be released into the wild.

In addition to the statutory animal welfare requirements, there are some self-regulated industry stipulations that may assist in safeguarding animal welfare. New Zealand zoos that are involved with wildlife display, breeding, education, or research for the ostensible purpose of conservation can become members of the Zoo and Aquarium Association (ZAA), an Australasian-wide nonprofit society with the stated mission to "harness the collective resources of zoos and aquariums to help conserve biodiversity in the natural environment."[24]

The ZAA has a code of ethics and code of practice for members, and this includes a position statement on animal welfare, available from its website. Larger zoos in New Zealand run by community organizations such as city councils and charitable trusts are members of the ZAA.

The ZAA has a code of ethics and code of practice for members, and this includes a position statement on animal welfare. Its website (www.zooaquarium.org.au) states that:

> Members of the Association share a commitment to animal conservation, welfare, collection sustainability and professional standards. The Association works with governments and the World Association of Zoos and Aquariums (WAZA) to facilitate its members in achieving excellence in wildlife conservation and animal welfare.[25]

Michael Gross[26] describes the way that zoos are having to make more convincing arguments to justify their survival in the face of mounting public opposition, and he concludes that it is an argument that circuses and dolphinaria have already lost. This can be seen in New Zealand after the closure in 2009 of New Zealand's last dolphinarium and last animal circus.

The US-based Association of Zoos and aquariums (AZA) have continued to justify zoos on the basis that they are looking after the animals well, and that they are required for conservation of endangered species. Michael Hutchins of the AZA has stressed that allowing the continuation of zoos requires a cost-benefit analysis, and stresses that AZA zoos can be justified because of their "dual goals of animal welfare and conservation provides a strong ethical justification for zoos and aquariums." Dr. Hutchins then compares the AZA zoos to nonaccredited zoos, which he appears to consider have a more questionable ethical basis.[27]

The AZA appears to be fighting a rearguard action to defend the continuation of zoos, and therefore it makes sense to assume that they would require strict adherence to animal welfare standards to prevent zoos getting a bad name among the public. The ZAA in New Zealand has a mission statement similar to the AZA, and both organizations are affiliated to the World Association of Zoos and Aquaria (WAZA).

To some extent the membership of WAZA through affiliated societies such as AZA and ZAA does appear to be a safeguard against the worst breaches of animal welfare, as shown for example by the way it threatened to expel the Japanese Association of Zoos and Aquariums (JAZA) from affiliation if they continued to procure captive dolphins from the dolphin slaughter at Taiji. As a result of this threat JAZA voted to discontinue this practice, which had provided a huge financial boost for the dolphin slaughter.[28]

THE CODE OF WELFARE FOR ZOO ANIMALS

The ZAA website lists twenty-four New Zealand zoos and wildlife parks as full or associate members (Table 4.1). Most of these have some conservation function, and two of these exist solely for conservation, being closed to the public. The official New Zealand government tourism website lists a further eight zoos that are promoted primarily as "entertainment," are not affiliated with the ZAA and therefore not subject to its requirements (Table 4.2). These zoos have a lesser stated commitment to conservation.

The ZAA therefore does appear to have some influence over the conservation ethos of its members. However, it has limited enforcement, its standards are not legally binding, and the worst sanction they can impose is to withdraw membership from noncomplying members, a sanction which may not be sufficient for some zoos to improve standards.

MPI inspections under the HSNO Act are restricted to exotic species enclosures and the inspectors would ignore other parts of the zoo, which often include native species, aquaria or children's "petting zoos," containing rabbits, hamsters, or farm animals.

So for most zoo animals in New Zealand, the only protection afforded is the Code of Welfare, and it is instructive to trace the regulatory steps in promulgating these regulations, and compare them to the way welfare codes for farm and laboratory animals were strongly watered down by industry interests.[29] Animals in zoos and aquaria are not a major part of the economy, and they are not suffering in secret in enclosed laboratories and barns—on the contrary, public display is the reason they are kept in

Table 4.1.   List of New Zealand zoos that are Members of the Zoo and Aquarium Association

Name	Ownership	Conservation initiatives	Main attraction	Other animal related attractions
Auckland Zoo	Auckland city council	DoC partner for captive breeding.	Elephants and other exotic megafauna	Exotic and native animals, including primates, felids, hippos, rhinos
Brooklands Zoo	District council	Part of ZAA breeding program for tamarins and some birds	Exotic animals	
Butterfly Creek, Auckland (associate member)	Private company	None given	Insects	Fish, crocodiles, monkeys
Dunedin Botanic Gardens	City council	Captive breeding programs for native birds	Native birds	
Esplanade Aviary	City council	Native bird recovery programs. Planned center for bird rehabilitation	Native birds	
Gibbs Wildlife Conservancy	Private	None given	Giraffes and zebras	
Hamilton Zoo	Hamilton city council	Funding, awareness	Exotic animals	
International Antarctic Centre	Private company	None given	Little blue penguins	
Kelly Tarleton's Sea Life Aquarium (associate member)	Private company	Turtle rehabilitation	Shark cages, walk-through aquarium	Penguins, other marine life

Name	Ownership	Conservation initiatives	Main attraction	Other animal related attractions
Kiwilife Bird Park	Private company	Kiwi recovery, wildlife breeding and rehabilitation, tuatara incubation	Kiwi, tuatara	Other native birds and reptiles, possums.
Kiwinorth: Kiwi House	Charitable trust	"Protect endangered native species," no details given	Kiwi, tuatara, gecko	
National Aquarium of New Zealand	City council	Research, "awareness"	Fish, penguins	
Natureland Wildlife Trust	Charitable trust	Captive breeding programs, wildlife rehabilitation	Native, exotic and domestic mammals and birds	
Nga Manu Nature Reserve	Charitable trust	Research	Nature reserve	Kiwi house, tuatara, aviary
Orana Wildlife Park	Charitable trust	Breeding programs for New Zealand birds, breeding exotics in captivity	Lions	Other African wildlife, Australian animals, kiwis
Otago Museum Tropical Forest	Statutory trust	None given for animals	Butterflies	Birds, fish, turtles
Otorohanga Kiwi House	Not for profit	Breeding kiwi for release.	Kiwi	Other birds
Peacock Springs/Isaac Wildlife Trust	Charitable trust.	Captive breeding of birds, tuatara, skinks, mudfish for release.	No entertainment function. Off limit to the general public.	No entertainment function. Off limit to the general public.
Pukaha Mt. Bruce National Wildlife Centre	Charitable trust	Captive breeding, habitat restoration	Native birds and tuatara	

Name	Ownership	Conservation initiatives	Main attraction	Other animal related attractions
Rainbow Springs Kiwi Wildlife Park	Iwi-affiliated company. Kiwi encounters run through a charitable trust.	Breeding kiwi for release, Operation nest egg	Kiwi	Fish, birds, tuatara
Te Puia (associate member)	Statutory institute	Kiwi breeding program	Maori cultural experience	Kiwi house
Ti Point Reptile Park	Private company	None given for animals	Native skinks and geckos	Exotic reptiles, including alligators
Wellington Zoo	Charitable trust	Captive breeding of skinks and birds, monitoring bird nesting sites, rehabilitation.	"Close encounters" with cheetah and other exotic mammals	Exotic animals
Westshore Wildlife Reserve	City council	Kiwi research and captive breeding. "Operation nest egg"	Kiwihouse not open to the public.	

Source: Zoo and Aquarium Association. http://www.zooaquarium.org.au. Further information was gained by accessing the official website for each zoo.

captivity in the first place. It should be expected therefore that they would be better protected than farm or laboratory animals.

The Code of Welfare for zoos has some positive provisions in place. For example, minimum standard #2 requires daily inspections, unless inspecting the animals may in itself impinge on their welfare. There are also minimum standards for hygiene (#4), overbreeding (#5), provision of food and water (#6), and physical environments (#7, 9, and 10). Live prey cannot be given to zoo animals, unless there is no alternative way of the predator gaining nutrition, and the harm to the prey is outweighed by the benefit to the predator.[30]

Of particular interest given that the requirements for allowing animals to express normal behavior is probably one of the most challenging facing zookeepers, are Minimum Standards requiring an appropriate social environment (#8), the requirement for behavioral enrichment programs (#11), and minimizing fear and distress (#12). Minimum standard #11 also prohibits the use of routine tethering, an improvement over previous

Table 4.2.   New Zealand Zoos that are Not Members of the Zoo and Aquarium Association

Name	Ownership	Conservation initiatives	Main attraction	Other animal related attractions
Agrodome	Private company	None given	Farm tours	Petting zoo
Willowbank Wildlife Reserve	Private company	Kiwi breeding, Operation nest egg.	Kiwi house	Tame farm animals. Other native and exotic animals.
Staglands Wildlife Reserve	Private company	Captive breeding programs for rare birds.	Deer park	Other tame animals for interaction. Eel pool.
Mill Creek Bird and Animal Encounters	Private company	None given	Birds	Farm park
The Parrot Place	Private company	None given	Bird zoo	Parrot sales
Hawkes Bay Farmyard Zoo	Private company	None given	Farm animals	Horse riding
Tame Wallaby Park EnkleDooVery Korma	Individual	Raising orphan wallabies	Petting wallabies	Other farm animals
Owlcatraz Native Bird and Wildlife Park	Private company	None given	Native owls not in enclosures	Other owls, petting zoo

Source: Names obtained from the Tourism New Zealand website (www .tourismnewzealand.com). Further information was gained by accessing the official website of each zoo.

codes. Minimum Standard #14 contains stipulations for facilities used in wild life rehabilitation that require among other things that the wildlife not be exhibited during the period of rehabilitation, unless this can be done in a way that the animal will not suffer distress.

The code disallows tethering, except for short-term and necessary use, but it still allows wing pinioning, an operation that restricts birds from flying. The code states that pinioning must be performed by a qualified veterinarian with appropriate pain relief, if it will involve "significant muscle, tendon or bone damage to the wing," but even where the operation itself is painless, as it is for many cases that only involve cutting feathers, it still deprives the birds of their freedom to display normal patterns of behavior. Pinioning would be an operation only useful to those keeping animals on display for entertainment. Birds being released for conservation purposes would not be crippled in any way.

In some ways therefore, zoo animals are better off than farm or laboratory animals, in that severe confinement and painful procedures are restricted and some allowances are made to prevent stress. However, as in the case when determining the Codes for farm[31] and laboratory animals,[32] NAWAC still took a disproportionate notice of industry desires and not those of the public.

The report by NAWAC accompanying the code describes in some detail the submissions on the code, and states that most submitters were opposed to the use of animals in zoos, especially for species that cannot adapt to a captive environment. There was particular opposition to the transfer of wild animals to zoos, the separation of social animals from companions and families, and the transfer of territorial animals to unfamiliar environments.

The functions of zoos were seen as an issue, with submitters questioning the standard defenses of zoo associations that they have a part to play in conservation and education. Submitters claimed that zoos had little or no educational value. Conservation efforts by zoos were considered to be minimal, and be diverting resources away from habitat preservation and preventing illegal hunting and smuggling. The main purpose of zoos was considered to be entertainment. A total of twenty-one submitters opposed all or some aspects of zoos, with sixteen of these opposing the display of wildlife. Five submitters were neutral, and one supported zoos.

NAWAC's response to all the submitters opposing zoos, and especially their entertainment and education function, was to dismiss them, on the grounds that the Animal Welfare Act does "not differentiate between the uses of animals." This is a novel interpretation of the legislative intent, because other parts of the Animal Welfare Act, do differentiate between the uses animals are put to. Part 6 (s.80–119) requires a cost-benefit analysis by Animal Ethics Committees before scientific experiments can be approved. The legislation also makes specific requirements for treatment of wild animals (Section 30A), permitted types of animal traps (s. 32), animal fights (s. 31), and animal exports (Part 3, s. 38–54). The system of Codes of Welfare was set up as an acknowledgement that different uses of animals may require separate justifications if operators are to be allowed to violate the principles of the Five Freedoms laid down in Sections 4 and 10.

Two more recent pieces of legislation show how the use animals are put to is a factor in determining what can be done to them. The first is a 2015 amendment to the Animal Welfare Act that prohibits using animals to test cosmetics (s.84A), and the second is a 2014 amendment to the Psychoactive Substances Act (2013) that prohibits using animal experiments to test psychoactive substances (aka "party pills" or "legal highs"), and that prohibits the regulatory body from evaluating results gained from animal experiments.

NAWAC also dismissed concerns over the capture of wild animals, on the grounds that all animals would have been wild at some stage in their ancestry. This shows a lack of understanding of basic biology, as animal behaviorists acknowledge that evolution does not suddenly stop once an animal is domesticated, but that domestic animals have very different behavior patterns that make them better adapted to captivity.[33] Indeed the NAWAC view is at variance even with standard observations, for example, that feral and domestic cats have a very different reaction to handling.

NAWAC dismissed suggestions that certain species such as big cats not be kept in zoos, using a conservation argument that with natural habitats being depleted at an increasing rates, zoos may be the only sanctuary left for endangered species. Here they are using the argument that the end justifies the means, a view inconsistent with their previous insistence that all animal uses are equally valid.

THE ROLE OF ZOOS IN CONSERVATION

The role of zoos in conservation and education are used by both the AZA[34] and NAWAC as justification to continue operating them. The educational function of zoos has come under a great deal of scrutiny, and their effectiveness is questionable, especially when compared to other means of teaching such as the use of wildlife reserves.[35]

The role of zoos in conservation is more equivocal, and therefore needs to be considered in more detail. There is also a statutory requirement for establishments to assist in conservation of endangered species both domestically and in developed countries. This is set out in Section 9 of the Convention of Biological Diversity, of which New Zealand is a signatory.

It is therefore necessary to evaluate just how effective zoos are at conserving endangered species, or whether the statutory obligations under the Convention may be better served through alternative strategies such as preserving habitat. This is especially the case given the number of submitters on the zoo and aquarium code who questioned the effectiveness of zoos for conservation.

The conservation roles of zoos can be divided into different functions. Zoos can act as places for sick and injured wildlife to recover. In New Zealand, the ZAA-affiliated Kelly Tarletons advertises its turtle rehabilitation program on its website, and Wellington Zoo rehabilitated "Happy Feet," the Emperor Penguin who was washed up on the Kapiti Coast in 2011 before being released into the wild.[36]

Other examples of these conservation roles are Auckland Zoo, which has a permit under the Marine Mammals Protection Act to keep injured seals. The Massey University oiled wildlife team also kept birds in temporary confinement prior to cleaning them and letting them recover after they were incapacitated by an oil spill when the *Rena* ran aground in 2011.

The second conservation function for zoos is their captive release programs, where animals are bred in the zoo for later release into the wild. In New Zealand, Operation Nest Egg, run by a trust set up by the Bank of New Zealand under the guidance of the Department of Conservation, iwi, and community groups, was established to protect kiwi eggs and chicks who were vulnerable to predation by introduced stoats. The participating zoos take kiwi eggs and chicks from the wild, and rear them in captivity until they are large enough to fend for themselves. Participating zoos need to adhere to guidelines for capture, rehabilitation, and release.[37]

Other capture-and-release programs include the Mt. Bruce wildlife center which releases kaka and kokako, and the Karori Wildlife Sanctuary (Zealandia). The latter is a sanctuary for New Zealand birds and tuatara and fish in a 225ha forest stream and wetland reserve, surrounded by a predator-proof fence, so it is debatable whether it could be described as a zoo in the conventional sense, though its website does mention native geckos kept in smaller enclosures.

A third stated conservation function for zoos are as "insurance" for species such as the tiger, which are severely threatened in the wild, and whose survival as a species may therefore depend on them being in zoos. The justification for keeping tigers is made on two levels, depending on degrees of optimism.

The optimistic view is that at some time in the future the tigers in zoos will be breeding stock that can be used to reintroduce the species to the wild once the outside environment becomes suitable. This can be seen as a kind of delayed version of Operation Nest Egg, only spreading over an indefinite time frame. The less optimistic view is that tigers can be kept in zoos in perpetuity even if they are unable to survive again in the wild.

For the optimistic view to have any credence, there needs to be more rigorous scientific evidence for the viability of long-term future releases. Operation Nest Egg appears to be showing some success in bringing back kiwi numbers.[38] However this initiative involving local experts, community, and iwi groups to rear a native species in a place close to its later release site is vastly different from the typical zoo conservation program for exotic species, where exotic species are kept in captivity for several generations in a place far removed from their eventual release point.

A review of the effectiveness of longer-term intergenerational rehabilitation programs cite cost as one of the reasons why these programs often fail, together with failing to achieving a self-sustaining population, disease, and genetic and behavioral change.[39] A study using ecological modeling together with mark-recapture studies of an endangered rodent population concludes that in the case of this species, rehabilitation efforts may further endanger the species, as removing individuals from their habitat for captivity harms the population more than it helps it.[40]

On the other hand, rehabilitation has been successful in some instances, such as the cases of the Californian condor, the blackfooted ferret, the Mauritius kestrel, and the Guam rail, which have been saved from extinction, at least in the short term.[41] When describing the use of captive facilities for the rehabilitation of primates in Indonesia, Cheyne et al.[42] acknowledge the concerns of the critics, but then go on to describe ways that rehabilitation procedures can overcome these objections. However many of these procedures involve keeping costs down by not using extensive viewable enclosures, keeping primates in seminatural settings close to the natural environment they will later be reintroduced to, and keeping human interaction to a minimum, partly to avoid the primates developing any dependency on humans. Such methods would be inimical to the standard zoo for exotic species in New Zealand, where the attraction for visitors is the sight of primates and other exotic animals in highly visible enclosures interacting with them in an urban environment far from their natural habitat.

The IUCN have recently published a review of successful reintroductions,[43] and this includes a chapter giving a detailed description on the successful translocation of the hihi in New Zealand.[44] The recovery project was conducted under the auspices of the Department of Conservation with support and sponsorship from corporate and commercial groups. In spite of being well resourced, the authors commented on how financial considerations were one of the barriers to a successful captive program, together with poor survival and breeding rates in captivity. The program eventually switched away from captive breeding and instead used translocations from established populations. As the authors put it: "Direct translocations have proven to be a more successful and cost effective translocation technique compared to captive breeding, which has now been discontinued."[45] Blue and Blunden[46] describe successful kiwi rehabilitation programs in Northland, of which Operation Nest Egg played a part. They describe the way that different stakeholders all had their role to play, and attribute their success to this "bottom-up" approach to conservation.

Under the optimistic view therefore, captive breeding can have a role to play in conservation management, but it requires financial resources, skilled staff, community input, extensive research on the species being rehabilitated, and facilities close to the rehabilitation site. When it comes to claims by New Zealand zoos that they are assisting with rehabilitation of exotic species the onus of proof is certainly on the zoos to prove that they have all the expertise, support, funding, and research capability.

Blanket statements not backed up by evidence should be discounted. This is particularly true of tigers and other big cats, and even proponents of captive rearing of tigers for eventual release[47] warn of the likelihood that artificial selection in the zoo environment will select for behaviors that would not enable the tigers to survive in the wild.

Certainly New Zealand zoos must provide convincing evidence to justify including big cats among their repertoire. Two New Zealand zoo-keepers have been killed after being attacked by captive tigers, one at Zion Wildlife Park near Whangarei in 2009, and one at Hamilton Zoo on September 20, 2015. The danger to zoo staff provides another reason for excluding these solitary predators from display.

Even if successful reintroduction of zoo animals is not possible, proponents of conservation can point to another function of zoos, which is to act as "genetic lifeboats" to preserve species that cannot be rehabilitated into the wild. The AZA openly admit in their introductions to a Species Survival Plan for tigers that rehabilitation is not their aim, but their function is rather to preserve genetic material in captivity.[48] There is little doubt that tiger breeding in captivity is proving successful,[49] so in this case zoos are succeeding in their stated aims. However, questions still need to be asked as to whether these aims are acceptable given the cost to the animals.

Firstly it is questionable whether the species being saved can be thought of as the same as that in the wild. All species are predominantly influenced by genes and environment, and these would both have changed irrevocably in captive animals. Natural selection would favor behavioral and other traits that are not advantageous in the wild,[50] and tigers as an ecological entity, interacting with other species and their physical environment would no longer exist.

The financial cost also needs to be considered, and whether preserving in a museum-like state a species that is doomed in the wild, is the best use of limited funds, especially in a country like New Zealand—a "biodiversity hotspot"[51] containing both a high degree of endemnicity and a high proportion of threatened and endangered species. Conservation funding may be better directed to saving species in their natural environment.

RECOMMENDATIONS FOR FUTURE CODES OF WELFARE

Keeping animals in captivity is an activity that by its nature impinges on an animal's freedom to express normal patterns of behavior, and therefore should only be excused only where this can be adequately mitigated through enrichment and where there are counterbalancing cost-effective, positive features such as education or conservation. So far, the evidence suggests that these countervailing factors are questionable or absent, and the burden of proof must be on the zoo community to provide evidence for the conservation of endangered species on a case-by-case basis, and to provide evidence that zoos are the best use of resources to educate about biodiversity.

Many submitters on the zoo code of welfare are totally opposed to zoos because the confinement of animals for human entertainment is totally unjustifiable. Submitters also questioned the use of zoos for education or conservation purposes. There were also concerns over specific practices such as capture of wild animals, breaking up of social and family units, overpopulation, overbreeding, pinioning, and hiring out animals for entertainment purposes such as the cheetahs at Wellington Zoo.

These concerns are echoed by animal rights and welfare groups in New Zealand. The largest animal advocacy group in New Zealand, the Royal New Zealand Society for the Prevention of Cruelty to Animals, supports the state animal welfare apparatus and has a member on NAWAC, and therefore can be described as part of the mainstream "center right" consortium of farmers, government officials, and their supporters, even while it also has a "center left" role in advocating for better treatment of animals.[52] This mainstream organization does not have an official policy on zoos, but it did put out a statement in 2010 strongly critical of the plans of Auckland Zoo to import more elephants into captivity. The reasons given were the detrimental effect captivity had on the welfare of elephants and the ineffectiveness of elephant captive breeding in contributing to conservation.[53]

The second-largest animal welfare group in New Zealand is Save Animals From Exploitation (SAFE), which has a policy of promoting veganism, and unlike the RNZSPCA does not support any part of the state animal welfare establishment. It is therefore part of the "center left" coalition of activists and academics supporting animal liberation.[54] SAFE goes further than the RNZSPCA in calling for an end to zoos. SAFE campaign director Mandy Carter, in an opinion piece for a national newspaper, states that "Even the best zoo doesn't compare to the natural ecosystems where wild animals belong," and "It's time to re-evaluate the role of zoos."[55]

The evidence presented above and the public submissions would suggest that the process of code review and formulation is not truly governed by "inclusiveness and science" as propounded by its supporters.[56] Unlike the case with farm and laboratory animals, there are few special interest groups that have a financial incentive to make money from animals, yet regulation of zoo animals is still subject to a heavy bias from NAWAC toward preserving the status quo.

The same can be found in regulations protecting companion animals, which also have little commercial value. The *Codes of Welfare* for cats and dogs provide better protection to these animals than farm, laboratory, or zoo animals, but there are also provisions in place clearly showing that human comfort takes priority over animal needs.

The *Code* for cats, for example, forbids killing by drowning, stipulates that food and water bowls must be "washed regularly" and states that kittens cannot be weaned younger than eight weeks old. However, the code also allows the painful practice of "declawing" (actually removing digits to the first joint). There are proposals that this should only be allowed where this is in the "best interests of the animal," but this is defined not as where the operation is required for therapeutic reasons, but simply because the owner finds the cats' behavior inconvenient.

The *Code* for dogs is a similar mixture. Dogs have to be walked every day, but "debarking" of dogs is allowed. In the case of both cats and dogs, "euthanasia" is allowed, not just as a mercy killing in the interests of the animal, but as a matter of convenience if it is in the interests of the owner.

Animals in zoos and in the household are therefore treated more like commodities to be enjoyed than sentient beings to be protected, and this attitude goes beyond simple economics.

A RIGHTS-BASED APPROACH

The view that animals should have rights has been supported by advocacy organizations in New Zealand and elsewhere. Advocacy organizations such as SAFE in New Zealand may support and seek to further animal welfare, as part of an overall strategy of furthering animal rights. An increasing number of academics and authors[57] also support the development of animal rights rather than an exclusive and limited focus on animal welfare.

A more rights-based approach to legal protection would certainly go a long way toward better treatment of animals in zoos. The most recent amendment to the Animal Welfare Act does specify in its title that one of the overall intents of the Act is to "recognise animals are sentient." There are therefore legal reasons to change the emphasis on animal protection to one that recognizes the interests of individual animals as sentient beings. Some recent changes in animal welfare legislation, specifically the ban on animal testing for cosmetics and psychoactive substances go some way along the welfare/rights continuum, in that the ban is absolute; the rights of the animals in these cases not to be tested on is not dependent on any cost-benefit equation.

There are fewer legislative provisions for the rights of zoo animals. However, in the meantime, if the process of code review and formulation is truly governed by "inclusiveness and science" as propounded by its supporters,[58] then the following restrictions on zoo operators need to be put into place. Such restrictions could advance the further development of rights for animals in zoos.

We recommend a complete phase-out of exotic primates, carnivores, and pachyderms. These animals are particularly difficult to keep in captivity, as discussed above, and their conservation function is also questionable. These animals should therefore not be brought into captivity, and should not be allowed to breed in captivity.

We also suggest a ban on the introduction of any other exotic animals where there is little known about how to best accommodate to their welfare under captivity. A recent systematic review[59] found that exotic primates, carnivores, and pachyderms are the most studied of zoo animals, in part because of their popularity in zoos. However as mentioned above, stereotypical behavior indicative of stress has been found in a number of species in zoos, including ungulates, caged rodents, fish, giraffes, and seals. The euthanasia of a depressed gibbon at Auckland Zoo[60] is another instance of the way zoos psychologically damage their inmates.

Indicators of stress are therefore widespread among zoo animals, and with the diverse range of animals being kept in captivity, all of which would have different behavioral requirements, the burden of proof should be on zoos to ensure that these are being adequately met. In addition, there are indications that the other Five Freedoms are also not being provided for in New Zealand zoos, shown for example in postmortem investigations of the five giraffes who died at Auckland Zoo, which showed that their diet had been inadequate.[61] The Standard for the HSNO Act requires different conditions for different types of zoo animals, so there is no reason why the Code of Welfare could not do the same.

A policy on how to look after existing primates, carnivores, and pachyderms should be created. Phasing out the breeding of animals that cannot exist in captivity will not solve the problem of animals already in zoos. Many of these animals have been institutionalized, and so release into the wild is not an option. Where funds are available, and where the animals can survive the journey, such animals could be released into sanctuaries, as has been done in New Zealand for many ex-circus animals for example.[62]

Where funding is not available, but the animals can be rehomed, there needs to be a public debate on whether funds should be diverted from zoo profits or from public funding to support this. The zoos and the public have been responsible for the animals' incarceration, so it would appear to make sense ethically to make funding from these sources available to mitigate a problem they caused.

Where the animals cannot be taken to a sanctuary, then a case-by-case decision needs to be made whether the animal should stay in the zoo. When considering the fate of the animals, the interests of the animal should be the only consideration. Even under a welfare-based system, euthanasia can only be considered if it is a true "mercy killing," and the only way of relieving physical and psychological torment. The animals should only be left to live their remaining lives in the zoo if the zoo can demonstrate that it has sufficient enrichment programs in place to allow them to express normal patterns of behavior, as well as have all their other needs met.

The fate of rescued animals such as the New Zealand fur seals being kept at Auckland Zoo under a permit needs to be examined in the same way, and a decision needs to be made, based on the welfare of the animals, whether they can eventually be released into the wild. If this is not possible, a decision needs to be made, based solely on the interests of the animal, whether it would be kinder to euthanize them rather than keep them in captivity.

We propose that conservation efforts should be restricted to rehabilitation of New Zealand species. The scientific research indicates that successful captive breeding and release is rare, and in the instances where it is successful, it needs to be carried out with the full backing of the local community in areas close to the release sites.[63] Projects should be further restricted to establishments that have a proven success rate, as shown by independent studies.

New Zealand would need to meet its obligations under the Convention on Biological Diversity to conservation in developing countries in another way. This could be done for example by providing donations to overseas conservation initiatives. Alternatively, the New Zealand government could move to ban the import of animal feed and palm oil that come from threatened habitats, or could reallocate its conservation priorities toward preserving habitats over industry profits. Any decisions on funding for conservation initiatives need to take into account the comparative cost effectiveness of all available measures, and would require cooperation between the New Zealand and overseas governments.

The educational functions of zoos should be restricted only to cases where this can be combined with genuine conservation efforts. The educational function of zoos is overstated and questionable, and even where learning does improve, it is unclear whether this could be equally well achieved by alternative, out of the classroom experiences such as visits to environmental parks. It would be better to put resources into developing wildlife reserves such as Zealandia and the Mount Bruce reserve, which serve both an educational and conservation function rather than continue to support urban-based zoos with smaller enclosures.

There should be much greater enforcement of the statutes. Enforcement of the Animal Welfare Act is the responsibility of MPI inspectors and the RNZSPA. However because only 0.07 percent of GDP is spent on animal welfare enforcement, the government agency is only able to follow up and prosecute a small percentage of complaints, leaving the RNZSPCA with most of the burden.

In 2011, 97 percent of animal welfare complaints were enforced by the RNZSPCA, not the MPI. This nongovernmental organization receives just 2 percent of its annual inspection budget through government funding, but is mostly reliant on charitable donations. This is the only case in New Zealand of a statutory enforcement body not having full funding from the state. As a result of the lack of resources allocated to animal welfare, in 2011, only 0.27 percent of animal welfare complaints led to a prosecution, compared with 60.3 percent of criminal cases overall.[64]

In summary, one of the issues with the animal welfare establishment in New Zealand is the way it is dominated by the same government agency that oversees agricultural production, together with its allies in academia, who are funded by the agricultural industries,[65] and this may constrain the possibility of developing rights for zoo animals. The MPI and its predecessor see animal welfare solely in terms of market access.[66] Animal welfare regulations have been drawn up to placate trading partners so they can buy New Zealand products with a clear conscience. In other words, animals will only be looked after when our trading partners are watching.[67] For animals in zoos with no economic value, this may even mean their needs are less scrutinized than those of farm animals. The dominance of an industry that sees animals in terms of commodities and market access could be one reason why this attitude prevails even in the promulgation of regulations for zoo and companion animals.

One solution that could further the development of rights for all animals in New Zealand is for a separate ministry or commissioner of animal welfare to oversee animal welfare legislation, which would have no affiliation to the farming industry. An independent ministry would report to a minister for animal welfare, who should not be the same person as the minister for primary industries. For a long time, the only opposition party to have an animal welfare portfolio was the Green Party. The New Zealand Labour Party now has a dedicated animal welfare spokesperson in their shadow cabinet, so there is a promise that this may change in a future Labour-led government.

A dedicated minister responsible for animals would put them on the same footing as other disadvantaged or marginalized groups; Maori, women, Pacific Islanders, and youth all have a ministry to promote their interests, and there is a commission set up for families.

A future ministry will need to allocate sufficient funding to enforce animal welfare offenses, to advise zoo operators on their responsibilities, and then to make follow-up inspection visits to ensure these have been complied with. Another factor this ministry will need to consider is whether the systems of codes of welfare, designed primarily for animals kept for agriculture, is the most appropriate regulatory framework.

The zoo of the future is unlikely to be totally abolished even under a regime that better reflects both the needs of the animals and the wishes of the public, but it will be more geared toward conserving New Zealand species, and many zoos will become more like wildlife parks, with enclosure sizes measured in hectares not square meters.

Management of these parks and wildlife reserves will require input from conservation experts, better funding from public sources, and involvement with community groups, private enterprise, and iwi.[68] These may be better managed by a new legislative framework that considers the requirements of all stakeholders, including the animals, as well as ensuring that conservation efforts are effective. This would need input not only from an animal welfare ministry but other government agencies such as the Department of Conservation, territorial and local councils, and possibly Te Puni Kokiri (Ministry for Maori affairs).

A legislative framework that incorporates these interests could still allow some space for an entertainment function of zoos, but only in so much as people find looking at our present wildlife reserves such as Zealandia and the Otorohonga Kiwi House an enriching experience. Human enrichment, animal welfare, education, and conservation could be brought together in a more integrated whole.

NOTES

1. We are grateful to Dr. John Hellstrom from the National Animal Welfare Advisory Committee, and to Dr. David Scobie, for reviewing this manuscript.

2. D. J. Mellor, and A. C. D. Bayvell, "New Zealand's inclusive science-based system for setting animal welfare standards," *Applied Animal Behaviour Science* 113 (2008): 313–29. Cheryl O'Connor and Kate Littin, "New Zealand animal welfare standards," paper presented at the Minding Animals Conference, Newcastle, NSW, July 2009.

3. Ruth Harrison, *Animal machines: The new factory farming industry* (Wallingford, UK: CAB International, 1964).

4. Marian Stamp Dawkins, "Animal welfare and the paradox of animal consciousness," *Advances in the study of behaviour* 47 (2015): 5–38.

5. Ibid.

6. J. Rushen and G. Mason, "A decade-or-more's progress in understanding stereotypic behaviour," in *Stereotypic Animal Behaviour: Fundamentals and Applications to Welfare*, G. Mason and J. Rushen, eds. (Wallingford, UK: CABI, 2006), 1–11.

7. Ros Clubb and Georgia Mason, *A review of the welfare of zoo animals in Europe: A report commissioned by the RSPCA* (Authors, 2002).

8. Ros Clubb and Georgia Mason, "Natural behavioural biology as a risk factor in carnivore welfare: How analysing species differences could help zoos improve enclosures," *Applied Animal Behaviour Science* 102 (2007): 303–28.

9. R. Bergeron, A. J. Badnell-Waters, S. Lambton, and G. Mason, "Stereotypic oral behavior in captive ungulates: foraging, diet and gastrointestinal function," in *Stereotypic Animal Behaviour: Fundamentals and Applications to Welfare*, G. Mason, and J. Rushen, eds. (Wallingford, UK: CABI, 2006), 19–57.

10. CAPS (Captive Animals Protection Society) *Suffering deep down: An investigation into public aquaria in the UK* (Author, 2004).

11. Colin Spedding, *Animal welfare* (London: Earthscan, 2000).

12. S. J. P. Garner, "Perseveration and stereotypy—systems level insights from clinical psychology," in *Stereotypic Animal Behaviour: Fundamentals and Applications to Welfare*, G. Mason and J. Rushen, eds. (Wallingford, UK: CABI, 2006), 121–52.

13. A. Mills and A. Luescher, "Veterinary and pharmacological approaches to abnormal repetitive behaviour," in *Stereotypic Animal Behaviour: Fundamentals and Applications to Welfare*, G. Mason and J. Rushen, eds. (Wllingford: CABI), 286–324.

14. Greg Mason and N. Latham, "Can't stop, won't stop: Is stereotype a reliable welfare indicator?" *Animal Welfare* 13 (2004): S57–S69.

15. Greg Mason, "Stereotypic Behaviour in Captive Animals: Fundamentals and Implications for Welfare and Beyond," in *Stereotypic Animal Behaviour: Fundamentals and Applications to Welfare*, G. Mason and J. Rushen, eds. (Wallingford, UK: CABI, 2006), 325–56.

16. E. J. Fernandez, M. A. Tamborski, S. R. Pickens, and W. Timberlake, "Animal-visitor interactions in the modern zoo: Conflicts and interventions," *Applied Animal Behaviour Science* 120 (2009): 1–8. This is also borne out by personal observations of Jiaqi Jiang, a visitor at Beijing Zoo (2015), who reports: "The worst thing I saw was a crowd of people hit the glass at different areas and the monkey in the cage seemed very anxious and angry. It kept climbing up the iron chain, jumping, punching and scratching the glass window of one side and then jumping to the other side and screaming. This monkey did these things again and again every time the crowd was excited and people cried, laughed, clapped, and kept enraging the monkey."

17. R. R. Swaisgood and D. J. Shepardson, "Environmental Enrichment as a Strategy for Mitigating Stereotypies in Zoo Animals: A Literature Review and meta-analysis," in *Stereotypic animal behaviour: Fundamentals and applications to welfare* (Wallingford, UK: CABI, 2006), 256–85.

18. Clubb and Mason 2007, "Natural behavioural biology."

19. Clubb and Mason 2002, *Welfare of animals in Europe.*

20. Arlene Peredes, "Elephant crushes zookeeper to death," *International Business Times*, April 26, 2012, http://www.ibtimes.com.au/elephant-crushes-zookeeper-death-1239879, accessed March 2017.

21. Michael Morris, "The use of animals in New Zealand: Regulation and practice," *Society and Animals* 19 (2011): 366–80.

22. Ibid.

23. Anon, "Marineland's last dolphin dies," *Dominion Post*, September 11, 2008, http://www.stuff.co.nz/life-style/cutestuff/623078/Marinelands-last-dolphin-dies.

24. Zoo and Aquarium Association website, http://www.zooaquarium.org.au/index.php/zaa-wildlife-conservation-fund/, accessed December 14, 2016.

25. Zoo and Aquarium Association.

26. Michael Gross, "Can zoos offer more than entertainment?" *Current Biology* 25 (2015): R391–94.

27. M. Kuehn, "Is it ethical to keep animals in zoos?" *JAVMA News* December 1, 2002.

28. Justin McCurry, "Japanese aquariums vote to stop buying Taiji dolphins," *The Guardian*, May 20, 2015, https://www.theguardian.com/world/2015/may/20/japanese-aquariums-vote-to-stop-buying-dolphins-hunt.

29. Morris, "The use of animals in New Zealand." Bourke, "The regulation of animal use."

30. This raises an interesting dilemma about the tension between the rights of predators and prey. A detailed discussion of this is outside the scope of this chapter, but this tension is explored by David Pearce, "The hedonistic imperative" (1995), http://www.hedweb.com/hedethic/tabconhi.htm, accessed June 13, 2016.

31. Peter Sankoff, "Five years of the 'new' animal welfare regime: Lessons learned from New Zealand's decision to modernize its animal welfare legislation," *Animal Law* 1 (2005): 7–38. Michael Morris, "The ethics and politics of animal welfare in New Zealand: Broiler chicken production as a case study," *Journal of Agricultural and Environmental Ethics* 22 (2009): 15–30. Michael Morris, and Peter Beatson, "Animal suffering in New Zealand: Can science make a difference?" *Kōtuitui: New Zealand Journal of Social Sciences online* 6 (2011), 124–32.

32. Sue Kedgley, "Lifting the veil of secrecy surrounding animal experimentation," in *Lifting the Veil: Finding Common Ground*, P. Cragg, K. Stafford, D. Love, and G. Sutherland, eds. (Wellington, NZ: ANZCCART, 2004), 27–32. Michael Morris, "Animal experimentation in New Zealand: The three 'Buts,'" in *Lifting the Veil: Finding Common Ground*, P. Cragg, K. Stafford, D. Love, and G. Sutherland, eds. (Wellington, NZ: ANZCCART, 2004), 137–44. Deidre Bourke, and Michael Morris, "Animal ethics committees and the protection of animals' interests" (paper presented at the New Zealand Bioethics Conference, Dunedin, February 10–14, 2006).

33. N .F. Snyder, S. R. Derrickson, S. R. Beissinger, J. W. Wiley, T. B. Smith, W. D. Toone, and B. Miller, "Limitations of captive breeding in endangered species recovery," *Conservation Biology* 10 (1996): 338–48.

34. Kuehn, "Is it ethical to keep animals in zoos?"

35. L. Marino, S. O. Lilienfield, R. Malamud, N. Nobis, and R. Broglio, "Do Zoos and Aquariums Promote Attitude Change in Visitors? A Critical Evaluation of the American Zoo and Aquarium Study," *Society and Animals* 18 (2010): 126–38. Eric Jensen, "Evaluating Children's Conservation Biology Learning at the Zoo," *Conservation Biology* 28 (2014): 1004–11. G. Kimble, "Children learning about biodiversity at an environment centre, a museum and at live animal shows," *Studies in Educational Evaluation* 41 (2013): 48–51.

36. Andrea O'Neil, "Penguin Happy Feet becomes a Wellington celebrity — 150 years of news," *Dominion Post*, July 16, 2011, http://www.stuff.co.nz/dominion-post/news/70229675/penguin-happy-feet-becomes-a-wellington-celebrity-150-years-of-news, accessed June 13, 2016.

37. Suzanne Bassett, *Operation nest egg incubation and chick rearing best practice and protocols* (Wellington, NZ: Department of Conservation, 2012).

38. Lyndsay Blue and Greg Blunden, "(Re)making space for kiwi: beyond 'fortress conservation' in Northland," *New Zealand Geographer* 66 (2010): 105–23.

39. Snyder et al., "Limitations of captive breeding."

40. R. McCleery, J. A. Hostetler, and M. K. Oli, "Better off in the wild? Evaluating a captive breeding and release program for the recovery of an endangered rodent," *Biological Conservation* 169 (2014): 198–205.

41. Snyder et al., "Limitations of captive breeding."

42. S. M. Cheyne, C. O. Campbell, and K. L. Payne, "Proposed guidelines for *in situ* gibbon rescue, rehabilitation and reintroduction," *International Zoo Yearbook* 46 (2011): 265–81.

43. P.S. Soorae, ed., *Global reintroduction perspectives 2013: Further case studies from around the globe* (Gland, Switzerland: IUCN/SSC reintroduction specialist group, 2013).

44. J. G. Ewen, R. Renwick, L. Adams, D. P. Armstrong, and K. A. Parker (2013), "1980–2012: 32 years of reintroduction efforts of the hihi (stitchbird) in New Zealand," in *Global reintroduction perspectives 2013: Further case studies from around the globe*, P. S. Soorae, ed. (Gland, Switzerland: IUCN/SSC reintroduction specialist group), 68–73.

45. Ibid., 72

46. Blue and Blunden, "(Re)making space for kiwi."

47. E.g., M. S. Szokalski, C. A. Litchfield, and W. K. Foster, "Enrichment for captive tigers (*Pantera tigris*): Current knowledge and future directions," *Applied Animal Behaviour Science* 139 (2012): 1–9.

48. Association of Zoos and Aquaria (AZA), *Management and conservation of captive tigers*, Panthera tigris (Author, 2006).

49. S. P. Saunders, T. Harris, K. Traylor-Holzerc, and K. G. Beck, "Factors influencing breeding success, ovarian cyclicity, and cub survival in zoo-managed tigers (*Panthera tigris*)," *Animal Reproduction Science* 144 (2014): 38–47.

50. Szokalski et al., "Enrichment for captive tigers."

51. N. Myers, R. A. Mittermeier, C. G. Mittermeier, G. A. B. da Fonseca, and J. Kent, "Biodiversity hotspots for conservation priorities," *Nature* 403 (2000): 853–58.

52. Morris and Beatson, "Animal suffering in New Zealand."

53. Reported in *World Animal Protection News* 2010.

54. Morris and Beatson, "Animal suffering in New Zealand."
55. Mandy Carter, "Animals deserve a life free of bars," *New Zealand Herald*, January 17, 2015, http://www.nzherald.co.nz/lifestyle/news/article.cfm?c_id=6&objectid=11392070, accessed June 13, 2016.
56. E.g., Mellor and Bayvel, "New Zealand's inclusive science-based system."
57. E.g., Gary Francione, *Rain without thunder: The ideology of the animal rights movement* (Philadelphia: Temple University Press, 1996). Tom Regan, *Empty cages: Facing the challenge of animal rights* (Lanham, MD: Rowman & Littlefield, 2004).
58. Mellor and Bayvel, "New Zealand's inclusive science-based system."
59. Swaisgood, and D. J. Shepardson, "Environmental Enrichment as a Strategy for Mitigating Stereotypes in Zoo Animals."
60. Martin Johnson, "Auckland zoo puts down 'unhappy and agitated' gibbon," *New Zealand Herald*, January 22, 2015, http://www.nzherald.co.nz/nz/news/article.cfm?c_id=111389939, accessed March 2017.
61. J. S. Potter and M. Clauss, "Mortality of captive giraffe (*Giraffa camelopardallis*) associated with serous fat atrophy: A review of five cases at Auckland Zoo," *Journal of Wildlife Medicine* 36 (2005): 301–7.
62. Martin Johnson, "Auckland zoo puts down 'unhappy and agitated' gibbon," *New Zealand Herald*, January 22, 2015, http://www.nzherald.co.nz/nz/news/article.cfm?c_id=111389939, accessed March 2017.
63. Ewen et al., "1980–2012: 32 years of reintroduction efforts of the hihi." Blue and Blunden, "(Re)making space for kiwi."
64. Danielle Duffield, "The enforcement of animal welfare offences and the viability of an infringement regime as a strategy for reform," *New Zealand Universities Law Review* 25 (2013): 1–46.
65. Morris and Beatson, "Animal suffering in New Zealand."
66. MAF (Ministry of Agriculture and Forestry), *Research in progress: 2005/2006 operational research objectives* (Wellington, NZ: MAF Policy Information Paper 06/02, 2006).
67. Peter Beatson (2008), *Falls the shadow: The animal welfare debate in New Zealand*, http://citeseerx.ist.psu.edu/viewdoc/download?doi=10.1.1.524.5421&rep=rep1&type=pdf, accessed July 2016.
68. Ewen et al., "1980–2012: 32 years of reintroduction efforts of the hihi." Blue and Blunden, "(Re)making space for kiwi."

BIBLIOGRAPHY

Anon. "Marineland's last dolphin dies." *Dominion Post*, September 11, 2008. http://www.stuff.co.nz/life-style/cutestuff/623078/Marinelands-last-dolphin-dies.
Association of Zoos and Aquaria (AZA). *Management and conservation of captive tigers, Panthera tigris* (Author, 2006).
Bassett, Suzanne. *Operation nest egg incubation and chick rearing best practice and protocols* (Wellington, NZ: Department of Conservation, 2012).
Beatson, Peter. *Falls the shadow: The animal welfare debate in New Zealand*. (Author, 2008.) http://citeseerx.ist.psu.edu/viewdoc/download?doi=10.1.1.524.5421&rep=rep1&type=pdf. Accessed July 2016.
Bergeron, R., A. J. Badnell-Waters, S. Lambton, and G. Mason. "Stereotypic oral behaviour in captive ungulates: foraging, diet and gastrointestinal function." In *Stereotypic Animal Behaviour: Fundamentals and Applications to Welfare*, G. Mason and J. Rushen, eds. (Wallingford, UK: CABI, 2006), 19–57.
Blue, Lyndsay and Greg Blunden. "(Re)making space for kiwi: Beyond 'fortress conservation in Northland." *New Zealand Geographer* 66 (2010): 105–23.
Bourke, Deidre and Michael Morris. "Animal ethics committees and the protection of animals' interests" (paper presented at the New Zealand Bioethics Conference, Dunedin, February 10–14, 2006).

CAPS (Captive Animals Protection Society). *Suffering deep down: An investigation into public aquaria in the UK* (Author, 2004).

Cheyne, S. M., C. O. Campbell, and K. L. Payne. "Proposed guidelines for *in situ* gibbon rescue, rehabilitation and reintroduction." *International Zoo Yearbook* 46 (2011): 265–81.

Clubb, Ros and Georgia Mason. *A review of the welfare of zoo animals in Europe: A report commissioned by the RSPCA* (Authors, 2002).

———. "Natural behavioural biology as a risk factor in carnivore welfare: How analysing species differences could help zoos improve enclosures." *Applied Animal Behaviour Science* 102 (2007): 303–28.

Dawkins, Marian Stamp. "Animal welfare and the paradox of animal consciousness." *Advances in the study of behaviour* 47 (2015): 5–38.

Duffield, Danielle. "The enforcement of animal welfare offences and the viability of an infringement regime as a strategy for reform." *New Zealand Universities Law Review* 25 (2013): 1–46.

Ewen, J. G., R. Renwick, L. Adams, D. P. Armstrong, and K. A. Parker. "1980–2012: 32 years of reintroduction efforts of the hihi (stitchbird) in New Zealand." In *Global reintroduction perspectives 2013: Further case studies from around the globe*, P.S. Soorae, ed. (Gland, Switzerland: IUCN/SSC reintroduction specialist group, 2013), 68–73.

Fernandez, E. J., M. A. Tamborski, S. R. Pickens, and W. Timberlake. "Animal-visitor interactions in the modern zoo: Conflicts and interventions." *Applied Animal Behaviour Science* 120 (2009): 1–8.

Francione, Gary. *Rain without thunder: The ideology of the animal rights movement* (Philadelphia: Temple University Press, 1996).

Garner, S. J. P. "Perservation and stereotypy—systems level insights from clinical psychology." In *Stereotypic Animal Behaviour—Fundamentals and Applications to Welfare*, G. Mason and J. Rushen, eds. (Wallingford, UK: CABI, 2006), 121–52.

Gross, Michael. "Can zoos offer more than entertainment?" *Current Biology* 25 (2015): R391–94.

Harrison, Ruth. *Animal machines: The new factory farming industry* (Wallingford, UK: CAB International, 1964).

Jensen, Eric. "Evaluating Children's Conservation Biology Learning at the Zoo." *Conservation Biology* 28 (2014): 1004–11.

Johnson, Martin. "Auckland zoo puts down 'unhappy and agitated' gibbon." *New Zealand Herald*, January 22, 2015. http://www.nzherald.co.nz/nz/news/article.cfm?c_id=111389939. Accessed March 2017.

Kedgley, Sue. "Lifting the veil of secrecy surrounding animal experimentation." In *Lifting the Veil: Finding Common Ground*, P. Cragg, K. Stafford, D. Love, and G. Sutherland, eds. (Wellington, NZ: ANZCCART, 2004), 27–32.

Kimble, G. "Children learning about biodiversity at an environment centre, a museum and at live animal shows." *Studies in Educational Evaluation* 41 (2013): 48–51.

Kuehn, M. "Is it ethical to keep animals in zoos?" *JAVMA News* December 1, 2002.

MAF (Ministry of Agriculture and Forestry). *Research in progress: 2005/2006 operational research objectives* (Wellington, NZ: MAF Policy Information Paper 06/02, 2006).

Marino, L., S. O. Lilienfield, R. Malamud, N. Nobis, and R. Broglio. "Do Zoos and Aquariums Promote Attitude Change in Visitors? A Critical Evaluation of the American Zoo and Aquarium Study." *Society and Animals* 18 (2010): 126–38.

Mason, Greg. "Stereotypic Behaviour in Captive Animals: Fundamentals and Implications for Welfare and Beyond." In *Stereotypic Animal Behaviour—Fundamentals and Applications to Welfare*, G. Mason and J. Rushen, eds. (Wallingford, UK: CABI, 2006), 325–56.

Mason, Greg and N. Latham. "Can't stop, won't stop: Is stereotype a reliable welfare indicator?" *Animal Welfare* 13 (2004): S57–S69.

McCleery, R., J. A. Hostetler, and M. K. Oli. "Better off in the wild? Evaluating a captive breeding and release program for the recovery of an endangered rodent." *Biological Conservation* 169 (2014): 198–205.

McCurry, Justin. "Japanese aquariums vote to stop buying Taiji dolphins." *The Guardian*, May 20, 2015. https://www.theguardian.com/world/2015/may/20/japanese-aquariums-vote-to-stop-buying-taiji-dolphins-hunt.

Mellor, D. J., and A. C. D. Bayvell. "New Zealand's inclusive science-based system for setting animal welfare standards." *Applied Animal Behaviour Science* 113 (2008): 313–29.

Mills, A. and A. Luescher. "Veterinary and pharmacological approaches to abnormal repetitive behaviour." In *Stereotypic Animal Behaviour—Fundamentals and Applications to Welfare*, G. Mason, and J. Rushen, eds. (Wallingford, UK: CABI, 2006), 286–324.

Morris, Michael. "Animal experimentation in New Zealand: The three 'Buts,'" in *Lifting the Veil: Finding Common Ground*, P. Cragg, K. Stafford, D. Love, and G. Sutherland, eds. (Wellington, NZ: ANZCCART, 2004), 137–44.

———. "The ethics and politics of animal welfare in New Zealand: Broiler chicken production as a case study." *Journal of Agricultural and Environmental Ethics* 22 (2009): 15–30.

———. "The use of animals in New Zealand: Regulation and practice." *Society and Animals* 19 (2011): 366–80.

Morris, Michael and Peter Beatson. "Animal suffering in New Zealand: Can science make a difference?" *Kōtuitui: New Zealand Journal of Social Sciences online* 6 (2011): 124–32.

Myers, N., R. A. Mittermeier, C. G. Mittermeier, G. A. B. da Fonseca, and J. Kent. "Biodiversity hotspots for conservation priorities." *Nature* 403 (2000): 853–58.

O'Connor, Cheryl and Kate Littin. "New Zealand animal welfare standards." Paper presented at the Minding Animals Conference, Newcastle, NSW, July 2009.

O'Neil, Andrea. "Penguin Happy Feet becomes a Wellington celebrity—150 years of news." *Dominion Post*, July 16, 2011. http://www.stuff.co.nz/dominion-post/news/70229675/penguin-happy-feet-becomes-a-wellington-celebrity-150-years-of-news.

Pearce, David. "The hedonistic imperative." (1995.) http://www.hedweb.com/hedethic/tabconhi.htm. Accessed March 2017.

Peredes, Arlene. "Elephant crushes zookeeper to death." *International Business Times*, April 26, 2012. http://www.ibtimes.com.au/elephant-crushes-zookeeper-death-1239879. Accessed March 2017.

Potter, J. S. and M. Clauss. "Mortality of captive giraffe (*Giraffa camelopardallis*) associated with serous fat atrophy: A review of five cases at Auckland Zoo." *Journal of Wildlife Medicine* 36 (2005): 301–7.

Regan, Tom. *Empty cages: Facing the challenge of animal rights* (Lanham, MD: Rowman & Littlefield, 2004).

Rushen, J. and G. Mason. "A decade-or-more's progress in understanding stereotypic behaviour." In *Stereotypic Animal Behaviour—Fundamentals and Applications to Welfare*, G. Mason, and J. Rushen, eds. (Wallingford, UK: CABI, 2006), 1–11.

Sankoff, Peter. "Five years of the 'new' animal welfare regime: Lessons learned from New Zealand's decision to modernize its animal welfare legislation." *Animal Law* 1 (2005): 7–38.

Saunders, S. P., T. Harris, K. Traylor-Holzerc, and K. G. Beck. "Factors influencing breeding success, ovarian cyclicity, and cub survival in zoo-managed tigers (*Panthera tigris*)." *Animal Reproduction Science* 144 (2014): 38–47.

Snyder, N. F., S.R. Derrickson, S. R. Beissinger, J. W. Wiley, T. B. Smith, W. D.Toone, and B. Miller. "Limitations of captive breeding in endangered species recovery." *Conservation Biology* 10 (1996): 338–48.

Soorae, P.S, ed. *Global reintroduction perspectives 2013: Further case studies from around the globe* (Gland, Switzerland: IUCN/SSC reintroduction specialist group, 2013).

Spedding, Colin. *Animal welfare* (London: Earthscan, 2000).

Swaisgood, R. R. and D. J. Shepardson. "Environmental Enrichment as a Strategy for Mitigating Stereotypies in Zoo Animals: A Literature Review and meta-analysis."

In *Stereotypic animal behaviour: Fundamentals and applications to welfare* (Wallingford, CABI, 2006), 256–85.

Szokalski, M. S., C. A. Litchfield, and W. K. Foster. "Enrichment for captive tigers (*Pantera tigris*): Current knowledge and future directions." *Applied Animal Behaviour Science* 139 (2012), 1–9.

FIVE

Ethical and Legal Rights for Zoo Animals in Southeast Asia

Govindasamy Agoramoorthy

Throughout human history, wild animals became the subject of amusement in circuses and other recreational venues.[1] Even modern zoos have their origins in royal menageries of ages past where animals provided entertainment for privileged societal elites.[2] The modern zoo concept does not allow displaying animals for public pleasure only. Instead, in Southeast Asia, most zoos directors feel that it plays a role in conservation, education, and research in addition to entertaining the public using various interactive sessions involving animals, keepers, and visitors.[3] This practice, however, is constantly under attack by activists who challenge their role in conservation, education, and research. Furthermore, whether zoos should even exist in the current civil society is likewise vigorously under debate.[4] The most controversial issues facing zoos are the procurement of animals for breeding, disposal of surplus animals, and use of animals in research and recreation.[5] This chapter will illustrate the significant problems with animal welfare and lack of legal rights for zoo animals in Southeast Asia. It will highlight the ongoing use of animals as entertainment in many countries. It suggests the possibility that this may increase among other commercial institutions. It reviews the current laws in several Southeast Asian countries and suggests areas where the laws need reinforcement.

THE IMPORTANCE OF ANIMAL WELFARE ORGANIZATIONS

Zoos in Southeast Asian countries are members of zoo accrediting associations. The data on the exact numbers of zoos that are functional in Southeast Asian countries are not available due to the lack of a centralized databank. In addition, not all zoos are members of the national or regional zoo associations. Once a zoo becomes a member of the national zoo association, however, it automatically adheres to the rules and regulations of the regional zoo association, which is the Southeast Asian Zoo Association. All regional zoo associations worldwide follow the ethical and welfare guidelines set by the World Association of Zoos and Aquariums. Nonetheless, both the World Zoo Association and the Southeast Asian Zoo Association are not involved in either creating new laws to enhance animal rights or providing advice to amend animal welfare laws. However, they do not object if national zoo associations work with government agencies to develop the necessary legal provisions. This is simply because the major objective of the global and regional zoo associations is to serve their members while allowing them to conduct their businesses more professionally. Individual zoos and their affiliated associations are often engaged in their internal politics of operating, managing, and upgrading standards to boost revenue.

Who then advocates for creating or amending laws to promote the rights for captive wildlife? The answer, of course, is animal right activists since their major objective is to make sure that animals get protection, both legally and morally. Government agencies on the other hand are not keen on thinking about the rights of captive wildlife since they are busy with their own priorities targeting people. Until enormous political pressure mounts on policy makers and leaders of government agencies, they will not indulge in creating any new laws favoring animals. Two decades ago, only a handful of animal right groups were active in Southeast Asian countries and they were involved in rescuing and caring mostly for domestic pets and farm animals. In recent years, however, several local and foreign animal right groups are actively pressuring government agencies to develop legislation protecting captive wildlife from abuse, as we shall see later in the chapter where I discuss individual countries. Therefore, whatever legislation came into existence to upgrade the rights of captive wildlife in Southeast Asian countries, it is mainly due to the pressure by various animal right groups.

Zoos in Southeast Asian nations in general acquire animals through various means that include exchange with other zoos using captive-bred stock, purchase from legal traders, and rescuing wild-caught/abandoned/smuggled animals confiscated by governments. Highly endangered large mammals such as the elephant herds often raid farms and palm oil plantations in Indonesia and Malaysia due to loss of natural habitat.[6] Some of those crop-raiding wild elephants end up in rescue operations and eventually reach zoos for long-term care. In addition, zoos can also get legal permits from the government to capture various species of native wildlife from forests. For example, zoos in Malaysia get permits to trap wild Malayan tapirs.

Nevertheless, there are cases in the past where some zoos used traders to get highly endangered animals illegally. An example is the import of gorillas by Malaysia from Nigeria that happened in 2002. The trafficked gorillas were returned to Africa under enormous pressure from numerous animal right groups.[7] Likewise, some zoos in the Philippines continue to get endangered endemic wildlife from hunters since the government is incapable of monitoring and microchipping all zoo animals throughout the country. For example, the Mantianak Zoo in Mindanao (Philippines) offered tiger cubs for sale in 2013.[8] Local newspapers in Manila continue to advertise tiger cubs for sale and some owners of zoos are apparently involved in this illegitimate venture. This situation shows the current problems of wild animal collection, trade, and management of zoos across the Philippines, which is a major biodiversity hotspot in Southeast Asia. Therefore, it needs to create new laws to stop the abuse of wildlife from further illegal exploitation.

Some of the newly created safari parks in the region received large numbers of rhinos, giraffes, and zebras in recent years alarming western zoo biologists. The Vinpearl Safari in Vietnam received numerous large mammals from South Africa and news reports indicated massive animal deaths in 2016.[9] This is an example of the enormity of the problems involving traders, zoological staff, and veterinarians working for the zoo. Although the zoo denied mass mortality, neither the World Zoo Association nor the regional zoo association investigated the issue.[10]

Why would a newly created safari park in Vietnam import large number of rhinos? Critics suspect the rhino horn trade to be behind the mass importation since the horn is so valuable. There is a huge ongoing illegal market for rhino horns in Vietnam and neighboring China. Therefore, the government of Vietnam needs to clarify reasons for allowing the legal importation of large numbers of rhinos from South Africa to enhance transparency in the zoo business involving highly endangered wild mammals, especially commercially important elephants and rhinos. Similarly, China's largest privately owned safari park, Chimelong imported two dozen baby elephants from Zimbabwe that created an international outcry. A report from *National Geographic* highlighted the physical abuse and mistreatment at the Qingyuan quarantine facility.[11] Moreover, the same park imported wild-caught Bornean elephants from the Sabah Wildlife Department in Malaysia a few years ago. Chimelong Safari is also the only zoo outside of Borneo to display the rarest pygmy elephant and that worries animal activists worldwide.

So, why did the Sabah Wildlife Department in Malaysia give legal permission to export the unique pygmy elephant to a new safari park in

China with a history of animal abuse? Why were they not shipped to a better zoo to a country in the European Union or the United States that have better facilities to provide care? This case illustrates the weakness in enforcing the Malaysian wildlife law. It also creates suspicion that Chimelong Safari may be stockpiling highly endangered species to corner the future commercial market of live wildlife trade. This zoo is not a member of the Southeast Asian Zoo Association so there is no mandate from the association to enforce any ethical policy.

As a membership-based organization, the Southeast Asian Zoo Association cannot demand members to disclose details of animal acquisition methods, background of animals, and trade facts. Historically, zoos tend to conduct their animal collection and trade more secretly and they seldom disclose information to anyone. When a national zoo becomes a member of the regional zoo association, it has the professional obligation to share data on animal stock, collection, breeding, surplus, trade, and other details with the association. Therefore, the Southeast Asian Zoo Association encourages its members to list all their animal collection and breeding data in the International Species Information System, which is a global database where all members can access data on zoos to make appropriate selection of animals for breeding.[12] Sadly, not all zoos have listed their animals in the database since they complain that the membership is expensive. It is true that some members cannot afford the high cost. Until the membership of the US-based International Species Information System becomes free, zoos in many Southeast Asian countries will not be able to share data with others. The International Species Information System therefore has become an obstacle for the already questionable zoos in Southeast Asia.

USING ANIMALS FOR ENTERTAINMENT

One of the largest problems of animal welfare in Southeast Asian zoos is the use of animals in entertainment. An important component of the modern zoo experience in Southeast Asia involves shows and photography featuring a whole array of wildlife. As public attitudes toward animal welfare and ethics have changed, remarkable worldwide charismatic species such as dolphins, seals, elephants, tigers, lions, monkeys, and apes receive increasing amounts of scrutiny for their use in entertainment.[13] Zoos and recreational parks in Southeast Asia are actively engaged in animal rides, breakfast or lunch with animals, and shows and photography to enhance visitors' experiences while most western zoos eschew these practices. Recognized zoos in Southeast Asia work diligently to improve standards of welfare and ethics.[14] Nevertheless, activists continue to point out that captive wild animals are often abused in zoos with fewer ethical and legal rights. In addition, resorts, recreational theme parks, restaurants, and even shopping malls are increasingly displaying wildlife while conducting animal shows and photography to attract customers.

Among the terrestrial mammals, primates are the most commonly exploited in such shows throughout Southeast Asia since their close evolutionary relationship with humans (Table 5.1). Most of the monkeys and apes used for shows are kept separately from their conspecifics on display, mostly in cages behind amphitheaters. Some animal trainers have voiced their concerns to welfare experts regarding the use of small and old cages to hold primates during and after shows, but not to their zoo owners out of fear and reprisal. Most monkeys and apes are hand-raised and trained from an early age for easier manipulation by their trainers. Animal trainers handle them daily and to ensure obedience to their commands. Most wild animals used in shows appeared to be profoundly imprinted on human trainers; hence, they interacted more with humans than conspecifics.

IMPACT OF ANIMAL TRAINING ON PRIMATES

Trained primates perform various acts that range from natural behaviors such as brachiating (gibbons), underwater diving to pick up food rewards (pigtail and long-tail macaques), and magic tricks of hiding a ball in their mouth (orangutans). Despicable circus acts recorded include rock-and-roll dancing (orangutans in Singapore), roller skating (chimpanzees in Thailand), boxing (orangutans in Thailand), playing golf (orangutans in Malaysia), and bicycling (orangutans in Malaysia, pigtail macaques in Thailand and Taiwan). Furthermore, trained pigtail macaques pluck coconuts from trees (Singapore, Malaysia, and Thailand). Most trainers use food rewards and verbal and/or nonverbal commands to make them to perform certain actions. Orangutans are the most commonly used primates in shows, followed by macaques and gibbons. Trainers are aware of public criticisms surrounding shows that involve physical punishment and abuse. Although zoo guests rarely witness physical abuse, it is likely that it occurs given that it is difficult to train and control strong and intelligent monkeys and apes without some level of fear and punishment. To take one example, the performing orangutans in Indonesia kept in cramped cages behind an amphitheater showed signs of distress. At another Southeast Asian zoo, macaques, gibbons, and orangutans blinked their eyes and tucked their head inward as an apparent sign of fear and distress that reaffirmed verbal or physical abuse from trainers. Visitors who do not know the behavioral repertoire of primates will not notice the quick reflex response on stage. Similarly, in Thailand a chimpanzee kept singly in a small cage for easier handling showed distress. When the above concerns were brought to the attention

of zoo directors by animal welfare advocates, some of the abusive practices stopped, suggesting the effectiveness of dialogue in convincing directors to enforce animal welfare standards. Some recreational parks in
Southeast Asian countries however do not listen to animal welfare suggestions and continue using primates in shows and photography. This
shows the need for more work in the region to educate zoo directors and
owners to upgrade animal welfare standards.

Unfortunately, this practice extends to lot of other small commercial
operations in the region. Under the Convention on International Trade in
Endangered Species of Wild Flora and Fauna, primate species are prohibited from trade unless it is for noncommercial purposes. Endangered
primates, however, are currently used in commercial operations including theme parks, resorts, restaurants and shopping malls across Southeast Asia. For example, a mini-zoo named Ark Avilon located in a shopping mall in Manila (Philippines) sells itself as equivalent of the biblical
Noah's Ark, by allowing visitors to hug animals and take photographs
with them.[15] The owner is also the President of the National Zoo Association. The ethical policy developed by the World Association of Zoos and
Aquariums strictly prohibits mini-zoos in shopping malls. Why then
does this mini-zoo continue to operate with the blessings of the national,
regional, and world zoo associations? To make matters worse, the zoo
exchanges animals with recognized zoos in Europe, which indicates that
the World Association of Zoos based in Europe sadly lacks the power to
enforce its own ethical policy.

There are many additional examples of animals used as entertainment. In Thailand, resorts and restaurants display captive wildlife. In
Vietnam, Vinpearl Land, the recently opened recreational park with an
aquarium, also displays reptiles and birds. In Malaysia, three popular
resorts such as Shangri-La resort in Kota Kinabalu, Bukit Merah resort in
Lake Town, and A'Formosa golf resort in Melaka use orangutans to at-
tract visitors. The Bukit Merah resort received rescued orangutans from
the Malaysian state of Sarawak many years ago and it continues to breed
them without any reintroduction plans. The resort has not released any
orangutans back into the wild. While visiting popular wildlife rehabilitation centers, business owners conceived the idea and then convinced
government agencies responsible for wildlife conservation that they want
to participate in conservation. Are these resorts legally zoological institutions? If not, how did they manage to get Asia's only great ape for display to please their guests? Do government agencies need resorts, restaurants, and shopping malls to promote wildlife conservation? These examples show only exploitation of apes by resorts to boost their revenue in
the name of wildlife rehabilitation, conservation, and education. Therefore, all nations in Southeast Asian countries should think about the consequences of business entities using captive wildlife to attract customers
by using the conservation brand name.

If resorts, restaurants, and mini-zoos in shopping malls are legally allowed to display captive wildlife, then gas stations and supermarkets may also apply for permits in future so that they could entertain customers while pumping gasoline and purchasing groceries. Will wildlife agencies in Southeast Asian countries entertain such ridiculous schemes? The law enforcement agencies must carefully scrutinize proposals on professional, legal, and ethical merits before final approval. It is imperative for politicians, policy makers, and the public to review existing laws regarding the use of captive wildlife—especially endangered primates—and take appropriate steps to make sure that our closest cousins are not exploited by the corporate industry in the name of tourism, education, rehabilitation, and conservation. To see what else the region can do to increase animal legal rights, we need to examine the extent of their rights in individual countries.

LEGAL RIGHTS OF ZOO ANIMALS IN SPECIFIC COUNTRIES

Singapore

In Singapore some animals are covered by the Animals and Birds Bill, which came into effect in 2002. Singapore also passed a new law in 2014 prohibiting cruelty to animals that prevents crimes that range from beating to abandonment. The law stipulates that animals must be provided with adequate and suitable food, water, and shelter without inducing pain and suffering. Those who violate the law will face a fine of USD 22,000 and/or a three-year jail term. In addition, those who run animal companies that disregard the law will face fines of up to USD 73,000 and/ or a three-year jail term plus the loss of their business license for a year.

Singapore's Agri-Food and Veterinary Authority has the law enforcement power to issue legal directives. However, it is primarily involved in solving public complaints about domestic animals, wild animals, illegal wildlife trade, pest and animal control, food animals, and various other problems. In 2016, an online petition site called Change.Org launched a petition to save the life of a long-tail macaque named Chippy with signatures from thousands of animal lovers worldwide. Activists argued that the imprinted macaque was not suitable for release into the wild so they demanded relocation to the Wales Ape and Monkey Sanctuary that agreed to provide long-term care. The Singapore government refused to release Chippy to the sanctuary and instead he spent over six weeks in a rescue center managed by a local politician and secretly released back into the wild. Sadly, details related to whereabouts of the released monkey are missing. Unfortunately, macaques are not safe in the wild because the government is actively culling them. In fact, Agri-Food and Veterinary Authority have already culled over 1,000 macaques in response to public complaints.[16] This case illustrates the distortion of the local legal process and the competing demands faced by animal agencies. In this case, the legal right of an individual captive wildlife was the last issue on the agenda, and it suggests that the imprinted monkey may have been safer at the UK-based rehabilitation center proposed by activists.

Malaysia

In Malaysia, the new Wildlife Conservation Regulations for zoos that came into effect in 2012 clearly define the minimum cage size and welfare standards to keep captive wild animals in zoos. The law regulates zoos, aquariums, and all other captive wildlife facilities systematically improving welfare standards. It replaced the Protection of Wildlife Act of 1972 that failed to increase welfare standards. As per the new law, zoo owners have a six-month grace period to comply with legal requirements. Anyone operating a zoo without a permit will be fined USD 18,000 and face a possible prison term of three years. It does not mean that all zoos in Malaysia are good in terms of upgrading or maintaining animal welfare standards, however. There are several small zoos where there are serious animal welfare concerns. Some private recreational parks also continue to use animals in entertainment. Therefore, Malaysia needs to enforce the law to improve ethical and welfare standards in all zoos. The new zoo regulations are part of the Wildlife Conservation law enforced by Malaysia's Department of Wildlife and National Parks that has the responsibility for managing national parks, captive facilities such as zoos, aquariums, safari and recreational parks, human-wildlife conflict issues, wildlife trade issues, pet animal issues, poaching, and all aspects of forest and wildlife. The department does not have enough workforces to either enforce the zoo animal welfare standards or monitor zoos regularly. Hence, they often rely on the national zoo association to monitor and upgrade zoos.

Taiwan

Taiwan's first animal protection law came into effect in 1998 and it extends to wildlife in captivity to some extent. Despite the law, legal enforcement continues to pose challenges for the government. Abuse of animals, including keeping captive animals in small cages with poor husbandry, happens in zoos, recreational parks, and government-run rescue centers across the country. A chained orangutan used for photography in Ba-Tao Zoo is an example. Primates such as pigtail macaques riding bicycles and performing acrobatic stunts in a private zoo (Leopard King Safari) still occur. The Leopard King Safari also displays ostriches and a restaurant owned by the zoo sells ostrich burgers to visitors.

In another case in in 2014, a hippopotamus named A Ho used for entertainment died after it was involved in two accidents. In one case it jumped from a moving truck and then got hurt again when the container it was traveling in dropped to the ground. The hippo's use for entertainment showed the sloppiness in enforcing animal welfare law in Taiwan. Realizing the negligence involved in the hippo abuse, the government toughened the law by adding a new clause dubbed by the media as "A Ho clause," which doubles the fine for intentionally causing injury/death to animals to USD 31,000, in addition to one year in jail. In a third case in 2016, an adult male giraffe died due to enormous stress induced during the capture operation while loading into a truck at a Taipei zoo.[17] An autopsy revealed later that the giraffe suffered pneumonia and nervousness due to capture and transport stress that triggered abnormal breathing and muscular damage.

Taiwan's Council of Agriculture is the country's law-enforcement agency. It also deals with various issues related to farmlands, farming, farmers, and crops. To please farmers, the Council allows the killing of macaques that raid farmlands thereby totally ignoring the legal and ethical implications of animal welfare for the country's only endemic nonhuman primate, the Formosan macaques. The Council also has a limited workforce that inspects zoos for animal welfare. There is a national zoo association, but it does not work with the Southeast Asian Zoo Association. This further impedes efforts to focus on animal welfare in zoos. To make matters worse, the United Nations does not recognize Taiwan as a country, so the zoo animal rights are low on their set of priorities. Therefore, Taiwan has a long way to go toward improving zoo animal welfare standards not only at Taipei Zoo, but also in other smaller zoos with long animal abusive histories.

Hong Kong

Animal welfare critics in Hong Kong call for new legislation to improve captive wild animal welfare issues since it lags behind the United States, Europe, and Australia. There is no law to ensure that zoo animals are provided with better environmental and behavioral enrichment. As a result, zoo animals are not at all protected by law beyond an outdated animal cruelty ordinance and a public health law enacted during the 1970s. Activists from the Society for the Prevention of Cruelty to Animals, Animals Asia, and Orangutan Aid complain that Hong Kong's only zoo located in the midst of the city displays animals in substandard conditions. The Hong Kong Zoo managed by the Leisure and Cultural Services Department must spend more money immediately for upgrading. If not, the already suffering zoo animals will continue to suffer in the future. The government has to implement a new law to guarantee zoo animal welfare as soon as possible.

Indonesia

The Criminal Code of Indonesia has eight key articles that address animal welfare. Nevertheless, critics argue that Indonesia needs a separate law to deal with captive zoo animal welfare issues since it is home to a large number of zoos and recreational parks. Although the national zoo association is doing some work to improve welfare standards among the institutional members, numerous complaints continue to plague zoos since local and exotic wildlife are often displayed in substandard conditions. The zoos also use captive wildlife in rides, shows, photography, and other entertainment activities.

The Ministry of Forestry is the agency responsible for enforcing the law regarding the rights of zoo animals and improving welfare standards. The ministry covers the entire country's forestry resources, so the zoo animal welfare work is the least priority in terms of urgency and national priority. As a result, the ministry relies on the academic experts from local universities and the national zoo association to assess zoos and to make improvements on welfare and ethics. However, the local zoo association was caught in a controversy recently related to large number of animal deaths when it managed the Surabaya Zoo. People for the Ethical Treatment of Animals called it the "zoo of death." Hence, Indonesia has to make serious efforts to upgrade all their zoos starting with amending the law to upgrading welfare standards of zoo animals.

Philippines

The first Animal Welfare Act of Philippines enacted in 1988 regulates breeding and holding facilities that house animals.[18] The act has some serious problems related to wildlife issues. For example, local animal activists filed a case against the Ocean Adventure Amusement Theme Park in 2001 for running a dolphin show without a legal permit. The court ruled in favor of the park stating that whales and dolphins were not covered by the welfare law because they were considered fish/fishery/ aquatic products covered by the Fisheries Code 1998. It reflects that it is not bad to be cruel to food animals and dolphins, which are not considered as animals according to existing laws. Hence, activists pushed for a change in the law to cover all animals inhabiting land, sea, and air and to include wildlife in entertainment, circuses, and confinement in cages.

The Philippines Animal Welfare Act amended in 2013 includes a jail term of one to two years and/or a fine up to USD 2,000 for animal death due to cruelty, ill treatment, or neglect. It also includes a jail term of one to one and a half years and/or a fine up to USD 1,000 when an animal survives an injury due to cruelty, ill treatment, or neglect needing human intervention. The law also imposes a jail term of six months to one year and/or a fine of up to USD 600 for subjecting any animal to cruelty, ill treatment, or neglect without injury and death.

The Philippines Department of Environment and Natural Resources is the agency responsible for enforcing the law to protect the rights of captive wild animals. The agency issues official permits to zoos and it monitors their collection, breeding, and export/import of wild animals. The agency unfortunately does not have enough funds or workforce to monitor all zoos since many of them are private zoos owned by rich people. For example, the oldest Manila Zoo owned by the city government continues to house animals in small cages where they exhibit abnormal behavior such as pacing, swaying their heads, and walking in circles. Due to lack of funds and human resources, the infrastructure has worsened in recent years. Hence, the Department of Environment and Natural Resources must take immediate legal action either to shut down the zoo or relocate the animals elsewhere. There is also a lack of any strong presence of international animal right groups in the Philippines so the monitoring of zoos and their collection is a serious problem.

Vietnam

A new Animal Health Law enacted in 2016 in Vietnam covers animal protection to some degree. Nonetheless, there are no regulations to enforce zoo animal welfare standards. Several new wildlife safari parks are coming up in Vietnam and all of them import numerous large mammals such as rhinos, giraffes and zebras from South Africa without legal restrictions or ethical scrutiny. This is a serious legal and ethical concern facing the zoo industry in Vietnam. Therefore, appropriate laws must be in place to protect the integrity, safety and welfare of captive wild animals.

Bear bile farms still exist in Vietnam and most of the wild caught bears come from the neighboring forest of Cambodia and end up on Vietnamese farms. Restaurants in Vietnam also serve soup made from bear body parts. As the economy of Vietnam is booming lately, rich business elites have the desire for exotic animals, both for food and medicine. Although Vietnam has started a new national zoo association, it has not initiated any evaluation of zoos to upgrade standards. The only zoo that underwent several animal welfare evaluations by the Southeast Asian Zoo Association is the Saigon Zoo and Botanical Gardens, which is the oldest zoo that came into operation in 1865.

The Prime Minister of Vietnam issued a directive in 2014 addressed to all ministries to combat illegal wildlife trade, especially trafficking of rhino horn and elephant ivory.[19] This shows the enormity of the illegal wildlife trade problem facing Vietnam and the lack of rights for wildlife. Sadly, there are not many activist groups fighting for the rights of zoo animals in Vietnam and the existing ones are afraid to go against the powerful government and business elites who own private safari parks. Hence, it will take many years to make some improvements to enhance the legal rights of captive wild animals in Vietnam.

Thailand, Myanmar, Cambodia, and Laos

The new animal cruelty law of Thailand came into effect in 2014 and it aims to enforce animal welfare issues thoroughly. Violators will face a jail term of two years and/or a USD 1,200 fine. Experts say that Thailand's animal welfare law is the shortest in terms of pages when compared to other countries. One of its articles states that no one can keep animals unnecessarily in cruel conditions. The animal right groups such as the Thai Society for the Prevention of Cruelty to Animals and Animal Activist Alliance of Thailand played a role in pushing the government to create the new law.

In general, animal issues are monitored by the Livestock Department that focuses primarily on pets, farm animals, and veterinary issues. The Department of National Parks is charged with recording, rescuing, and releasing wildlife. Animal welfare law enforcement has now become an extra activity for the department since they have to monitor the legal status of all captive wildlife while inspecting welfare standards in zoos. The enforcement however will be difficult at the beginning so the government must allocate extra funding and additional staff to tackle the new legal task.

There are no statistics available on the exact numbers of zoos in Thailand. The government-owned Zoological Parks Organization of Thailand manages eight captive facilities with numerous wild animals in their collections. It has established a system of evaluating animal welfare standards and the zoos tend to have better welfare standards than other private zoos. Hence, it has the potential to assist small zoos in the country to upgrade welfare standards. Some zoo directors however complain that they do not have the legal right to euthanize seriously sick and painfully suffering animals since the Buddhist religious mandate prohibits them from killing any animals. So, a legal provision should be included to give exceptions for humane euthanasia in some special cases involving seriously sick animals suffering pain approved by ethics committee in Thailand zoos.

In Myanmar, animal right groups have recently criticized the oldest Yangon Zoo for forcing elephants to perform circus acts in hot weather. Myanmar has an Animal Health and Development Law, but the country does not have a specific law protecting captive wild animals from abuse. It has several zoos and captive facilities with a huge diversity of wildlife. Therefore, Myanmar needs to develop a new law to extend protection to zoo animals. It also must upgrade welfare standards in all zoos.

Myanmar has recently conducted an open democratic election so it will need time to improve human rights. Therefore, legal rights for animals is not at all the priority for the newly elected government. It will take more time for animal rights activism to evolve slowly so the country has a long way to go before upgrading any legal rights for captive wildlife. The same goes to the neighboring Cambodia and Laos that do not have any recognized zoos. They have no laws presently to protect captive wild animals from abuse. The lawlessness then will continue until activism forces the government to develop new laws in favor of captive wildlife.

INCREASING LEGAL RIGHTS FOR ZOO ANIMALS

The Singapore Zoo was the first in the region to utilize great apes for entertainment, and popularized their use that was later copied by other countries such as Malaysia, Thailand, Indonesia, Philippines, Taiwan, China, and elsewhere. Use of chimpanzee photography was terminated in a Singapore zoo following an outcry when a keeper disciplined a chimpanzee. Using wild animals in shows may educate the public to understand their behavior and conservation so that visitors can learn more to save forest and biodiversity. But, shows and photography should maintain high welfare standards without compromising the rights of animals.

When best welfare standards cannot be maintained, it is recommended that the use of iconic species such as monkeys, apes, dolphins, seals, large cats, and elephants in entertainment in zoos and recreation parks affiliated with the local, regional, and global zoo associations should be tapered off because public pressure against these practices is likely to intensify. This can be done only by incorporating a legal provision in animal welfare laws that prohibits the use of animals in shows, photography, and rides. In the meantime, zoos that use animals must keep them in appropriate habitats with conspecifics, and not permanently in small cages to serve the sole purpose of holding them until next the show. Alternatively, future shows may be conducted in exhibits avoiding direct physical contact using operant conditioning to express natural behaviors using applied animal behavior techniques.

Elephant rides are common in countries such as Thailand, Cambodia, Laos, Indonesia, Malaysia, and Myanmar. Tourists from Australia, New Zealand, East Asia, Europe, and North America visit these countries to enjoy elephant rides since it is not available in their countries. This provides economic benefit through revenue so impoverished nations will object to banning them. Most zoos in Southeast Asian countries handle elephants so keeping the rides is a better way to keep them cooperative toward keepers. Zoos and recreational parks therefore will resist banning animal rides. Handling elephants using hooks and making them carry people around reaffirms the physical and psychological abuse to some extent. Hence, most western zoos stopped this practice long ago. However, foreigners are lining up to go for rides in Southeast Asian countries so a central question that critics of zoos and recreational parks must address is that of how to stop this tourism. One possibility, although it is unlikely, is that all countries in the region create a total legal ban on the use of captive wild animals in entertainment including elephant rides.

NEW LAWS AND AMENDMENTS

In terms of regulations, all countries in Southeast Asia must strengthen existing laws to make sure captive wildlife have the right to share the human environment without compromising welfare. What is more worrying is that some countries such as Hong Kong, Myanmar, Cambodia, and Laos need to come up with totally new laws on captive wild animal rights. Countries such as Singapore, Taiwan, and Malaysia that have better animal welfare legislation need to enforce their laws seriously. Having better laws without enforcing it is like holding on to a world map and not traveling outside the country. Blaming the lack of funds and human resources is an excuse not to impose the law. Once a law is enacted, the public expects the government to enforce it. They believe in government agencies and their employees should do their duties and sincerely uphold the rights of captive wildlife. Countries such as Indonesia, Thailand, and Philippines need to amend their laws to provide better rights for captive wildlife.

In countries such as Taiwan, Thailand, Malaysia, Singapore, Indonesia, and Philippines that have basic animal welfare laws, captive wild animals displayed at resorts and restaurants suffer the worst abuse. Even the famous Shangri-La Resort continues to display rehabilitated orangutans in its nature reserve. The Sabah Wildlife Department in Malaysia allows this unprofessional act in the name of conservation and education. When owners of other resorts see orangutans at Shangri-La, they are naturally inspired to obtain endangered animals to entertain hotel guests. That is how the abuse goes on spreading across the region like an epidemic. The only way to stop this misuse is to amend a new legal provision in the existing Wildlife Conservation (Operation of Zoo) Regulations of Malaysia preventing resorts, restaurants, and commercial businesses from owning or displaying captive wildlife. This way, only zoos, safari parks, and aquariums with an objective to educate and conserve wildlife would be legally permitted to display wildlife. If this provision comes into effect, it will stop the exploitation of captive wildlife in commercial ventures.

All countries in Southeast Asia need appropriate laws to guarantee large enough enclosure space for animals in captivity. In addition, they need more environmental and behavioral enrichment to make sure animals enjoy some freedom and are not cramped into small cages. New laws must include the exact cage size information according to species and groups of animals recommended by internationally respected subject specialists. Thus, the Malaysian law has the potential for use as a model for other countries in the region.

After Malaysia enacted the law, the Zoo Melaka owned by the law enforcement agency, the Department of Wildlife and National Parks, failed to upgrade their animal enclosures to accommodate the minimum cage requirements. As a result, the government disowned the zoo and contracted it out to a private company. After the ownership changed, the zoo animal welfare situation sadly deteriorated.

Critics argue that the Department of Wildlife and National Parks should have allocated more funds to renovate enclosures by upgrading the zoo to enhance animal welfare standards. That gesture would have shown that the government cares for the right of captive wild animals kept under its care. Now, it is unclear whether other zoo owners will look into the possibility of spending more money for upgrading zoos. This shows that governments tend to follow the easier option of "all or nothing" so contracting it out appears to be better than risking responsibility to uphold welfare standards.

Zoos in the region should also give equal weight to the welfare of endangered and nonendangered animals. Most zoos in Southeast Asia serve as rescue and rehabilitation centers for confiscated animals. The Taipei Zoo obtained large number of confiscated and highly endangered lizards from Madagascar that it exhibited. In contrast, it prefers not to provide shelter for the locally rescued Formosan macaques, which are a common monkey. This double standard suggests that the rights of captive wild animal are important as long as they have an endangered status, in which case the zoo will care for them dearly. A legal provision should be added to the existing animal welfare law clearly stating that zoos cannot discriminate against captive wildlife based on their commonality or rarity. Zoos should treat all captive wildlife equally since they have the responsibility to provide housing for all confiscated wildlife using taxpayer money.

Another issue with rescue and rehabilitation operations is the lack of legal clarity on their specific role. These centers are supposed to exist temporarily, but all countries in Southeast Asia run rescue and rehabilitation centers for decades. Therefore, a new legal provision should be included by separating the short-term rescue and rehab centers from long-term care shelters for captive wildlife. This way, when rescued animals go through rehabilitation, they can end up being released into the wild. The unreleasable animals can be relocated to zoos. Once the operations are over, the respective rescue and rehab centers will cease to exist. The long-term care center on the other hand can continue to provide humane care for the handicapped, aged, and other animals that lack the opportunity for release into the wild or relocation to zoos. Now, there is no legal distinction even in developed countries to separate these ideologically complicated concepts of rescue and rehabilitation and long-term care.

At present, the existing animal welfare laws do not define criteria for keeping captive wild animals with conspecifics. This is a critical issue since most animal abuse happens when captive animals are isolated. Therefore, introducing new legal provisions that require all captive wild animals be kept together with their species and social animals be kept in large open enclosures in groups is crucial. At present, the national zoo associations and the Southeast Asian Zoo Association are trying to enforce this mandate informally, but it is not easy to impose since most zoos have single animals in enclosures. That is how complaints from visitors start since people do not like to see a single chimpanzee in an enclosure. When they see this, they protest that zoos do not care about the rights of animals. Unfortunately teaching zoo managers that this practice is bad has not seemed to work. Changing the individual country's law is the only option that will prevent zoo directors from housing social animals by themselves.

Most zoos in Southeast Asia make a profit from tickets, but it is not enough to upgrade enclosures to provide better space and enrichment for animals. At present, there are no laws to make sure zoos generate sufficient revenue to upgrade for the welfare of the animals. Nor is there any requirement that a percentage of ticket sales be diverted to law enforcement agencies that work for animal welfare in zoos. Therefore, it would be good to create a new law aiming at generating income for law enforcement protecting zoo animals. For example, the enforcement of animal welfare laws in most Southeast Asian countries is weak due to the lack of human resource and funds. Some zoo staff, especially senior managers with better educational qualification and expertise in animal welfare could play a leading role in inspecting zoos on behalf of law enforcement agencies. This way, the deputized zoo staff while inspecting other zoos could levy fines for welfare violations. It is similar to the honorary game warden status given to citizens who live around national parks in which they have the legal right to apprehend lawbreakers and hand them over to the nearest police station for action.

A legal provision to empower the experienced zoo curators and managers would certainly fill the gap of worker shortage in animal agencies that enforce zoo laws. If the government cannot handle the law enforcement part of captive animal welfare, it could also delegate it to local animal right groups who could do the job efficiently. Empowering zoo managers and activists would enhance the efficiency of law enforcement. Ultimately, the government has the power to decide on these radical options. No country in Southeast Asia has tested these creative approaches to animal welfare highlighted in this book. However, if they adopt and adapt to these ideas, it will increase legal rights for zoo animals while empowering compassionate animal lovers.

STAKEHOLDERS OF WILDLIFE WEALTH

The wildlife conservation industry involves three major stakeholders: conservationists, zoo owners/managers, and animal right activists. These three peculiar bands seldom work amicably due to their ideological agendas. Conservationists restrict themselves to wildlife protection issues. As they tend to prioritize conservation of highly endangered species, they end up approving the culling of common or pest animals with the justification of scientific management. But, they work with governments to create laws to preserve nature and wildlife. Though they are not fond of zoos, they are sometimes loath to go against them since some zoos operate multimillion dollar conservation funds. An example is the Bronx Zoo's Wildlife Conservation Society that keeps numerous wildlife scientists worldwide in their payroll.

Zoo managers confine themselves to the status quo of captive animals and they seldom venture out to create laws to protect the rights of wildlife. They leave this legally challenging agenda to activists. But, they respect conservationists for their knowledge on the natural history of animals. The zoo folks are often not fond of activists since they dislike hearing complaints on abuse.

In Southeast Asian countries, only a few animal right groups deal with wildlife and they often run wildlife rescue centers. An example is the Animals Asia Foundation that runs bear rescue centers in China and Vietnam. Also, most animal right groups primarily deal with domestic animal issues. They play a key role in pushing new laws targeting domestic, farm, food, and pet animals, but have left captive wild animal laws unaddressed. That's why specialized legal advocacy addressing the needs of captive wild animals is often missing from all animal welfare laws that exist in the region. In order to fill the gap, more balanced captive wild animal rights groups are needed in the region.

In some rare cases, some animal right groups treat domestic and wild animal issues equally. An example is the former Buddhist monk, Wu Hung, who played a decisive role in forcing the Taiwanese law enforcement agency, the Council of Agriculture, to draft a new law to uphold the rights of captive wildlife. Eating wildlife is a delicacy in Taiwanese tradition. Wu Hung however, is an unusually compassionate activist who continues to fight while heading the Environment and Animal Society as an Executive Director.[20] Whatever little legal rights captive wild animals have in Taiwan, it is because of activists like Wu Hung. All nations in Southeast Asia need such compassionate souls to work to upgrade rights for captive wildlife.

FUTURISTIC ZOOS WITH BETTER LEGAL RIGHTS FOR WILDLIFE

When zoo associations receive complaints, they launch an investigation and try to assist zoos to improve standards. All zoo associations follow this standard operating procedure since they are obligated to assist and not abandon their members. Nevertheless, associations do not have legal powers to shut down bad zoos. They can revoke their membership when public complaints increase, but that is all they can enforce. Associations are therefore legally toothless to enforce either the law or the standards forcefully. They can only advise zoo owners and directors to make changes and the change happens at a snail's pace.

The closing of bad zoos is the responsibility of the law enforcement agencies in each country and it rarely happens in Asia. India however, is an unusual exception. India's Central Zoo Authority has legally closed down 150 bad zoos so far, which is the highest recorded in the Asia Pacific region. Sadly, India does not have a single excellent and iconic modern zoo. Most zoos are government-owned and their employees do not have overseas exposure to famous zoos and safari parks. Besides, they have low animal diversity and the level of management has remained poor. However, they are very good at shutting down bad zoos. So, all Southeast Asian countries must think about starting an independent law enforcing entity for zoos by adopting India's Central Zoo Authority model, and arming them with legal powers to close down badly managed zoos. This is the only legal option to minimize captive wild animal abuse in Southeast Asian zoos.

Southeast Asia has a long list of numerous wildlife species listed as highly vulnerable for extinction if habitat loss continues with expanding human populations. An example is the Sumatran orangutan, which faces an enormous struggle to survive in the rapidly dwindling forests on the island of Sumatra, Indonesia. The Asia Pacific region's forest cover has now fallen below 27 percent, but it holds over 60 percent of the global human population. The pressure through deforestation, development, agriculture, plantation, forest fires, and hunting will intensify in the near future threatening the survival of many wildlife species. In this murky scenario, how will the futuristic zoos evolve in the region?

Zoos have progressed tremendously over a century, from confined cages of menageries to moated enclosures, to safari parks. Popular zoos have excellent naturalistic exhibits, be it the Bronx Zoo's Congo gorilla exhibit or Singapore Zoo's river safari exhibit; all these multimillion-dollar enclosures are made of concrete, cement, and stone with huge glass panels and artificial trees. How would a futuristic zoo look in Southeast Asia while augmenting the legal rights for wildlife? To answer this question, one has to look at the wilderness. Look at the Nairobi National Park in Kenya and Kruger National Park in South Africa for instance. These nature reserves harbor numerous rare wildlife and they

Table 5.1.   Use of Primates in Entertainment in Southeast Asian Zoos and Recreational Parks

Name of captive facility/ country	Name of primates used in entertainment	Specific act(s) performed by primates
Singapore Zoo, Singapore	Orangutan	Shows and photography
	Gibbon	Swinging
	Long-tail macaque	Diving underwater
	Pig-tail macaque	Coconut plucking
Sentosa Island, Singapore	Pig-tail macaque	Circus acts
Surabaya Zoo, Indonesia	Orangutan	Riding bike, circus acts, photography
Gembira Loka Zoo, Indonesia	Orangutan	Bipedal walking on the road, photography
Ragunan Zoo, Indonesia	Orangutan	Riding bike
Bandung Zoo, Indonesia	Long-tail macaque	Circus acts
	Orangutan	Bipedal walking around the zoo
	Pig-tail macaque	Dressing up and riding bike
Taman Safari, Indonesia	Orangutan	Magic tricks, photography
Dusit Zoo, Thailand	Gibbon	Swinging
Safari World, Thailand	Orangutan	Boxing, playing golf, circus acts
	Chimpanzee	Roller skating, circus acts, photography
Khao Kheow Open Zoo, Thailand	Chimpanzee	Circus acts
	Gibbon	Swinging
Phuket Zoo, Thailand	Orangutan	Circus acts
	Pig-tail macaque	Riding bike
Chiang Mai Zoo, Thailand	Gibbon	Swinging
Mae Rim Monkey School, Thailand	Pig-tail macaque	Plucking coconut, riding bike, diving under water, circus acts, photography
Johore Zoo, Malaysia	Orangutan, Gibbon	Circus acts, photography
	Pig-tail, Long-tail macaque	Chained to the ground for contact
Zoo Melaka, Malaysia	Orangutan	Photography
Bao-Da Forest Park, Taiwan	Orangutan	Photography
Leopard King Safari Zoo, Taiwan	Pig-tail macaques	Circus acts

are already fenced to restrain megaherbivores and -carnivores from rampaging farms. Thus, the creation of the futuristic megazoos has already started before we comprehend the concept of future zoos.

Most national parks in Southeast Asia have become forest islands surrounded by towns, cities, farms, and plantations riddled with millions of humans. Elephants have lost their traditional migrating routes so they often stumble onto villages, farms, and plantations increasing the frequency of human-wildlife conflict daily. If legal rights for wild animals started to take strong foothold in Southeast Asia, most zoos will naturally die out since they simply cannot implement stringent legal requirements. So, the future concept of zoos will move inside national parks occupying 5 to 10 percent of forest areas by creating new megazoos. This novel concept would reunite the three competing shareholders of wildlife wealth under one roof intertwining the megazoo concept. Conservationists will provide insights into selection of species while zoo experts supported by veterinarians will manage the *ex situ* wildlife population under the watchful eyes of animal activists. All three groups will abandon their animosities and amiably work for the first time in history. These futuristic megazoos will operate in far-reaching transparency with public-private partnership so that animals will have their maximum legal rights to roam free in confined large track of forests. This way, people have the choice to observe both *in situ* and *ex situ* activities while passing through national parks in Southeast Asia. The next century's visionary megazoo concept has the potential to change the hearts and minds of future generations and beyond.

NOTES

1. Robert J. Hoage and William A. Deiss, *New Worlds, New Animals: From Menagerie to Zoological Park in the Nineteenth Century* (Baltimore: Johns Hopkins University Press, 1996).

2. Eric Baratay and Elisabeth Hardouin-Fugier, *Zoo: A History of Zoological Gardens in the West* (London: Reaktion Books, 2003).

3. John E. Fa, Stephan M. Funk, and Donnamarie O'Connell, *Zoo Conservation Biology* (Cambridge: Cambridge University Press, 2011).

4. Dale W. Jamieson, "Against Zoos," in Peter Singer, ed., *In Defense of Animals* (New York: Harper & Row, 1986), 108–77. Stephen St. C. Bostock, *Zoos and Animal Rights: The Ethics of Keeping Animals* (London: Routledge, 2014).

5. Sonya P. Hill and Donald M. Broom, "Measuring Zoo Animal Welfare: Theory and Practice," *Zoo Biology*, 28 (2009): 531–44. Terry L. Maple and Bonnie M Perdue, *Zoo Animal Welfare* (London: Springer, 2013).

6. Philip J. Nyhus and Ronald L. Tilson, "Agroforestry, Elephants, and Tigers: Balancing Conservation Theory and Practice in Human-Dominated Landscapes of Southeast Asia," *Agriculture Ecosystems and Environment*, 104 (2004): 87–97.

7. The "Taiping Four" are young gorillas who had the misfortune to be caught up in the international live animal trade. See "The Taiping Four Gorilla Scandal," Anonymous, *Animal Welfare Institute News*, Winter 2004 (https://awionline.org/awi-quarterly/2004-winter/taiping-four-gorilla-scandal, accessed on September 8, 2016). Govindasa-

my Agoramoorthy, "Ethics and Welfare in Southeast Asian Zoos," *Journal of Applied Animal Welfare Science*, 7 (2004): 189–95. Govindasamy Agoramoorthy, *Animal welfare: Assessing animal welfare standards in zoological and recreational parks in South East Asia* (Delhi: Daya Publishing House, 2008).

8. Three tiger cubs at the Mantianak Park for sale due to the high cost of sustaining the 3-month cubs (http://www.gmanetwork.com/news/photo/39677/news/misamis-park-offers-to-sell-tiger-cubs, accessed on September 8, 2016).

9. The Vietnamese conglomerate Vingroup has denied allegations of 1,700 creatures died at their new safari saying the death toll was just 100. See "Vin Group Denies Denies Zoo Experts' Claims of Massive Animal Deaths at its Park," Anonymous, *Thanhien News* (http://www.thanhniennews.com/education-youth/vingroup-denies-zoo-experts-claims-of-massive-animal-deaths-at-its-park-59476.html, accessed on September 8, 2016).

10. Safari park dismisses claims of endangered species deaths. The government issued a statement on behalf of Kien Giang Province's department of agriculture and rural development that no endangered animal has died at the safari. See "Vin Group Denies Denies Zoo Experts' Claims of Massive Animal Deaths at its Park," Anonymous, *Thanhien News* (http://www.thanhniennews.com/education-youth/vingroup-denies-zoo-experts-claims-of-massive-animal-deaths-at-its-park-59476.html, accessed on September 8, 2016).

11. New photographs and video exclusive to *National Geographic* suggest that two dozen young elephants flown to China from Zimbabwe were mistreated and slipped into poor health, according to analysts who examined the images. See Christina Russo, "Young Elephants in China Show Signs of Abuse," *National Geographic*, September 25, 2015 (http://news.nationalgeographic.com/2015/09/150925-elephants-china-zimbabwe-cites-joyce-poole-zoos-wildlife-trade, accessed October 12, 2016).

12. International Species Information System, also known as Species360, is a non-profit entity that maintains a global database on zoo animals (https://www.isis.org/Pages/default.aspx, accessed October 12, 2016). Nathan R. Flesness, "International Species Information System (ISIS): Over 25 years of compiling global animal data to facilitate collection and population management," *International Zoo Yearbook*, 38 (2003): 53–61.

13. James K. Kirkwood, "Welfare, husbandry and veterinary care of wild animals in captivity: Changes in attitudes, progress in knowledge and techniques," *International Zoo Yearbook*, 38 (2003): 124–30. Eduardo J. Fernandez, Michael A. Tamborski, Sarah R. Pickensc, and William Timberlake, "Animal-visitor interactions in the modern zoo: Conflicts and interventions," *Applied Animal Behavior Science*, 120 (2009): 1–8. Peter Singer *Animal liberation: The definitive classic of the animal movement,* (New York: Harper Perennial Modern Classics, Reissue edition, 2009).

14. Joseph Barber, Denny Lewis, Govindasamy Agoramoorthy, and Miranda Stevenson, "Setting standards for evaluation of captive facilities," in Devra G. Kleiman, Katerina V. Thompson, and Charlotte Kirk Baer, eds., *Wild mammals in captivity: Principles and techniques for zoo management*, Second Edition (Chicago: University of Chicago Press, 2010), 22–36. Govindasamy Agoramoorthy, "Animal welfare and ethics evaluations in Southeast Asian zoos: Procedures and prospects," *Animal Welfare*, 11 (2002): 295–99. Govindasamy Agoramoorthy and Bernard Harrison, "Ethics and animal welfare evaluations in Southeast Asian zoos: A case study of Thailand," *Journal of Applied Animal Welfare Science*, 5 (2002): 1–13. Govindasamy Agoramoorthy, *Wildlife welfare in zoos: Case studies from South East Asia* (Berlin: Lap Lambert, 2011).

15. The Ark Avilon is an indoor interactive zoo in Frontera Verde shopping mall near Manila, Philippines. Visitors interact with orangutans, parrots, pythons, tortoises, binturongs, and other wildlife (http://www.avilonzoo.ph/ark-avilon-zoo, accessed October 12, 2016). Ronnel Almazan, Roberto Rubio, and Govindasamy Agoramoorthy, "Welfare evaluations of nonhuman animals in selected zoos in the Philippines," *Journal of Applied Animal Welfare Science*, 8 (2005): 59–68.

16. "Misamis Park Offers to Sell Tiger Cubs," Anonymous, GMA News Online, June 25, 2013 (http://www.gmanetwork.com/news/photo/39677/news/misamis-park-offers-to-sell-tiger-cubs, accessed September 8, 2016). Rachel Middleton, "Wales Petition to Rescue Chippy the Macaque from Singapore Gathers Pace," *International Business Times*, July 1, 2016 (http://www.ibtimes.co.uk/wales-petition-rescue-chippy-macaque-singapore-gathers-pace-1568380, accessed October 12, 2016).

17. Zachary Toliver, "Panicked and Terrified Giraffe dies at Taiwanese Zoo," Peta.org, August 12, 2016 (http://www.peta.org/blog/panicked-terrified-giraffe-dies-taiwanese-zoo/, accessed October 12, 2016).

18. Republic Act 8485 or the Animal welfare Act 1998 of Philippines enacted by the Senate and House of Representatives (http://www.paws.org.ph/animal-welfare-act-ra-8485.html, accessed October 12, 2016).

19. The Prime Minister issued a directive to ministries to crack illegal wildlife trade to cut trafficking of rhino horn and ivory trade. See "Vietnam Declares Action to Tackle Illegal Wildlife Trade," SavetheRhino.org, March 12, 2014 (https://www.savetherhino.org/latest_news/news/938_vietnam_declares_action_to_tackle_illegal_wildlife_trade, accessed October 12, 2016).

20. Former monk leads fight for animal rights in Taiwan through his nonprofit agency. See Chen Wei-tzu and Jake Chung, "Former monk leads fight for animal rights," *Taipei Times*, December 27, 2012 (www.taipeitimes.com/News/taiwan/archives/2012/12/27/2003551130, accessed October 12, 2016).

BIBLIOGRAPHY

Agoramoorthy, Govindasamy and Bernard Harrison. "Ethics and animal welfare evaluations in Southeast Asian zoos: A case study of Thailand." *Journal of Applied Animal Welfare Science*, 5 (2002): 1–13.

Agoramoorthy, Govindasamy. "Animal welfare and ethics evaluations in Southeast Asian zoos: Procedures and prospects." *Animal Welfare*, 11 (2002): 295–99.

———. "Ethics and Welfare in Southeast Asian Zoos," *Journal of Applied Animal Welfare Science*, 7 (2004): 189–95.

———. *Animal Welfare: Assessing Animal Welfare Standards in Zoological and Recreational Parks in South East Asia* (Delhi: Daya Publishing House, 2008).

———. *Wildlife welfare in zoos: Case studies from South East Asia* (Berlin: Lap Lambert, 2011).

Almazan, Ronnel, Roberto Rubio, and Govindasamy Agoramoorthy. "Welfare evaluations of nonhuman animals in selected zoos in the Philippines." *Journal of Applied Animal Welfare Science*, 8 (2005): 59–68.

Ark Avilon (http://www.avilonzoo.ph/ark-avilon-zoo, accessed on October 12, 2016).

Barber, Joseph, Denny Lewis, Govindasamy Agoramoorthy, and Miranda Stevenson. "Setting standards for evaluation of captive facilities." In Devra G. Kleiman, Katerina V. Thompson, and Charlotte Kirk Baer, eds., *Wild Mammals in Captivity: Principles and Techniques for Zoo Management*, Second Edition (Chicago: University of Chicago Press, 2010), 22–36.

Baratay, Eric and Elisabeth Hardouin-Fugier. *Zoo: A History of Zoological Gardens in the West* (London: Reaktion Books, 2003).

Bostock, Stephen St. C. *Zoos and Animal Rights: The Ethics of Keeping Animals* (London: Routledge, 2014).

Fa, John E., Stephan M. Funk, and Donnamarie O'Connell. *Zoo Conservation Biology* (Cambridge: Cambridge University 2011).

Fernandez, Eduardo J., Michael A. Tamborski, Sarah R. Pickensc, and William Timberlake. "Animal-visitor interactions in the modern zoo: Conflicts and interventions." *Applied Animal Behavior Science*, 120 (2009): 1–8.

Flesness, Nathan R. "International Species Information System (ISIS): Over 25 years of compiling global animal data to facilitate collection and population management." *International Zoo Yearbook*, 38 (2003): 53–61.

Hill, Sonya and Donald M. Broom. "Measuring Zoo Animal Welfare: Theory and Practice." *Zoo Biology*, 28 (2009): 531–44.

Hoage, Robert J. and William A. Deiss. *New Worlds, New Animals: From Menagerie to Zoological Park in the Nineteenth Century* (Baltimore: Johns Hopkins University Press, 1996).

International Species Information System (https://www.isis.org/Pages/default.aspx, accessed October 12, 2016).

Jamieson, Dale W. "Against Zoos." In Peter Singer, ed., *In Defense of Animals* (New York: Harper & Row, 1986), 108–77.

Kirkwood, James K. "Welfare, husbandry and veterinary care of wild animals in captivity: Changes in attitudes, progress in knowledge and techniques." *International Zoo Yearbook*, 38 (2003): 124–30.

Maple, Terry L. and Bonnie M. Perdue. *Zoo Animal Welfare* (London: Springer, 2013).

Middleton, Rachel. "Wales Petition to Rescue Chippy the Macaque from Singapore Gathers Pace." *International Business Times*, July 1, 2016 (http://www.ibtimes.co.uk/wales-petition-rescue-chippy-macaque-singapore-gathers-pace-1568380, accessed October 12, 2016).

"Misamis Park Offers to Sell Tiger Cubs." Anonymous, GMA News Online, June 25, 2013 (http://www.gmanetwork.com/news/photo/39677/news/misamis-park-offers-to-sell-tiger-cubs, accessed on September 8, 2016).

Nyhus, Philip J. and Ronald L. Tilson. "Agroforestry, Elephants, and Tigers: Balancing Conservation Theory and Practice in Human-Dominated Landscapes of Southeast Asia." *Agriculture Ecosystems and Environment*, 104 (2004): 87–97.

Republic Act 8485 or the Animal Welfare Act 1998 of Philippines enacted by the Senate and House of Representatives (http://www.paws.org.ph/animal-welfare-act-ra-8485.html, accessed October 12, 2016).

Russo, Christina. "Young Elephants in China Show Signs of Abuse." *National Geographic*, September 25, 2015 (http://news.nationalgeographic.com/2015/09/150925-elephants-china-zimbabwe-cites-joyce-poole-zoos-wildlife-trade, accessed October 12, 2016).

"Safari park dismisses claims of endangered species deaths." Anonymous, Vietnam News, February 25, 2016 (http://vietnamnews.vn/society/282791/safari-park-dismisses-claims-of-endangered-species-deaths, accessed October 12, 2016)

Singer, Peter. *Animal liberation: The definitive classic of the animal movement*, Reissue edition (New York: Harper Perennial Modern Classics, 2009).

"The Taiping Four Gorilla Scandal." Anonymous. *Animal Welfare Institute News*, Winter 2004 (https://awionline.org/awi-quarterly/2004-winter/taiping-four-gorilla-scandal, accessed September 8, 2016).

Toliver, Zachary. "Panicked and Terrified Giraffe dies at Taiwanese Zoo." Peta .org, August 12, 2016 (http://www.peta.org/blog/panicked-terrified-giraffe-dies-taiwanese-zoo/, accessed October 12, 2016).

"Vin Group Denies Denies Zoo Experts' Claims of Massive Animal Deaths at its Park." Anonymous. *Thanhien News* (http://www.thanhniennews.com/education-youth/vingroup-denies-zoo-experts-claims-of-massive-animal-deaths-at-its-park-59476.html, accessed September 8, 2016).

"Vietnam Declares Action to Tackle Illegal Wildlife Trade." SavetheRhino.org. March 12, 2014 (https://www.savetherhino.org/latest_news/news/938_vietnam_declares_action_to_tackle_illegal_wildlife_trade, accessed October, 12 2016).

Wei-tzu, Chen and Jake Chung. "Former monk leads fight for animal rights." *Taipei Times*. December, 27, 2012 (www.taipeitimes.com/News/taiwan/archives/2012/12/27/2003551130, accessed October 12, 2016).

SIX

Sanctuaries

Zoos of the Future?

Ron Kagan

Zoos (for brevity this term includes aquariums henceforth) and animal sanctuaries are places of great ethical inconsistency and complexity as human and nonhuman exotic/wild animals are cohabitating in close quarters. These situations bring forward a balancing act of meeting human desires and needs with those of the nonhuman animals that are cared for, captive, and/or confined.

"Animal sanctuaries" are different than protected wild areas called "wildlife sanctuaries." Although the term *sanctuary* signifies a clear purpose (though it is often hijacked by those who would exploit animals and label their activities as "sanctuary"), *zoo* continues to mean different things over time and in different cultures. The single, most essential challenge that has confronted zoos since their earliest iterations may be defined by the quality of life afforded captive animals.[1] Animal welfare is at the heart of considering whether there is justice (is it fair for the individual) on the ark.

Both of these animal islands are places where mostly nondomestic animals are kept, held captive (as harsh as that can sound). "In human care" is how zoo professionals now characterize and view the paradigm of captivity. The assumption is that zoos will keep animals (or send them to other zoos if needed) for their entire lives and that this is what's not only of interest and enjoyment to the public, but also in the best interest of the animals and their species. While "freedom" sounds nice and zoos offer only some dimensions of freedom (e.g., freedom from starvation and predation), life in the wild is not easy for any animal.

At times, zoos and sanctuaries have been burdened with skeptical audiences, turbulent histories, and the need to cope with rapidly evolving societal values. The best zoos and sanctuaries provide almost natural, physical and social environments for animals in their care (though obviously without affording animals several freedoms like the ability to leave). They are mostly staffed with well-trained and humane professionals and they provide *safe* places—a foundational element of "sanctuary"—that offer a lifetime of relative peace and security. Many sanctuaries are modest in scope, scale, resources, and ability. Despite best efforts, they can only provide limited and basic facilities and many only have volunteer help to care for the animals.

In this chapter, we will cover the diversity of care and welfare within sanctuaries and zoos as well as fundamental comparisons between zoos and sanctuaries that may inform our understanding of whether captive exotic animals in zoos and sanctuaries are afforded a "just" life. Perhaps even more significant is the question of whether they can be afforded a just life. Though some confiscated and rescued animals may find a home in a credible sanctuary or zoo, many do not. Extremely challenging situations emerge where euthanasia is considered by some as the most humane outcome.[2, 3]

Considerations about societal values with regard to the origins, living conditions/situations, and the destinies of animals living in sanctuaries will primarily focus on exotic and wild animals (as opposed to domestic, companion and/or farm animals) so that zoos and sanctuaries are properly compared.

Seeking justice for captive exotic animals, and defining that concept in a relevant way within zoos and sanctuaries, is an important task currently given little attention outside of animal rights circles. Genuine zoological profession aspirations of saving both individual animals and entire species are laudable and often resourced with well-trained and passionate professionals in the best zoos. However, there's seemingly never enough appropriate space or financial resources available given the magnitude of the challenge that animals face in the wild and in captivity.

These entities are supported by private and/or public financial support. Zoos are more and more engaged in major scientific initiatives in order to advance animal health, animal care, animal welfare, and wildlife conservation. Most sanctuaries tend to be solely focused on rescuing (including accepting confiscated animals) and caring for individual animals that often come from impoverished or abusive situations. Yet, both motives and results of both entities are at times suspect in academic and professional circles, and by animal protection and welfare groups. Even society, especially in Western cultures and nations, often wonders whether these places provide good lives for the animals.

In no small way, this set of circumstances has led to an ironic paradigm. Those who aim to do good are at times under fire. The credibility of truly good zoos and sanctuaries, those that are genuine and effective champions of individual animals and/or species conservation, is often undermined by bad practices, and indeed exploitation of animals by unaccredited "roadside" zoos and unaccredited "pseudo" sanctuaries. Both of these types of facilities are essentially exploitative animal compounds where commerce is the prime activity and animal welfare is only considered in the context of keeping and breeding animals in order to make a profit.

The public is unclear about the quality of life in some zoos and sanctuaries, though often the human fascination with, and desire to be near, to touch and hold animals, can at times sweep aside reservations someone might have. In that situation, people conveniently overlook the potential hardship of captivity. Ironically, "biophilia" (and human selfishness) fuel this exploitive animal exhibitionism.

Where do captive exotic animals come from? Aside from captive births, both zoos and sanctuaries take in animals from an astounding array of situations. Historically, zoos have been reluctant to take animals with unknown genetic backgrounds because those individuals would take up space and other resources without being able to contribute to the gene pools of captive populations. In recent years, more zoos have adopted a more balanced approach to rescues with consideration of both captive breeding and compassion as elements to weigh. This may be in part because zoos (including accredited zoos) historically overbred exotic animals either to sell or to ensure ample surplus animals so that natural sex ratios were attainable (many species live in harems so more females than males are needed). It also appears that some zoos recognize the significance of their unique skills and assets as well as the need to factor in a compassionate philosophy.

Additionally, circuses, the entertainment (film) industry, private commercial breeders, exotic pet holders, drug dealers, and more all held, bred, and dispersed exotics. And there is massive international illegal trade in exotic animals (and their "parts").[4] When discovered, confiscated animals are either placed in a zoo or sanctuary or destroyed. Much of this trade is also connected with organized crime. Many of the illegal US-sourced exotic animals ultimately are confiscated or abandoned. Zoos have taken in nonreleasable wild-born and some "entertainment world" chimpanzees, bears (e.g., grizzlies, black bears, brown bears, and the occasional polar bear), as well as nonreleasable bald eagles and seals. Over the past twenty-five years, the Detroit Zoo has rescued ten lions and tigers, five grizzly bears (and several other bears including a circus polar bear), numerous seal species (e.g., harp, grey, and harbor), lemurs, and even racehorses. The basic problem is that animals that have simply (and unfortunately) been considered "exotic" property generally cannot be properly cared for by nonprofessionals[5] and are not afforded concern beyond their commercial value.

Though accurate statistics regarding the numbers and types of exotic pets in private hands is extremely difficult to document, from several sources we may estimate that there are roughly a staggering 79 million in the United States and another 82 million in Europe—half of those in the United Kingdom[6, 7] Those estimates include an estimated 15,000 primates and 18,000 large carnivores in the United States.[8] and the numbers worldwide (depending on what one includes in the category of exotic/nontraditional pet) are simply unknown. The sheer scale of the injustice for most of these millions of animals is difficult to comprehend. Rescue, freedom, and sanctuary, whether in the wild or placed at a zoo or a sanctuary, is clearly impossible for almost all of them.

Among the alarming results of widespread exotic pet ownership is the enormous threat to human safety given both zoonotic disease transmission and animal attacks. At least seventy people in the United States have been killed over the past twenty-five years from exotic pet attacks. Disease and incidents of injuries dwarf this number. Pet shops that sell exotics are often a serious breeding ground for many diseases (especially salmonella) that present both great risk to many other animals, as well as to animal caregivers, pet owners, and the general public.

ZOO VERSUS SANCTUARY

There is a legal framework for operating any US facility that holds, breeds, and/or exhibits animals. The United States Department of Agriculture (USDA) enforces the Animal Welfare Act. Many would argue it's an almost impossible task given the vagaries of the law's language, the bureaucracy and limited budget of the agency and perhaps most importantly its contradictory mandate. The USDA must both advance agribusiness and protect farm, pet, domestic and exotic animals. While it monitors and regulates the "quality" and safety of animals as food for human consumption (a concern that is clearly about human, not nonhuman, welfare), it is also supposed to ensure the welfare of animals including licensing zoos and sanctuaries. Imagine the banking industry federally mandated to both promote itself and regulate itself. The Animal Welfare Act almost exclusively regulates conditions for captive mammals, leaving care and welfare conditions of other taxa much less regulated.

In addition to the Animal Welfare Act, the Endangered Species Act, and the Marine Mammal Protection Act also regulate activities (the latter especially with respect to the acquisition and disposition of covered species) thereby affecting zoo and aquarium "collections." There are many loopholes and unclear regulations in these federal laws and agencies.[9]

Numerous animal welfare and protection groups are concerned with, monitor, and sometimes critique conditions at zoos (rarely at sanctuaries) worldwide. These include: In Defense of Animals (IDA), which, among other activities, issues annual "10 worst zoos/aquariums" reports with respect to the welfare of captive elephants and cetaceans; the Humane Society of the United States (HSUS); People for the Ethical Treatment of Animals (PETA); ZooCheck (Canada); Born Free Foundation (US and UK); World Society for Protection of Animals (WSPA); and the International Fund for Animal Welfare (IFAW).

There are also professional accreditation systems for both zoos and sanctuaries. They are essentially association-based self-monitoring schemes that involve peer-to-peer reviews. The Association of Zoos and Aquariums (AZA) in the United States and the Global Federation of Animal Sanctuaries (GFAS) have developed extremely comprehensive and rigorous sets of rules related to governance, safety, transparency, commercial activity and accountability, facilities, policies and procedures, animal care and welfare standards, and more. These two are generally considered to be the "gold standard" of accreditation systems.

Accreditation — Standards that Include
Ensuring Good Care, Welfare, Proper Policies, and Facilities

In the United States, zoos are accredited by the Association of Zoos and Aquariums (AZA). This association now represents over 230 zoos and aquariums, the vast majority in the United States. In addition, the World Association of Zoos and Aquariums (WAZA) supports accreditation programs worldwide through regional and national affiliates like AZA. Among the many WAZA association members are Canada's Accredited Zoos and Aquariums (CAZA), the European Association of Zoos and Aquaria (EAZA), the Pan-African Association of Zoos and Aquaria (PAAZA), the South East Asian Zoo Association (SEAZA), Zoo and Aquarium Association Australasia (ZAA), Latin American Zoo and Aquarium Association (ALPZA), the Central Zoo Authority (CZA/India), and the Japanese Association of Zoos and Aquariums (JAZA).

Zoos are generally financed by public monies, philanthropic support, and earned revenue. They are mostly visited and financially supported by their local communities. Most have long histories and deep relationships with their region's residents, offering an escape of sorts from urban/ suburban lives that have become disconnected from natural experiences and places. And of course, zoos have always appealed to humans because of our fascination with animals. Sanctuaries are entirely supported by private, foundation, and corporate gifts. Their funding is usually a fraction of that of public zoos, but that is partially offset by not needing to expend large sums on visitor considerations and related amenities.

For sanctuaries, the bonafide accrediting entity is the Global Federation of Animal Sanctuaries (GFAS). GFAS "defines" legitimate sanctuaries based on several key principles. It established a matrix of physical and
operational elements that are defined as either required (e.g., lifelong
care—the so-called cradle to grave philosophy), recommended (e.g.,
chemical restraint of animals by a veterinarian only), allowed (e.g., species-specific birth control), discouraged (use of water barriers for containment due to risks of drowning), or prohibited (e.g., breeding).

Similarly, AZA accreditation covers many areas and is generally more
prescriptive especially when it comes to financial sustainability, staffing,
contingency and emergency plans, educational programs, quarantine,
and governance, among others. Basic accreditation categories include 1)
animal care, welfare, and management, 2) veterinary care, 3) conservation, 4) education and interpretation, 5) research, 6) governing authority,
7) staff, 8) support organization, 9) finance, 10) physical facilities, 11)
safety/security, 12) guest services, 13) other programs, and 14) miscella-
neous.

To clarify what respectively defines and differentiates between a zoo
and a sanctuary, it's informative to compare the accrediting systems, both
of which employ guidelines that significantly surpass the USDA's limited
(and often vague) standards. Primary distinctions between sanctuaries
and zoos revolve around different principles and operating models regarding commercial activity, conservation, research, breeding, animal
disposition, staffing, and public participation. There are many other distinctions though that may appear subtle yet they reflect some underlying
philosophical differences and help clarify what "true" sanctuary is. For
example, a GFAS-accredited sanctuary must assume lifelong care for
each rescued animal. AZA accreditation is silent on this issue. In addition, while culling (often incorrectly referred to as euthanasia by zoos) is
allowed in accredited zoos, it is prohibited in accredited sanctuaries.

To be eligible for GFAS Accreditation or Verification, organizations
must have nonprofit/noncommercial status and endorse/follow several
policies:

- No captive breeding (with a potential exception for those organizations having a bona fide release/reintroduction program to return
  wildlife to the wild).
- No commercial trade of any kind in animals or animal parts.
- No tours allowed that are not guided and conducted in a manner
  that minimizes the impact on the animals and their environment,
  does not cause them stress, and gives them the ability to seek un-
  disturbed privacy and quiet.
- Animals are not exhibited or taken from the sanctuary or enclo-
  sures/habitats for nonmedical reasons, with some limited excep-

tions for certain animal species, such as horses, under approved circumstances.

- The public does not have direct contact with wildlife (with some limited exceptions: for example, in conjunction with adoption/ foster programs for some birds and small reptiles as allowed by law).

In addition, organizations must demonstrate:

- Adherence to standards on animal care including housing, veterinary care, nutrition, animal well-being, and handling policies, as well as standards on physical facilities, records, and staff safety, confirmed by an extensive questionnaire, periodic site visit (at least every three years), and interviews.
- Ethical practices in fundraising.
- Ethical acquisition and disposition of animals.
- Restrictions on research, limited to noninvasive projects that provide a health, welfare, or conservation benefit to the individual animal and/or captive animal management and/or population conservation.
- The existence of a contingency plan if the property where the sanctuary is located is not owned by the sanctuary or its governing organization.

Table 6.1 below illustrates the primary accreditation areas covered (and compared) by the Association of Zoos and Aquariums and the Global Federation of Sanctuaries.

The primary differences between zoos and sanctuaries in how they operate are not only reflected in the ultimate priority given in zoos to exhibition, care, conservation, and education (as compared to sanctuaries being[10] almost solely devoted to the care of individual animals and advocacy), but more fundamentally, true (as opposed to "pseudo") sanctuaries are consumed with and committed to each animal regardless (generally) of its status in the wild, health, genetic importance/background, reproductive status, social abilities/status, and age. Many, if not most roadside zoos and "pseudo" sanctuaries fundamentally exploit their animals. Photo ops, animal handling, taking animals out for fairs/shows are but a few activities that compromise the animals' well-being. Table 6.2 reflects a subjective comparison of the best zoos and sanctuaries (accredited in both cases) with respect to justice (is it fair to the individual) for the animals cared for in each. This often connects to the fundamental question of what quality of life captive animals experience. Efforts to answer this for each species and individual through a comprehensive welfare framework have been recently employed.[11]

Table 6.1.   Primary Characteristics Embedded in AZA and GFAS Accreditation Systems

	AZA	*GFAS*	*Comments*
Government/Board	Mostly public/civic leaders	Often small and limited skillset	Sanctuaries may not have sufficient oversight.
Public Contact/ Access	Often in the millions	None or limited	Sanctuaries are much less expensive to operate as a result and animals are less stressed.
Animal Care	Highest/extensive training	Variable	Both can be excellent.
Financial Solvency/ Transparency	Generally secure and transparent	Can be tenuous	Both zoos and sanctuaries have struggled but zoos usually have a safety net.
Education	Extensive programs	Limited in part due to limits on public access	Education can be critical to changing laws and having a more compassionate public.
Staff/Volunteers	Usually sufficient to needs and well-trained	Can be variable though enormously committed to animal well-being	Sanctuaries need more financial resources to afford more expert staff.
Safety policies, protocols, and procedures	Very robust	Limited	Could be a sanctuary weakness.
Animal acquisition, disposition, and breeding	Often extensive investment	Varies but usually limited or none	GFAS sanctuaries are more focused on advocacy work that advances conservation.

Source: Created by the author.

If we consider the thousands of unaccredited sanctuaries and zoos that reflect the vast majority of these types of animal facilities, the table would be quite different.

The fact that thousands of exotic large cats are in private hands in the United States while "only" hundreds are in accredited zoos is but one example of the unfortunate plight of many legally unprotected animals. It

Table 6.2. Key Factors Affecting Animal Welfare in AZA and GFAS Accredited Facilities

	AZA	GFAS	Comments
Social environment	Often many species and many individuals; focus on genetic pairing	Careful attention to each *personality*	Due consideration especially in sanctuaries, but still challenging for animals in both.
Space requirements	Still too focused on minimums	Very variable	Very challenging in all but the best of circumstances for both.
Welfare focus	Balanced with conservation (species welfare)	It's all about each animal!	Zoos should focus more!
Public stress potential	Can be significant	Minimal or none	Zoos should be more *patient-centered.*
Health care	The best there is	Can be limited	Sanctuaries need more resources.
Staff expertise/ number	Seasoned and stable	Variable but devoted	Zoos should help sanctuaries more.
Climate suitability	Poorly addressed too often	Well-considered	Zoos should pay attention!

Source: Created by the author.

also illustrates the massive disparity between "supply" and the availability of qualified and humane options for these animals. Other entities like pet shops, private/pet ownership, animal auctions, petting zoos, and animal circuses fuel this continued crisis.

Aside from GFAS-accredited sanctuaries that handle companion (pet) animals, farm animals, and exotic/wild animals, there are untold numbers of other sanctuaries around the world. They range from an individual who may occasionally rescue local wildlife (and possibly rehabilitate for release) to major facilities often with hundreds or thousands of diverse types of animals like the Four Paws (seven sanctuaries) in Eastern Europe, Borneo, and Africa; Tigers in America (thirteen sanctuaries) holding more tigers than all AZA zoos combined; the Performing Animal Welfare Society (PAWS) sanctuaries in California; and the Black Beauty Ranch in Texas. There are also many taxa-specific sanctuaries for animals such as great apes, big cats, bats, or elephants. Among larger, noteworthy ones in the United States are Project Chimps in Georgia; Save the Chimps and the Center for Great Apes sanctuaries in Florida; Chimp Haven in

Louisiana; Born Free's Primate Sanctuary in Texas; Tigers, Lions and Bears in California; Big Cat Rescue in Florida; Wildcat Sanctuary in Montana; Carolina Tiger Rescue in North Carolina; Exotic Feline Rescue in Indiana; Bat World Rescue in Texas; and the Elephant Sanctuary in Tennessee. New, ambitious sanctuaries are also under development to assist with rescue situations involving captive elephants in South America (Global Sanctuary for Elephants in Brazil) and Europe (Elephant Haven) as well as captive cetaceans in North America (the Whale Sanctuary and the National Aquarium's Dolphin Sanctuary).

Sadly, some sanctuaries are not sufficiently resourced/sustainable and fail, resulting in a crisis as hundreds, even thousands, of animals suddenly need new sanctuary. Such was the case in 2010 with the Montana Large Animal Sanctuary and Rescue.

In Europe, the European Alliance of Rescue centres and Sanctuaries (EARS) currently serves as a support network of sixteen facilities. Some, like sanctuaries in Greece, Romania, Kosovo, and Bulgaria, are caring for over one hundred rescued European brown bears, and others like the Foundacion Neotropica and the Mona Foundation Sanctuary in Spain focus on primates.[12]

There are also unusual sanctuaries around the world that are engaged not only in "traditional" sanctuary activities but also extensive conservation and wildlife protection work. AZA awarded the 2016 International Conservation Award to the Grauer Gorilla Rehabilitation and Education Center (GRACE) in the DRC. This collaborative effort on the part of several US-accredited zoos, the International Fund for Animal Welfare, Holtzman Wildlife Fund, Disney's Conservation Fund, and the Fossey Fund has rescued dozens of one of the most endangered primates in the world while educating the local population and advancing protection and conservation efforts. All this despite being located in one of the worst genocide areas of the world in recent times.

Similarly, the Chimpanzee Sanctuary and Wildlife Conservation Trust in Uganda rescues, rehabilitates, and conserves apes; Wildlife SOS assists wild and captive animals in India; and Animals Asia runs bear sanctuaries in both China and Vietnam while actively engaged in powerful animal welfare advocacy and education work in both countries.

Occasionally zoos work with humane and animal protection groups, especially with some rescues for which zoos may be most and/or uniquely qualified to assist. The Humane Society of the United States and PETA have collaborated with a number of zoos and aquariums even as they at times clash with others (most notably over cetaceans and elephants in captivity). In 2009 PETA, the Society for the Prevention of Cruelty to Animals (SPCA) of Texas, the Detroit Zoological Society, and law enforcement collaborated on the confiscation, rescue, care, and placement of over 26,400 animals including amphibians (4,567), wallabies, chinchillas, lemurs, sloths, coatis, prairie dogs, short-tailed opossums, flying squirrels, agoutis, kinkajous, snakes (1681), lizards (7,755), turtles (6,635), and various other small vertebrates and invertebrates. Over 70 percent of the confiscated animals died within six weeks from injuries, disease, and poor health associated with their warehouse living conditions.[13]

Law enforcement authorities and protection groups generally turn to sanctuaries for placement of rescued animals. The Humane Society of the United States (HSUS) operates its own sanctuaries including the Cleveland Amory Black Beauty Ranch in Texas with over 1,300 large domestic and exotic animals, the South Florida Wildlife Center, Cape Wildlife Center in Massachusetts, and Duchess Sanctuary of Oregon. The animal protection organization Born Free USA operates a primate sanctuary in Texas with over 600 primates. Most of the animals at these sanctuaries either lived in roadside zoos, were research subjects in medical test facilities, were confiscated or abandoned "exotic pets," or were rescued from circuses.

The Global Federation of Animal Sanctuaries (GFAS) was in part born from an earlier association called The Association of Animal Sanctuaries (TAOS) and the Captive Wild Animal Protection Coalition (CWAPC). GFAS currently has 130 accredited/verified sanctuaries, rescue centers, and rehabilitation centers in the United States and 18 more globally. GFAS sanctuaries are taking in on average well over 1,000 animals every year. These sanctuaries must meet strict standards ensuring proper animal care and welfare. Over 50 are exclusively for equines. There are other sanctuaries that could meet GFAS standards but for various reasons have not (yet?) sought accreditation. In fact, it is estimated that there are over 130 primate sanctuaries (caring for more than 10,000 primates) in Africa, Asia, and the Americas alone.[14] Most are not GFAS accredited so the level of care is unknown in many.

ACCREDITATION VERSUS VERIFICATION: WHAT IS THE DIFFERENCE?

In addition to meeting the requirements described above, accreditation involves an additional rigorous screening of compliance with GFAS operational standards regarding matters such as: governance, staffing, finance, education, and outreach as well as safety policies, protocols, and training.

Other alliances and associations of exotic/wild animal sanctuaries exist in the United States and elsewhere, ostensibly in order to bind sanctuaries together. They may or may not have accreditation schemes and if they do, they generally are significantly less comprehensive/rigorous than GFAS standards. Among these are the American Sanctuary Alliance (ASA), the North American Primate Sanctuary Alliance (NAPSA), the loosely organized Humane Outreach for Wolves League (HOWL), the

European Alliance of Rescue Centres and Sanctuaries (EARS), the Federation of Indian Animal Protection Organizations (FIAPO) and the Pan African Sanctuary Alliance (PASA).

CONCLUSION

Given the incomprehensibly large number of captive wild and exotic animals in conditions that are inadequate and mostly inhumane, we are left with a pragmatic question of how many could be rescued and what would be possible as real sanctuary for them. One wonders whether the accredited zoos could shift focus to breeding strictly for conservation-related purposes (e.g., for release) rather than for sustaining populations of nonendangered animals for continued exhibition. Along with corresponding messaging and education, the exhibitions and stories of rescues and need for better public policy that protects the environment and non-human animals would blur some of the differences making zoos more sanctuary-like, and through the massive visitation (almost 200 million a year just in the United States) it's likely legislative advocacy relating to advancing responsible and healthier relationships between human and nonhuman animals would be greatly enhanced.

The space and resources currently available that meet GFAS or AZA standards are miniscule compared to the many tens of thousands of animals in need of sanctuary. And that's obviously not including millions of animals in the wild that almost certainly will suffer and die without habitat protection (or rescue) due to habitat loss and fragmentation, hunting, climate change, pollution, and numerous other human-caused pressures.

Is it just to stand by as the Anthropocene proceeds to erase individuals and species? Can zoos and sanctuaries provide a better life for the exotic animal refugees? Even as accredited zoos continue to integrate welfare into their values, the possibilities seem limited. There may be less than a few hundred substantial, viable, self-sustaining sanctuaries worldwide that can provide more than basic requirements to the influx of wild or exotic animals destined to end up in their care. At best, there may be twice as many accredited zoos as this with the ability to provide thriving environments. These highly impactful and professional zoos can share invaluable advice and training to less resource-rich sanctuaries (and smaller accredited zoos) as well as engage in far more advocacy and legislative efforts as they employ the experts in what is good for wildlife in general and individual animals in human care in particular. This is essential knowledge to those who must both write laws like the Animal Welfare Act (or possible amendments to it) and to those who enforce it.

In addition, it is those top zoos, aquaria, and sanctuaries that could provide a better path for enforcement agencies often confronted with little or no viable destination to place confiscated animals. Were zoos and aquaria to be even more restrictive and selective about which animals to breed, there could be more (though clearly not sufficient) resources and space for rescues and confiscations. Often the stereotypical behavior associated with these refugees makes integration into zoo populations extremely challenging.

Ultimately, prevention is far more important. The United States could move enforcement of the Animal Welfare Act from the Agriculture Department to the Department of Justice. In addition, the United States could enact a zoo and sanctuary license act that would allow very specific control over this on-going problem. Laws which effectively prevent securing and owning exotic animals for anything other than true conservation, protection, and welfare (e.g., rescue) reasons could be dramatically impactful and reduce the number of animals facing injustices. Heavy financial penalties (though technically they are already part of the law) and enforced financial guarantees for nonaccredited zoos and sanctuaries (perhaps all should be covered even if accredited) may dissuade some bad practices.

The math is simple. Almost all captive nondomestic animals in need will have a slim chance of a "good" captive life. For those lucky few, a real sanctuary, and a zoo or aquarium that aspires to focus on individual animals first and foremost, may well be the most "just" destiny any animal could hope for. As more and more zoos do head toward an agenda centered on animal welfare and compassionate conservation they may well become the best of future sanctuaries.

NOTES

1. Ron Kagan and Jake Veasey, "Challenges of Zoo Animal Welfare," in Deva Kleiman, ed., *Wild Mammals in Captivity: Principles & Techniques,* Second Edition (Chicago: University of Chicago Press, 2010), 11–21.

2. Michael Moore, Greg Early, Kathleen Touhey, and Randall Wells, "Rehabilitation and release of marine mammals in the United States: Risks and benefits," *Marine Mammal Science* 23(4) (2007): 731–50.

3. Scott Carter and Ron Kagan, "Management of Surplus Animals," in Deva Kleiman ed., *Wild Mammals in Captivity: Principles & Techniques,* Second Edition (Chicago: University of Chicago Press, 2010), 263–67.

4. R. Henriksen, A. Kreilhuber, D. Stewart, M. Kotsovou, P. Raxter, E. Mrema, and S. Barrat, eds., 2016, "The Rise of INTERPOL Environmental Crime—A Growing Threat To Natural Resources Peace, Development and Security. Rapid Response Assessment."

5. Carl D. Soulsbury, Graziella Lossa, Sarah Kennell, and Stephen Harris, "The welfare and suitability of primates kept as pets," *Journal of Applied Animal Welfare Science* 12(1) (2009): 1–20.

6. Catherine A. Schuppli, D. Fraser, and H. J. Bacon, "Welfare of non-traditional pets," *Rev Sci Tech* 33(1) (2014): 221–31.

7. Clifford Warwick, Phillip C. Arena, Caterina Steedman, and Mike Jessop, "A review of captive exotic animal-linked zoonoses," *Journal of Environmental Health Research* 12(1) (2012): 9–24.

8. Carl D. Soulsbury, Graziella Lossa, Sarah Kennell, and Stephen Harris, "The welfare and suitability of primates kept as pets," *Journal of Applied Animal Welfare Science* 12(1) (2009): 1–20.

9. Carney Anne Nasser, "Welcome to the jungle: How loopholes in the federal Endangered Species Act and Animal Welfare Act are feeding a tiger crisis in America," *Albany Government Law Review* 9 (2016): 194–239.

10. Gina M. Ferrie, Kay H. Farmer, Chris W. Kuhar, and Tammy L. Bettinger, "The social, economic, and environmental contributions of Pan African Sanctuary Alliance primate sanctuaries in Africa," *Biodiversity and Conservation* 23(1) (2014): 187–201.

11. Ron Kagan, Scott Carter, and Stephenie Allard, "A Universal Animal Welfare Framework for Zoos," *Journal of Applied Animal Welfare Science*, 18 (2015): sup1, S1–S10.

12. Miquel Llorente, David Riba, Sandra Ballesta, Olga Feliu, and Charles Rostán, "Rehabilitation and Socialization of Chimpanzees (Pan troglodytes) Used for Entertainment and as Pets: An 8-Year Study at Fundació Mona," *International Journal of Primatology* 36(3) (2015): 605–24.

13. Shawn Ashley, Susan Brown, Joel Ledford, Janet Martin, Elizabeth Nash, Amanda Terry, Tim Tristan, and Cliff Warwick, "Morbidity and mortality of invertebrates, amphibians, reptiles, and mammals at a major exotic companion animal wholesaler," *Journal of Applied Animal Welfare Science* 17(4) (2014): 308–21.

14. Hannah R. Trayford and Kay H. Farmer, "Putting the Spotlight on Internally Displaced Animals (IDAs): A Survey of Primate Sanctuaries in Africa, Asia, and the Americas," *American Journal of Primatology* 75(2) (2013): 116–34.

BIBLIOGRAPHY

Ashley, Shawn, Susan Brown, Joel Ledford, Janet Martin, Elizabeth Nash, Amanda Terry, Tim Tristan, and Clifford Warwick. "Morbidity and mortality of invertebrates, amphibians, reptiles, and mammals at a major exotic companion animal wholesaler," *Journal of Applied Animal Welfare Science* 17(4) (2014): 308–21.

Carter, Scott and Kagan Ron. 2010. "Management of Surplus Animals." In Devra Kleiman, ed., *Wild Mammals in Captivity: Principles & Techniques*, Second Edition (Chicago: University of Chicago Press, 2010), 263–67.

Ferrie, Gina M., Kay H. Farmer, Chris W. Kuhar, and Tammy L. Bettinger. "The social, economic, and environmental contributions of Pan African Sanctuary Alliance primate sanctuaries in Africa," *Biodiversity and Conservation* 23(1) (2014): 187–201.

Kagan, Ronald and Jake S. Veasey. "Challenges of Zoo Animal Welfare." In Devra Kleiman, ed., *Wild Mammals in Captivity: Principles & Techniques*, Second Edition (Chicago: University of Chicago Press, 2010).

Kagan, Ronald, Scott Carter, and Stephanie Allard. "A Universal Animal Welfare Framework for Zoos," *Journal of Applied Animal Welfare Science* 18 (2015): sup1, S1–S10.

Moore, Michal J., Grey Early, Kathleen Touhey, and Randall Wells. "Rehabilitation and release of marine mammals in the United States: Risks and benefits," *Marine Mammal Science* 23(4) (2007): 731–50.

Nasser, Carney Anne. "Welcome to the jungle: How loopholes in the federal Endangered Species Act and Animal Welfare Act are feeding a tiger crisis in America," *Albany Government Law Review* 9 (2016): 194–239.

Llorente, Miquel, David Riba, Sandra Ballesta, Olga Feliu, and Charles Rostán. "Rehabilitation and Socialization of Chimpanzees (Pan troglodytes) Used for Entertainment and as Pets: An 8-Year Study at Fundació Mona," *International Journal of Primatology* 36(3) (2015): 605–24.

Schuppli, Catherine A., D. Fraser, H. J. Bacon. "Welfare of non-traditional pets," *Rev Sci Tech* 33(1) (2014): 221–31.

Soulsbury, Carl D., Graziella Lossa, Sarah Kennell, and Stephen Harris. "The welfare and suitability of primates kept as pets," *Journal of Applied Animal Welfare Science* 12(1) (2009): 1–20.

Trayford, Hannah R., and Kay H. Farmer. "Putting the Spotlight on Internally Displaced Animals (IDAs): A Survey of Primate Sanctuaries in Africa, Asia, and the Americas," *American Journal of Primatology* 75(2) (2013): 116–34.

Warwick, Clifford, Phillip C. Arena, Catrina Steedman, and Mike Jessop. "A review of captive exotic animal-linked zoonoses," *Journal of Environmental Health Research* 12(1) (2012): 9–24.

Conclusion

Beyond Personhood: Legal Rights for Zoo Animals

Jesse Donahue

In the United States in the mid-1970s and 1980s the Association of Zoos and Aquariums (then known as the AAZPA) had a staff that actively championed welfare for animals both inside and outside of zoos. The animal welfare measures they proposed for animals inside zoos were not perfect and reflected the reality they faced trying to help their members survive and in that way keep the exotic animals alive as well. Nonetheless they advocated for minimum standards of animal welfare care that were eventually adopted by the USDA as formal regulations and later expanded by the AZA's own internal accreditation requirements. During this period the executive director and key members of the organization of the AAZPA also actively pushed for animal welfare outside of zoos. They submitted testimony to Congress that supported the Endangered Species Act and the Marine Mammal Protection Act, for example. This was a political organization that actively involved itself in the larger goals of the animal welfare movement.

Unfortunately, however the AZA's continuing political advocacy today is largely lost in their focus on increasing accreditation standards for zoos and creating the structures for species preservation. To that end they created elaborate animal welfare requirements that far exceeded the minimal standards of the AWA. And they developed state-of-the-art veterinary care to keep animals healthy in their homes. They also set about trying to save endangered species through species conservation programs and reintroductions. They created numerous committees and organizational structures for sharing information designed to preserve the lives of some species within zoos and hopefully work to send them out of zoos and back to the managed wild. And as we can see from our chapter on reintroductions, they and their partners in the US Fish and Wildlife Service had some success with a small number of animals. Zoos have had mixed success in reintroducing animals in part because they have not actually structured their institutions to house and breed the most endangered animals. They have participated in the conservation of endangered species *in situ*, but this remains a task that zoos should be strongly en-

gaged in for the future.[1] Even when they do more reintroductions, however, they have faced and will continue to face a fundamental problem
for many species which is that legal hunting in particular is a significant
impediment to reintroducing endangered species. A world that still allows hunting means that at best reintroduced animals are going to face
enormous odds when returning unprotected spaces. If we took in human
refugees and then placed them back in their war-torn homes, we would
not expect them to thrive but this is what we see in the case of species
conservation programs implemented by zoos and the Fish and Wildlife
Service.

At the same time zoo's focus on species reintroductions necessitated
the increased turn to professional biologists. While biologists with bache-
lor's degrees had been part of the zoo profession from relatively early on
in the United States and western Europe, now zoos needed highly trained
biologists with doctoral degrees. They promoted the conservation of animals in zoos, but also used a language that was very clinical and designed to help them work with one another, not with politicians, animal
welfare groups, or the public. They talked about "species," not refugees
or animals who need rescuing in loving homes. They referred to biological "collections" rather than to individually named animals who reside at
the refuge that is the zoo. They facilitated animal exchanges to increase
"genetic diversity" for the ultimate goal of endangered species conservation through reintroductions in the wild. Their overriding goals was to at
least help end the large scale animal extinction happening on our planet.[2]
All of this is noble in the grand sense, but clinical and cold in the particu-
lars and clearly created a sense of unease for activists about the animals
involved. Would we want scientists manipulating us? Would we want to
be in a "collection?" All of this new rhetoric was layered on top of the
older vocabulary of the zoo world that drew from their analogy to natural history museums. As a result, zoo animals were placed in what are
still called "exhibits" rather than in homes. This language also fit well
with the attempts to get money for zoos from national museum funding
sources, but as a result we got a strange combination of an institution that
combined the language of theater with the coldness of biological termi-
nology and ceded the language of rescuing and care to sanctuaries.

Also lost in this discussion was the fact that these biologists were so
focused on the biology of animal welfare at zoos or in species preservation groups, that they were not as involved in the politics as they should
have been. This oversight is likely to hurt zoos significantly in the future.
The AZA should have been and should be today a relentless opponent of
hunting. We should see their testimony against most hunting measures
in most places most of the time, and yet we do not. The organization
should also be a constant advocate for listing new species under the
Endangered Species Act to protect them from future extinction in the
wild. And its counterparts around the world should do so as well. Al-

though the AZA does a lot to fund some programs that help some endangered species in the wild, they are remarkably silent about pushing to identify endangered species. In contrast, the Humane Society of the United States and other political animal welfare groups are routinely petitioning the US Fish and Wildlife Service to list endangered species and in that way try and preserve them in the wild before they become so critically endangered that they need the safety of the zoo to even exist. What is the difference? The AZA still champions significant pieces of conservation legislation that help animals in the wild. They are currently urging visitors to support the National Endowments for the Ocean Act, the Southern Sea Otter Recovery Act, the Marine Turtle Conservation Act, and the Multispecies Conservation Funds Reauthorization Act, among others.[3] The problem is that their advocacy on these issues is one among many of the roles that they and zoo directors play. Zoo directors who are more politically engaged seem focused primarily on creating new and better zoos or sanctuaries because they recognize the desperate need for more space for more needy animal refugees. But this is a never-ending cycle if the causes of the animal refugee status is not stopped.

As several of the contributors to this volume have argued, the United States, New Zealand, and Southeast Asia (and really all countries around the world) need a public agency that focuses solely on exotic captive animal refugees. The closest we have come to this in the United States was congressman William Whitehurst's Federal Assistance for Zoos and Aquariums bills in 1973. Because one of the major stated goals of both the AZA and animal welfare organizations is zoo animal welfare, it is possible that these groups could come together and work with an agency whose primary mission was to protect endangered species in the wild before they got to zoos. Together they might also recognize zoos and sanctuaries as refuges, mainly temporary, but sometimes permanent for animals who cannot be reintroduced. This would naturally incorporate the existing AZA focus of species conservation and reintroduction at the same time that it recognized these institutions for what they should be— the arks, lifeboats, and refuges that are supposed to protect exotic animals first and ferry these animals back to some kind of stability in the wild when they can. As our Southeast Asian specialist suggested, this agency could be funded by a tax on ticket sales to zoos. In that way all patrons would have to contribute to preserving refuges for exotic captive animals when needed. A tax on ticket sales that automatically went to conservation and species reintroduction would allow zoos to spend less time on fundraising for these goals. And if guests were explicitly told that they were paying for conservation, they would likely feel a sense of participation in the larger animal preservation movement. In the United States this would potentially deromanticize the connection between hunting and habitat preservation that occurs because of the Pittman-Robertson Act (1937). Currently, state fish and wildlife agencies receive millions of dollars in aid distributed from the Department of Interior from the receipt of an excise tax on firearms and ammunition. State wildlife agencies get that money for research and habitat protection for some endangered species. Unfortunately, however, it has made hunters into one of the largest funding sources for habitat preservation.

Abandoning the false promises of sanctuaries is also a crucial first step in increasing zoo animals' legal rights. At the moment scholars and activists are too focused on the mythology of sanctuaries rather than on the reality. There are good sanctuaries and bad sanctuaries. Many sanctuaries today, moreover, are much more like zoos than people understand. They allow visiting paying guests just as zoos do because they cannot afford to take care of their rescued animals without the stream of revenue that guests bring in. Many of them are not the expansive retreats that advocates might like. Animals in big cat sanctuaries, for example, often live in cages rather than in the large parklike settings that the word "sanctuary" connotes.[4] Even if every sanctuary lived up to the hype about their fitness to house exotic captive animals, there are simply not enough of them to address all of the need. The exotic pet trade alone means that it is extremely difficult to stop private citizens from breeding them. As a result, we will need as many safe spaces as possible to house these animals. The name of the institution is not as important as the quality of life that the animal receives when it lives there. Assuring the best home should be the goal of the animal welfare movement. The US Fish and Wildlife Service recently decided against sending some research chimpanzees from the Yerkes National Primate Research Center to a sanctuary in the United States and instead allowed them to go to the Wingham Wildlife Park, an unaccredited zoo in England, that was creating a 12,700 square foot home for the eight animals.[5] Space-wise this was the best home for the animals compared to the other possible options. If animal welfare is the goal, as we hope that it always is, then public agencies should be open to all options for the animals.

Another good step to increasing zoo animal legal welfare is to avoid the privatization fantasies of activists and scholars. Here we see writers calling up the image of significant parks such as the Kruger Park in South Africa. The panacea is that these will be expanded as more such tracts of land are somehow purchased and preserved for wild animals (it is always vague which ones will be there). At their most realistic we do have the actual cases where a large interest group or donor purchases an area in the American West or South America to preserve the animals in that area. William Conway, one of the late directors of the Bronx Zoo, imagined "zoo reserves" located in important animal wildlife areas "tied to the fabric of SSPs," that could serve as ecotourism locations, venues for research, and places to train local conservationists and rangers.[6] In other cases we have wealthy land owners such as Ted Turner proposing to create a wildlife refuge for the very wealthy who can afford to buy houses that rim the edge of the refuge so that they alone can see the animals from the peace and privacy of their living rooms. These kinds of places will help animals who exist easily in these particular geographic climates and who are not dangerous. But that still leaves the vast majority of animals in need of homes and help because these refuge sites are not offering to take all of the current zoo or sanctuary animals. To help these animals we need to refocus on the law.

Reforming the Animal Welfare Act and its counterparts in New Zealand and the Southeast Asian countries would certainly increase zoo animals' legal rights. Because any agency that enforces the law is likely to lack the staff necessary for frequent and effective surprise inspection visits, incorporating a citizen suit provision into these laws would help in some cases. This would give concerned citizens and activists legal standing to sue for violations of animal welfare when they believe they see it. Currently almost all animal welfare activists' attempts to get standing in court in the United States have failed so this would give these groups the legal tool they need to help the agencies that enforce these laws do their job. Some of the laws in Southeast Asia are so new that they may face less resistance there to basic change. Unfortunately, however, the Animal Welfare Act in the United States has proved impervious to change and thus this is an unlikely tool for increasing legal rights for zoo animals in this country, even if it may work in others.

Granting nonhuman primates personhood has potential as a means of securing at least one group of exotic captive animals' rights. Peter Singer's Great Ape Project and Steven Wise's legal advocacy in the US courts are drawing attention to captive animals and at a minimum forcing legislatures and courts to ask important questions about why any group of animals should not have their freedom. In 2008 the Spanish Parliament passed a nonlegislative measure that granted rights to nonhuman primates, specifically chimpanzees, orangutans, gorillas, and bonobos, and made it illegal to experiment on them or to arbitrarily confine them. It is important to note, however, that even this law allowed apes to remain in captivity for conservation purposes.[7] The Barcelona Zoo, for example, houses orangutans. Similarly, Germany is one of the most progressive animal welfare countries because it protects animals in its national constitution, but there are a large number of zoos in Germany that are home to many nonhuman primates, suggesting that even when these animals get the highest level of constitutional protection in a country they are likely to remain in zoos or sanctuaries if they are not in reintroduction programs of some sort.[8] As a result, even if animals are granted personhood, it is highly likely they will not be granted the exact same legal status as humans and will need additional and different laws that apply to them just as we apply different laws to children even though they are people. Thus the animals are likely to remain in zoos or sanctuaries. Given that status, it seems best strategically to focus on other laws at the same time.

This approach is a lot less glamorous and attention-grabbing, but likely to yield more legal protections for zoo animals. It will also require the many small steps that David Favre suggests all animals need for increased representation in the legal system.[9]

Animal welfare interests groups and activists have their best shot at increasing zoo animal legal rights through local laws, and this is where animal rights interest groups should focus their work. American states are adopting more animal laws than Congress at the moment and this trend seems likely to continue because the partisan makeup of state legislatures has not changed since some of these laws were enacted. States with Republican-dominated legislatures seem just as likely to enact these kinds of bills. The North Carolina legislature, for example, recently passed (N.C.G.S.A.§ § 114–8.7), a bill that required the Attorney General to create a hotline to receive reports about animal cruelty or violations of the AWA by private animal owners.[10] Tennessee, another Republican-dominated legislature, passed the first bill that allows families to recover up to $4,000 in noneconomic damages for emotional damages (not just fair-market value) when their companion animals are seriously injured or killed. The idea behind the T-Bo Act (2000) was that companion animals are valuable to their families beyond the price they paid for bringing the animal home.[11] Service animals who serve law enforcement officers seem poised to get increasing rights because of their work for humans. And states typically also have equine liability laws that could be refashioned for zoos as well. In these laws horse owners are protected from guests who might claim injury after visiting the premises. The equine liability laws state that spending time around horses is inherently dangerous and therefore guests can expect significant potential injury. In that way the law protects the horse owner and indirectly the horse because families do not lose their farms when someone sues them because they were, say, bitten by a horse as they walked by its stall. These same state laws could be rewritten in appropriate ways for zoos and thereby protect some animals from euthanasia when guests decide not to honor the privacy of an animal's home and break through protective barriers designed to protect them.

Another way in which zoo animal rights can be expanded is through states' increasing willingness to expand animal cruelty laws and compensation for injury to animals. At the most basic level, zoo animals need laws that stop animal performances, many of which rely on physical cruelty to get the animals to behave as requested. There is nothing wrong with asking animals to engage in a few behaviors that are healthy in exchange for simple treat rewards, particularly to help them in some way, but physically abusive behavior needs stiffer criminal penalties, both in the United States and around the world. Currently Minnesota, Mississippi, and Oklahoma do not have any exemptions for zoo animals in their animal cruelty laws. Other states, however, frequently exempt zoos from cruelty statutes, so zoo animal welfare advocates should think about expanding these laws. Similarly, the anti-exotic pet laws in states could be strengthened to prevent people from owning those animals. It seems that the political timing to expand these laws might be soon.

Both zoos and animal welfare groups now have an opening to work on increasing zoo animal welfare. Some of the past interest group protectors of animal cruelty are now losing their battles. Biomedical research institutions that used chimpanzees in research, for example, were some of the most vociferous and regular opponents of any attempt to revise legislation that might impact them, but their use of the great apes in research is now significantly less prevalent in the United States, the Netherlands, the United Kingdom, and Germany among other countries. Their newfound lack of interest in defending the cruel treatment of captive exotic animals in their research facilities suggests that animal welfare activists focused on exotic captive animals in other contexts will have one less foe. Similarly, circus interests are sufficiently weakened so that the large organizations are no longer going to use elephants in their shows. This suggests that there is a potential opening now for lobbying for state anticruelty laws that would include zoo animals and thereby get rid of many of the so-called roadside zoos that serve as poorly equipped homes to many animals.

All of these proposed laws would help accredited zoos and sanctuaries and could potentially significantly harm or even possibly put the bad versions of those institutions out of business. A zoo or sanctuary that had to pay significant anticruelty fines would both generate bad publicity and start to cut into its profits. A poorly funded roadside zoo that had to have a trust fund for each animal could not afford to exist. Zoo guests who hurt animals when they visit might be significantly less likely to act out in that way if they faced significant animal cruelty fines and jail time.

There is a significant chance that these protections could be extended to zoo animals across the United States and if adopted here, they could serve as a model for other countries. Unlike farm interests that may extend across multiple statehouse districts within a state, a zoo is located in just one district. Even when the zoo has a great deal of political clout because of its size, it is still only located in one district and therefore limited in how much opposition it can generate to political regulation. But zoos must engage animal welfare activists, politicians, and lawyers in this effort. Accredited zoos in the United States and around the world will need to be far more politically engaged about animal welfare than they have been in the past if they are to avoid losing the animals in their care. As others have noted "zoos have been poor at actively participating in politics, often hesitant to be seen as political organizations. Yet the future of biodiversity is intimately tied to the political process. Zoos ignore that process at their peril."[12] William Conway also argued that it was time for "focused legislator, lawyer, and conservation support exhibits at least as specialized and imaginative as those for children."[13] We would add that the future of animal welfare is just as closely tied to the political process and the very existence of zoos could be on the chopping block if they do not actively engage in promoting legal changes that benefit the welfare of their animals.

Part of the struggle to increase zoo animal rights, however, will certainly also involve a reevaluation of zoos by animal welfare activists. Zoo animals fill the same emotional role at the community level that companion animals serve in homes. When longtime recognizable animal residents of zoos die, they are frequently keenly missed by the citizens of that community.[14] When Willi B a lowland gorilla at the Atlanta Zoo died in 2000, seven thousand people attended his memorial service and hundreds of others sent sympathy notes to the zoo. More recently people held a vigil for Harambe, the seventeen-year-old silverback gorilla who was euthanized because a child crawled through the protective barriers of his home. The participants emphasized that they were not protesting against the zoo, but rather expressing their sadness about the killing.[15] Animal welfare activists sometimes seem oblivious to this human sympathy for animals at zoos instead preferring at times to refer to people who go to visit them as "ill-educated."[16] It will be difficult to increase the legal rights of zoo animals, however, with this kind of rhetoric. These animals need a much more sophisticated sense of advocacy and a better understanding of our interconnectedness with them. They need activists who seek any institution that is best for them and who pursue the best possible legal rights for our fellow co-citizens. We owe them that.

NOTES

1. For a discussion on the ways that zoos contribute to species reintroductions, see Mark R. Stanley Price and John E. Fa, "Reintroductions from zoos: A conservation guiding light or a shooting star?" in Alexandra Zimmerman, Mathhew Hatchwell, Lesley A. Dickie, and Chris West, eds., *Zoos in the 21st Century: Catalysts for Conservation?* (New York: Cambridge University Press, 2007), 155–77.

2. For statistics on animal extinction and the zoo profession's response, see William Conway, "Entering the 21st Century," in Alexandra Zimmerman, Mathhew Hatchwell, Lesley A. Dickie, and Chris West, eds., *Zoos in the 21st Century: Catalysts for Conservation?* (New York: Cambridge University Press, 2007), 12–21.

3. For AZA conservation advocacy, see https://www.aza.org/conservation-legislation. Accessed November 20, 2016.

4. Jesse Donahue, "Back to the Future: The New Politics of Elite Access to Exotic Animals," paper presented at Zoo Studies and New Humanities: A Workshop, Hamilton, Canada, November 2–3, 2016.

5. James Gorman, "Plan to Export Chimps Tests Laws to Protect Species," *New York Times*, November 14, 2015, http://www.nytimes.com/2015/11/15/science/plan-to-export-chimps-tests-law-to-protect-species.html. Accessed November 15, 2016.

6. William Conway, "Entering the 21st Century" in Alexandra Zimmerman, Mathhew Hatchwell, Lesley A. Dickie, and Chris West, eds., *Zoos in the 21st Century: Catalysts for Conservation?* (New York: Cambridge University Press, 2007), 18.

7. See www.projetogap.org for this work. Accessed September 5, 2016. For a brief discussion of this law and European animal welfare politics in general, see Nicholas Pedersen, "Detailed Discussion European Animal Welfare Laws 2003–the Present: Explaining the Downturn," 2009, The Animal Legal and Historical Center, https://www.animallaw.info/article/detailed-discussion-european-animal-welfare-laws-2003-present-explaining-downturn; Stephanie J. Englesman, "A Look at Lagging American Protection Laws," 22 *Pace Entl. Law Review* 329 (Fall 2005), https://www.animallaw.info/article/world-leader-what-price-look-lagging-american-animal-protection-laws.

8. Stephanie J. Englesman, "World Leader At What Price: A Look at Lagging American Protection Laws?" 22 *Pace Environmental Law Review* 329 (Fall 2005), https://www.animallaw.info/article/world-leader-what-price-look-lagging-american-animal-protection-laws. Accessed March 7, 2017.

9. David Favre, "Integrating Animal Interests into Our Legal System," *Animal Law*, 10, 87 (2004): 87–97. Favre proposes an additional animal tort law in this piece which could also potentially help zoo animals.

10. See https://www.animallaw.info/ for this bill. Accessed November 18, 2016.

11. William C. Root, "Man's Best Friend: Property or Family Member? An Examination of the Legal Classification of Companion Animals and its Impact on Damages Recoverable for their Wrongful Death or Injury," *Villanova Law Review*, 47 Vill L. Rev. 423 (2002), https://www.animallaw.info/article/mans-best-friend-property-or-family-member-examination-legal-classification-companion. Sept. 2, 2016.

12. Bengst Holst and Lesley A. Dickie, "How do national and international regulations and policies influence the role of zoos and aquariums in conservation?" in Alexandra Zimmerman, Mathhew Hatchwell, Lesley A. Dickie, and Chris West, eds., *Zoos in the 21st Century: Catalysts for Conservation?* (New York: Cambridge University Press, 2007), 30.

13. William Conway, "Entering the 21st Century," in Alexandra Zimmerman, Mathhew Hatchwell, Lesley A. Dickie, and Chris West, eds., *Zoos in the 21st Century: Catalysts for Conservation?* (New York: Cambridge University Press, 2007), 14.

14. See Jesse Donahue and Erik Trump, *Political Animals: Public Art in American Zoos and Aquariums* (Lanham, MD: Lexington Books, 2007), 102.

15. Sarah V. Schwig, "Gorilla Killed at Zoo is Honored by Heartbroken Public," May 31, 2016, http://www.thedodo.com. Accessed June 1, 2016.

16. Jaqueline B. Ramos, "Gorilla Escapes London Zoo Looking for Freedom." This is a curious article all around because the gorilla did not actually escape the London Zoo for example. For the article, see http://www.projetogap.org.br/en/noticia/gorilla-escape-in-london-zoo-looking-for-freedom/. Accessed November 21, 2016.

BIBLIOGRAPHY

Conway, William. "Entering the 21st Century," in Alexandra Zimmerman, Mathhew Hatchwell, Lesley A. Dickie, and Chris West, eds., *Zoos in the 21st Century: Catalysts for Conservation?* (New York: Cambridge University Press, 2007), 12–21.

Donahue, Jesse. "Back to the Future: The New Politics of Elite Access to Exotic Animals." Paper presented at Zoo Studies and New Humanities: A Workshop, Hamilton, Canada, November 2–3, 2016.

Donahue, Jesse and Erik Trump. *Political Animals: Public Art in American Zoos and Aquariums* (Lanham, MD: Lexington Books, 2007).

Englesman, Stephanie J. "A Look at Lagging American Protection Laws," 22 *Pace Entl. Law Review* 329 (Fall 2005), https://www.animallaw.info/article/world-leader-what-price-look-lagging-american-animal-protection-laws.

———. "World Leader At What Price: A Look at Lagging American Protection Laws?" 22 *Pace Environmental Law Review* 329 (Fall 2005), https://www.animallaw.info/article/world-leader-what-price-look-lagging-american-animal-protection-laws.

Favre, David. "Integrating Animal Interests into Our Legal System," *Animal Law* 10 (2004): 87–97.

Gorman, James. "Plan to Export Chimps Tests Laws to Protect Species." *New York Times*, November 14, 1015, http://www.nytimes.com/2015/11/15/science/plan-to-export-chimps-tests-law-to-protect-species.html. Accessed November 15, 2016.

Holst, Bengst and Lesley A. Dickie. "How do national and international regulations and policies influence the role of zoos and aquariums in conservation?" in Alexandra Zimmerman, Mathhew Hatchwell, Lesley A. Dickie, and Chris West, eds., *Zoos in the 21st Century: Catalysts for Conservation?* (New York: Cambridge University Press, 2007), 22–33.

Pedersen, Nicholas. "Detailed Discussion European Animal Welfare Laws 2003–the Present: Explaining the Downturn." 2009, The Animal Legal and Historical Center, https://www.animallaw.info/article/detailed-discussion-european-animal-welfare-laws-2003-present-explaining-downturn.

Price, Stanley, Mark R., and John E. Fa. "Reintroductions from zoos: A conservation guiding light or a shooting star?" in Alexandra Zimmerman, Mathhew Hatchwell, Lesley A. Dickie, and Chris West, eds., *Zoos in the 21st Century: Catalysts for Conservation?* (New York: Cambridge University Press, 2007), 155–77.

Ramos, Jaqueline B. "Gorilla Escapes London Zoo Looking for Freedom." http://www.projetogap.org.br/en/noticia/gorilla-escape-in-london-zoo-looking-for-freedom/. Accessed November 21, 2016.

Root, William C. "Man's Best Friend: Property or Family Member? An Examination of the Legal Classification of Companion Animals and its Impact on Damages Recoverable for their Wrongful Death or Injury," *Villanova Law Review*, 47 Vill L. Rev. 423 (2002).

Schwig, Sarah V. "Gorilla Killed at Zoo is Honored by Heartbroken Public." May 31, 2016, http://www.thedodo.com. Accessed June 1, 2016.

Zimmerman, Alexandra, Mathhew Hatchwell, Lesley A. Dickie, and Chris West, eds., *Zoos in the 21st Century: Catalysts for Conservation?* (New York: Cambridge University Press, 2007).

Index

About the Contributors

Govindasamy Agoramoorthy currently serves as distinguished research professor at the College of Environment and Health Sciences, Tajen University, Taiwan. He also serves in the executive board of the South East Asian Zoos Association (SEAZA). His research includes integrated aspects of *in situ* and *ex situ* conservation of endangered species. He has carried out field research in the tropical forests of Asia, Africa, and South America over the last three decades to study wildlife including monkeys and apes. Between 1989 and 1993, he served as visiting scientist at the Conservation and Research Center, National Zoological Park, Smithsonian Institution (Washington, DC). He is the founding chairman of Ethics and Welfare Committee of South East Asian Zoos Association. He led the committee from 1998 to 2012 and upgraded all major zoos and safari parks in the region. He has authored 25 books and 250 articles related to wildlife, zoo biology, and environment conservation in various peer-reviewed journals with impact factor.

Jesse Donahue is the chair of the Political Science department at Saginaw Valley State University where she teaches a course on animal politics and law. She has coauthored three books about zoos, *American Zoos During the Depression: A New Deal for Animals*, *Political Animals: Public Art in American Zoos and Aquariums*, and *The Politics of Zoos: Exotic Animals and Their Protectors*. She has written additional chapters of books on zoos and presented many conference papers on the topic as well.

Ron Kagan is CEO of the Detroit Zoological Society and an advocate for compassionate conservation, animal welfare, and humane education. He has worked at and consulted for numerous zoos and aquaria over the past thirty-five years and lectures at universities and conferences around the world. Ron has authored numerous contributions to scientific journals, encyclopedias, and books on museums, zoos, and animal ethics/welfare. Kagan created, cowrote, and produced ten internationally award-winning wildlife conservation and welfare documentaries and established both the Academy for Humane Education and the Center for Zoo Animal Welfare. He has led the development of unique and award-winning facilities including the Gorilla Conservation Research Center, the "Wilds of Africa," the "Wildlife Interpretive Gallery" (a museum exploring the relationship between humans and animals over time and in different cultures), the National Amphibian Conservation Center, the "Arctic Ring of Life" (the largest polar bear facility in the world), the Ford Education Center, the Wild Adventure Simulator (a motion-based cabin simulator that builds empathy for other species as people experience life through animals' senses), and the Polk Penguin Conservation Center.

Susan Margulis is an associate professor of animal behavior, ecology and conservation, and biology at Canisius College. She did a postdoctoral fellowship that involved work at the Brookfield Zoo, and she has written articles related to zoo science including, "Establishing a Keeper-Based Behavioral Monitoring Program: A Top-Down/Bottom-Up Approach," in *Proceedings, 2001 AZA Annual Conference*; "Linking observation and conservation: Baboon research and conservation at the Brookfield Zoo," in *Bison*, 11: 10–19; and "The Sexual behavior and hormonal estrus cycles in captive aged lowland gorillas *(Gorilla gorilla)*," in *American Journal of Primatology*.

Donald E. Moore III is currently director of the Oregon Zoo. He was formerly a senior scientist with the Smithsonian National Zoo and has more than forty years of experience in animal welfare and wildlife conservation. As associate director for Animal Care at the Smithsonian zoo he placed increased focus on animal welfare. He has made significant contributions to global efforts to conserve rare species. His field research experience includes work in "El Tapado" Estancia, Uruguay (1987–1996, 2002, 2010); the Northeast seal census (2004–2006); the Adirondack Wood Turtle Atlas (2005); the New York State "Herpotology Atlas" (1995–1997); and work at the Huntsman Marine Biology Research Lab, St. Andrews (1976).

Michael Morris is a vegan activist. He has written articles on animals and society including "Animal Suffering in New Zealand: Can Science Make a Difference?" in the *New Zealand Journal of Social Sciences*. He received his PhD in zoology from the University of Auckland and has a master's degree in environmental law, policy, science, and education. He is the author of *Factory Farming and Animal Liberation in New Zealand*. He has written several articles on about animals in New Zealand for *Society and Animals*.

Mary Murray's paid and volunteer work, before becoming an academic sociologist, included social services for youth and the elderly, factory and office work, and community work, as well as work for the environmental organization Friends of the Earth. Since becoming an academic, Mary has also contributed to Trade Union organization and Animal Rights organizations, and has worked as a volunteer counselor. Mary lives in a household which includes cats, dogs, turtles, and birds, all of whom would otherwise have been euthanized or homeless.

Lightning Source UK Ltd.
Milton Keynes UK
UKHW011939131119
353477UK00001B/63/P